Damnable Heresy

Portrait of William Pynchon.
Used by permission of the Peabody Essex Museum, Salem, Massachusetts.

Damnable Heresy

William Pynchon, the Indians,
and the First Book Banned (and Burned) in Boston

David M. Powers

Foreword by David D. Hall

For All Saints Church, Springfield

Faithfully,

David M. Powers

September 9, 2015

WIPF & STOCK · Eugene, Oregon

DAMNABLE HERESY
William Pynchon, the Indians, and the First Book Banned (and Burned) in Boston

Copyright © 2015 David M. Powers. All rights reserved. Except for brief quotations
in critical publications or reviews, no part of this book may be reproduced in any
manner without prior written permission from the publisher. Write: Permissions,
Wipf and Stock Publishers, 199 W. 8th Ave., Suite 3, Eugene, OR 97401.

Wipf & Stock
An Imprint of Wipf and Stock Publishers
199 W. 8th Ave., Suite 3
Eugene, OR 97401

www.wipfandstock.com

ISBN 13: 978-1-62564-870-9

Manufactured in the U.S.A.

To the memory of my teachers,
George Huntston Williams
C. Conrad Wright

Contents

Illustrations[1]

---

1. Unless otherwise noted, illustrations are by the author.

Foreword

BE IT AS FOUNDER of a Massachusetts town or be it as lay theologian, William Pynchon (1590–1662) complicates the stories we like to tell about the "Puritan" founders of New England in the seventeenth century. He is in good company, for the complexities of his life were repeated many times over among the people who chose to come to New England in the 1630s. How can we weave so many strands of thought, action, and identity into a single narrative that encompasses entrepreneurs and idealistic theocrats, the heterodox and the orthodox, the English and the Native Americans, local circumstances and what was happening in the Atlantic world? From day one, the organizers of the Massachusetts-Bay Company (1629) were acutely aware that every step they took was being scrutinized in England by their enemies—and for that matter, by their friends. Were they friends or foes of the government of the English monarch Charles I? Were they so critical of the Church of England, the state church to which all of them officially belonged, that they were really "Separatists" (the most radical wing of the Puritan movement)? From day one, the organizers of the Massachusetts-Bay Company, with John Winthrop at its head, struggled to control an untidy process of emigration and settlement that disrupted their initial plans for where people would live. And, from day one, the ambition of many of the colonists to create "pure" churches on this side of the Atlantic brought into play all of the contradictions that had developed within the Puritan movement since its beginnings in the middle of the sixteenth century. Should local congregations be generously inclusive, or admit only those who were "visible saints"? Should local congregations defy the civil state, or allow it to regulate some aspects of religion? Should lay people be allowed to speak out on matters of theology, or must they defer to the expertise of university-educated ministers? Behind these questions lay the challenge of creating a consensus strong enough to keep the new society from falling apart, as had happened at Jamestown in the Chesapeake.

There is much to learn from the life of William Pynchon as David Powers has reconstructed it, for Pynchon sat astride several of the forces that could have wrecked the Puritan colonies. He reached out to the Native Americans and was notably fair in his dealings with them; his skills as a merchant and fur trader helped the colonists find their footing, but not at the price of giving up religion; he supported Winthrop and other magistrates in their efforts to keep the lid on religious and social dissent; and when, as a lay theologian, he speculated about a fairly abstruse point of doctrine and got into trouble for doing so, he never repudiated other aspects of mainstream theology. No wonder, then, that historians have disagreed on how to locate him within the wider story of Puritan New England. Now, in this new biography, we can see more clearly than ever before that Pynchon was not as much of an outlier as others have suggested. Here, for the first time, we are provided the fullest possible account of Pynchon's activities as a Puritan and entrepreneur before he emigrated and after he returned to England. And here, we see him as a man of the Atlantic world. So were many of the colonists who remained in New England, and the alarm bells that went off in Boston about Pynchon's theology are best seen as a response to "Atlantic" circumstances—in particular, the extraordinary proliferation of heterodox or divergent theologies among lay people (and some clergy) in Civil War England. In the 1640s, the leadership in Massachusetts had been singed by accusations from abroad that their system of "congregational" governance was responsible for much of the turmoil in England. Taking a stand against Pynchon was part and parcel of a program intended to demonstrate to English and Scottish Puritans that, on the contrary, orthodoxy was in good hands in New England—indeed, faring better in New England than in their homeland.

Much that is unexpected awaits the careful reader of *Damnable Heresy*. We may still feel challenged by the presence of someone as distinctive as Pynchon, but we finally have a full telling of his life on which to base any larger narrative.

David D. Hall
Bartlett Research Professor of New England Church History
Harvard Divinity School

Acknowledgments

I COULD NOT HAVE brought my "Project Pynchon" to this completion without the assistance of many others. My deep thanks for their expertise, encouragement, and willing help in so many ways go to:

David D. Hall, Bartlett Research Professor of New England Church History, Harvard Divinity School, always unfailingly supportive and generous with encouragement, wisdom, and advice;

Glynis Morris, Archive Assistant, Deputy Librarian at the Essex Record Office, Chelmsford, United Kingdom (1994–2014), and researcher extraordinaire;

Margaret Bendroth, Executive Director of the Congregational Library and Congregational Christian Historical Society, Boston, Massachusetts, and an ever-dependable advisor;

Maggie Humberston, Head of Library and Archives, and Cliff McCarthy, Archivist, Lyman and Merrie Wood Museum of Springfield History, Springfield Museums, Springfield, Massachusetts, who provided ready access to original sources;

Margaret Baker of Brentwood, Essex, United Kingdom, translator of the Latin record of William Pynchon's fealty at the Springfield Dukes manorial court in 1622;

Raymond John Brown, Rector of All Saints' Church, Springfield, Chelmsford, United Kingdom;

Simon Douglas Lane, Vicar of St. Andrews Church, Wraysbury, United Kingdom (2005–2013);

Dennis Pitt, historian, Wraysbury, United Kingdom;

Barbara Wells, Assistant Librarian, Dennis Memorial Library, Dennis, Massachusetts;

Linford D. Fisher, Assistant Professor of History, Brown University;

ACKNOWLEDGMENTS

Kevin McBride, David Naumec, and Laurie Pasteryak Lamarre of the Mashantucket Pequot Museum and Research Center, Mashantucket, Connecticut;

Gloria Korsman, Research Librarian, Andover Harvard Library, Harvard Divinity School;

Ted Korbel, Douglas K. Showalter, and Karen Wren, who kindly read the manuscript and made useful suggestions;

Matthew Wimer, Assistant Managing Editor, and Alex Fus, Copyeditor, at Wipf & Stock Publishers;

Brenna McLaughlin, Director of Marketing and Communications at the Association of American University Presses, and my daughter-in-law, for her suggestions regarding publication;

Alan W. Powers, Professor Emeritus, Bristol Community College, Fall River, Massachusetts, and my brother, whose linguistic skills greatly helped to sharpen my prose;

And Sally E. Norris, a welcome companion in research as in so many other adventures, whose valuable advice and encouraging support I have cherished throughout the many months I have spent creating this book.

Introduction

THE CHALLENGE OF INTERRACIAL misunderstandings in the midst of intercultural hostilities. Anxieties from living in a time of war in one's own land. Charges of entrepreneurial profiteering when food was scarce. Unruly residents in a remote frontier community. Harsh accusations for speaking the unspeakable and publishing the unprintable. All this and more figured in the life of one seventeenth-century man—William Pynchon, the Puritan entrepreneur and founder of Springfield, Massachusetts.

Two things in particular stand out. Pynchon enjoyed uniquely positive relationships with Native peoples.

And, he wrote the first book banned—and burned—in Boston.

For those two achievements alone, the William Pynchon saga warrants our attention, though his story is far richer than that. Arriving in New England in 1630, Pynchon plunged into the import-export business, and also into service as Massachusetts' "Mr Treasurer" from 1632 to 1634. To secure more beaver pelts to trade in England, in 1636 he moved closer to the source of furs on the Connecticut River frontier. His phenomenal accomplishments as a fur trader mark Pynchon as a notable figure in the economic development of New England. The inhabitants of his frontier community of Springfield legitimated his governance in an innovative way, with a popular election. His administration of the Springfield magistrate's court, with his goal of evenhanded justice for Indians as well as English, left an important legacy.

Unlike most of his contemporaries, the pragmatic Pynchon believed in treating Native peoples with caution and respect. By seeking to understand Native cultures, he consistently avoided escalating irritations into conflicts. His 1636 deed to Springfield, for instance, included Algonquian words, names of women in the Agawam tribe's matriarchal society, and specific rights requested by the Indians. Pynchon's insistence on purchasing land from Native peoples and guaranteeing them the rights they sought differed from the practices of other Puritans. His irenic and positive relationships with Native peoples and his unfailing call for calm and reason offer a model for intercultural connections, though the example he provided was sadly not copied by others.

But Pynchon's wholly unexpected book was his undoing. His treatise on *The Meritorious Price of our Redemption*, published in 1650, proved to be problematic. Pynchon was not a theological scholar. He was self-taught—clearly an accomplishment in and of itself—but probably in part for that very reason his work was not well received. In his maverick treatise on the atonement, Pynchon claimed that Christ did not suffer "hell-torments" because God would never "impute" punishment to an innocent person. When copies of the book arrived during the Massachusetts legislature's meeting, Pynchon was caught in a political bind. His book was instantly condemned. He tried to defend himself, but felt forced to retreat to England in 1652. There he wrote four more increasingly lengthy books, largely on the same theme.

It was in fact the charge of heresy that brought William Pynchon to grief as well as to the notice of subsequent generations.

Far from being an outmoded notion, heresy as an unwelcome, variant conviction is an ever-present threat. To speak of the unacceptable, and even the forbidden, and to do so deliberately has the capacity to create confrontations that can prove devastating. Over the years, many topics have perched dangerously on the borderlines of public conversation and at the risky edges of acceptable discourse. In the seventeenth century, undisciplined theological conjecture about the atonement was deemed heresy, and it put its proponents severely at odds with acceptability. Today, unguarded political speculation about the righteousness of revolutionaries, for example, or tolerance of terrorist plots, might produce the same results. Champions of the insufferable inevitably present a threat. They threaten those in charge as well as the shared public conversation that creates the community. Nobody wants heresy, except the heretics.

The story of William Pynchon, a colonial entrepreneur, Puritan magistrate, and unorthodox theologian, is not only a study in heretical discourse. It also highlights factors that proved formative in shaping community in early New England. The Pynchon case illuminates the development of polities, both ecclesiastical and political—the forms of governance that Puritans developed on these shores. Francis J. Bremer has identified as one of the Puritan enterprise's basic challenges "how and where to position the perimeter fence dividing what was acceptable from what was not."[1] Set loose from the traditional givens of monarchial government, the state-sanctioned Episcopal Church, and centuries-old village institutions in England, the immigrants to New England had to take on the task of establishing a godly society of their own devising. William Pynchon spent much of his life in America doing just that, helping to define the boundaries of that society—until one day he found himself on the wrong side of the fence. His story culminated in his condemnatory treatment at the hands of the Massachusetts legislature, and in his subsequent responses to public censure.

A handful of relatively concise publications in past decades have presented portions of William Pynchon's story. Ezra Hoyt Byington's "Sketch of William Pynchon" appeared in the *Andover Review* in 1886; it summarized the scholarship then available and was included in rewritten form as the chapter "William Pynchon, Gent." in Byington's 1897 *The Puritan in England and New England*. Samuel Eliot Morison presented a lecture in the 1930s on "William Pynchon, the Founder of Springfield," which he later recast as a supplemental chapter in *Builders of the Bay Colony*. Ruth A. McIntyre's 1961 booklet for the Connecticut Valley Historical Museum, *William Pynchon: Merchant and Colonizer, 1590–1662*, paid particular attention to commercial aspects of his life. More recently, Philip F. Gura included a chapter in his 1984 volume, *A Glimpse of Sion's Glory: Puritan Radicalism in New England, 1620–1660*, entitled "William Pynchon," in which he sought to identify Pynchon's intellectual antecedents and connections. Michael P. Winship's 1997 article, "Contesting Control of Orthodoxy among the Godly: William Pynchon Reexamined," detailed the tensions between and among Puritan thinkers that were exemplified by Pynchon's case. Marty O'Shea's 1998 article on "Springfield's Puritans and Indians: 1636–1655" in the *Historical Journal of Massachusetts* highlighted unusual factors in Pynchon's relationships with Native peoples. These works all offered either basic introductions to Pynchon's life or insights into his theology; none exceeded forty pages. In addition to these articles, Peter A. Thomas' unpublished 1979 dissertation for the University of Massachusetts, "In the Maelstrom of Change: The Indian Trade and Cultural Process in the Middle Connecticut River Valley, 1635–1665," provided much helpful information

---

1. Bremer, *First Founders*, 5.

on economic and intercultural factors at work in the Connecticut River Valley in the seventeenth century. And Stephen Innes' 1983 book, *Labor in a New Land: Economy and Society in Seventeenth-Century Springfield*, applied anthropological and sociological insights to William Pynchon's story, as well as to the much longer story of his son John.

While past studies have laid down a foundation and have also suggested various possible directions for the lines of inquiry I have pursued, my approach to the Pynchon story has required concentrated focus on primary sources. Reconsidering the original data has led to several adjustments and revisions in the received interpretation of Pynchon's achievements. I have examined a wide array of documents from that era. An untranslated Latin theological treatise, English manorial court minutes, land transfers, official Colony records, bills of lading, minutes of British Parliamentary maneuvers, as well as a paper trail of Pynchon's writings, his Springfield Court record, and his personal letters all came into play and served to situate Pynchon and his intriguing story in its own time and place. Other details helped to complete the picture: Puritan booksellers in London and their wares, the exchange rate for wampum, changes in the local price of corn, or the weight of a beaver's hide.

Part I on "A Puritan's Journey" presents Pynchon's experiences through a series of chapters; each begins with an incident that exposes an arena of Pynchon's life. From his origins in Essex County during the waning days of Elizabethan England, the story winds through his involvement with the Massachusetts Bay Company and immigration to America in 1630. It then traces Pynchon's emergence as a respected leader and businessman in the Bay Colony and as the founder of a plantation at the western frontier of the English presence, the Connecticut River. It considers Pynchon's relationships with Native peoples, which were unusually constructive for the era. Then, following the appearance of Pynchon's problematic theological treatise and its fiery condemnation, the account charts his struggles with the Massachusetts General Court, his return to England, and his subsequent writings.

Part II, "The Plight of William Pynchon," offers an analysis of the various ecclesiastical and political dynamics at work around his case. Pynchon's aristocratic assumptions, for one, led him to form a divergent view on the nature of the church; he assumed a single national church structure as the norm, with a privileged role for magistrates like himself in ecclesiastical affairs. His lack of involvement with the colony's political processes resulted in a growing distance from emerging democratic trends that led to expansion of the franchise. Though Pynchon was an opponent of "liberty of conscience," in an ironic twist he was charged with publishing unacceptable ideas of his own—yet a minority in the Massachusetts legislature voted to support him.

As a native of Springfield, I have long had an interest in its earliest days, and particularly the part the Pynchons played in shaping its life. From a map of Pynchon's early settlement in a book by Springfield historian Harry Andrew Wright that I discovered in the attic of my uncle's home on Westfield Street in West Springfield, to a paper for C. Conrad Wright's American church history class at Harvard Divinity School, to extensive research since retirement in both New England and Old, I have explored as much of the story as I could, wherever the trail might lead. I am pleased to share the results of that journey with you.

A Note on Usage

QUOTATIONS FROM SEVENTEENTH-CENTURY SOURCES have been reproduced largely with original spelling where the meaning remains clear, though words contracted by superscriptions have been expanded to modern usage. Except in one note, I have replaced the letter "thorn," written as "y," with its pronunciation, "th." Dates are given in old style (Julian calendar); years are in new style (Gregorian calendar), with January 1 rather than March 25 treated as the first day of the year.

Abbreviations

CCR	*The Public Records of the Colony of Connecticut*, J. Hammond Trumbull
CN	*Covenant of Nature*, William Pynchon
CR	*The Pynchon Court Record*, Joseph Smith
ERO	Essex Record Office, Chelmsford, United Kingdom
FD	*A Farther Discussion*, William Pynchon
JS	*The Jewes Synagogue*, William Pynchon
MBCR	*Records of the Governor and Company of the Massachusetts Bay*, Nathaniel B. Shurtleff
MHS	Massachusetts Historical Society
MP	*The Meritorious Price*, William Pynchon
NEHGS	New England Historic Genealogical Society
NEQ	*The New England Quarterly*
ODNB	*Oxford Dictionary of National Biography*, H. C. G. Matthew and Brian Harrison
WP	*Winthrop Papers*, Allyn B. Forbes

Prologue

THURSDAY, OCTOBER 17, 1650. As the weekly Lecture ended and people began to stroll down the street from the Meetinghouse, the colony's hangman, Thomas Bell, dropped a book onto a fire. He had kindled the flames late that morning near the crossroads where the street leading up from the waterfront widened into an open space. Here was the Boston marketplace, and because it served as the commercial center of the settlement—and indeed, the entire Bay colony—this area was frequented by everybody. Open-air markets had been scheduled here on Thursdays since 1634. They coincided with the midweek worship service just yards away to the north.[1]

The book Bell dropped onto the fire was a thin volume, just 169 pages long. It had been printed earlier that year in London, probably in June, and had just arrived in Massachusetts. In the style typical of the era, the title went on at some length: *The Meritorious Price of Our Redemption, Iustification, &c. Cleering it from some common Errors; and proving* . . . quite a number of things, all of which were laid out on the first page. The author, too, was listed: "William Pinchon, Gentleman, in New-England."[2]

1. Bell is named in Shurtleff, *MBCR*, 2:271 (May 2, 1649). Market day in Boston was set on March 4, 1634 (ibid., 1:112). In time, the site where Pynchon's book was burned would host Boston's first government building, the Town-house of 1658, and after that structure burned down, the Old State House, which is still standing.

2. A notation on the title page of British Museum's original copy gives the publication date as June 2, 1650 (Pynchon, *Meritorious Price of Our Redemption*, lvii).

For a book that was publicly destroyed, the first edition of Pynchon's notorious volume has actually flourished nicely over the last couple of centuries. In 1885, Joseph Pynchon reported that there were "but three of these books extant": the British Library copy, plus two in private hands in New York City and Suffield, Connecticut (Pynchon, *Record of the Pynchon Family*). In 1931, Harry A. Wright noted on the title page of his photostat reproduction that there were "but four copies . . . known," these being in the British Library, New York Public Library, Connecticut Historical Society, and the Congregational

1

The onlookers that day were witnessing the first instance of book burning in English North America.

In the events that preceded this moment there lies the story of a remarkable Puritan's journey. William Pynchon's commitments had brought him from Old England to the New as one of the Commonwealth's founding generation. A man who was prominent in business and government, he played vital supporting roles in planting the colonies of Massachusetts and Connecticut. He had extended the Bay colony westward to the Connecticut River, where he developed the community of Springfield. But in the aftermath of this incident in the marketplace, Pynchon's own life irreversibly changed, and significant aspects of a new ethos emerging in New England came to light. Pynchon's case illumined the tensions of an incipient democracy, with its struggles over diversity versus conformity in public life, flexibility versus firmness, and asserting independency versus maintaining colonial ties to the motherland.

What led to such a hostile reaction that day in the marketplace, when an unpretentious book was considered so dangerous that it had to be burned? What was so unacceptable about what William Pynchon had written? And what resulted afterwards, when the flames died down?

Library in Boston. (Wright's reproductions were made from the last of these.) In 1961, Joseph H. Smith named the locations of eight copies. In 1992, the Worcester Polytechnic Institute Studies in Science, Technology, and Culture reprint noted that "nine copies . . . have been noted by bibliographers": the British Museum, New York Public Library, Springfield History Library and Archives of the Lyman and Merrie Wood Museum of Springfield History, the Congregational Library, as well as the Bodleian Library and the Balliol College at Oxford University, Newberry Library in Chicago, Huntington Library in San Marino, California, and the Free Library of Philadelphia.

This book will be cited hereafter as *The Meritorious Price* in the text, and *MP* in the notes.

Part I

A Puritan's Journey

1

The Rear Admiral under a Chilly Sun

FRIDAY, APRIL 23, 1630. A clear spring day on the north Atlantic—not really warm, but at least the landlubber passengers were recovering from the storms of the previous week. Some were on deck, gingerly testing their abilities to manage at sea. Staving off seasickness had been a challenge when the journey began. Now the brisk winds of the morning were dying down as the little fleet sailed west. The three ships in the vanguard sat becalmed just north of the forty-fifth parallel of latitude, sails hanging motionless from spars, hulls gently rising and falling on the slow sea swells. The company had nick-named their vessels: the *Arbella* was known as "The Admiral," the *Talbot* as the "Vice-Admiral," and the *Ambrose* as the "Rear-Admiral." Towards noon, Peter Milborne, master of the flagship *Arbella*, sent his skiff around to the *Ambrose* and the *Jewel* to collect the captains for a mid-ocean midday meal together. They would gather in the *Arbella*'s roundhouse, the captain's own uppermost cabin overhanging the stern. Their wives and other female relatives would be relegated to the "great cabin" on the deck just below.

The *Arbella* was a 350-ton merchant ship formerly known as the *Eagle*. She had been refitted for passengers and re-christened to honor Lady Arbella, daughter of the Earl of Lincoln and wife of Isaac Johnson. The Johnsons were on board and would be joining the captain for dinner. Transporting such a large number of persons and so many tons of freight across the Atlantic was an expensive business, and Lady Arbella acted as a very welcome and deeply appreciated financial patron of the voyage. The *Jewel*'s captain, Nicholas Hurlston, was ferried to the lead vessel. From the *Ambrose* they fetched Capt. John Lowe—and William and Ann Pynchon.

William Pynchon, Gentleman, had earned a seat at the captain's table. Now thirty-nine years old, William was the son of John and Frances Brett Pynchon. He was born in 1590, possibly on October 11, and probably at Writtle, a picture-perfect village a few miles west of the Essex County shire town of Chelmsford.[1] He married Ann Andrew sometime between 1615 and 1618. Ann was the daughter of William Andrew from Twywell, a village near Northampton in Nottinghamshire, eighty miles northwest of Springfield. The couple became parents of three daughters and a son. Anna was their firstborn, perhaps in 1620 or 1621; then came Mary, born around 1622; then Margaret, born sometime in 1624; and finally John, born in 1625 or 1626. Now the whole family was among the first wave of a huge undertaking which shared the goal of founding in New England a permanent outpost based on Puritan Reformation principles.

The English Reformation created an era of heady controversy in which religious disputes ran parallel to heated arguments about public values and the nation's governance. As Reformation convictions spread from their beginnings on the continent and deepened throughout the population in sixteenth-century Britain, new expectations developed for both church and society. Various emerging religious and political visions were in sharp competition with one another. Pynchon's home county of Essex was particularly alive with Puritan sentiments.

The name "Puritan" has acquired many dismissive and negative overtones during the centuries since their era. It is important, however, to peel away all the parodies in order to relocate the original nature of the Puritans' project. Their objective was an ambitious one: they aimed at nothing less than sweeping renewal throughout church and nation. They wanted to cultivate a deeper knowledge of the Bible across all segments of society. They sought to enforce stricter attention to morality through the application of Bible norms in both private and public life. They encouraged a wider role for citizens in communal affairs. In churches, Puritans worked for a more serious, more holy environment. Where they could, they initiated streamlined worship, which in their opinion echoed the practices of the early church. They rejected long-standing Christian traditions that they considered human inventions—so much for saints' days, liturgical seasons, and Christmas. In acts that earned them a reputation for aesthetic barbarism and vandalism, they removed

---

1. For a timeline of William Pynchon's life, see Appendix 1.

works of art in churches, including some stained glass windows, because they found them distracting to worship. Puritans pressed for university-educated pastors. The movement was particularly attractive to residents of cities and villages, which were home to an incipient middle class of self-employed craftsmen and merchants. It was a time when democratic aspirations were on the rise and feudal institutions held little appeal.[2]

A high proportion of those who led this cause came from East Anglia, the extensive region spanning Great Britain's eastern seaboard. Perhaps the greatest concentration came from Essex.[3] And at the heart of Essex, Chelmsford developed into a major center for the Puritan movement. The community had a history of feistiness. Centuries before, the June 1381 Peasants' Revolt (also known as Wat Tyler's Rebellion) emerged in large part out of Essex; Richard II dealt it a fatal blow in Chelmsford when he ordered thirty-one capital sentences to be carried out on the leaders. They were hanged on Primrose Hill in what one historian called "the grim theatre of royal vengeance."[4] By the early 1600s, Chelmsford was a growing community with probably somewhat more than 1,500 residents. The number of households prosperous enough to be taxed had risen 26 percent over the previous half-century, from 124 households in 1587 to 157 in 1642. In 1643 communicants numbered an estimated 2,000. As a market and legal center, the town provided numerous places where people could gather. The ancient Crown Inn, later known as the Great Black Boy, on the corner of Roman Road (Springfield Road) and the High Street, had served as a social center since the early 1300s. The George Inn at the center of town was a short walk up the road from the cathedral, St. Mary the Virgin, and next to the grammar school on Duke Street. It boasted six hearths and had provided hospitality ever since its founding as the Chequer in 1536.[5]

In the midst of this lively commercial hub, Puritan preaching and teaching abounded. One prominent voice was the Cambridge-educated Rev. Thomas Hooker (1586–1647), who proved to be an imaginative,

---

2. For a description of the essential features of the Puritan undertaking, see "Puritanism, Its Essence and Attraction," in Bremer, *Puritan Experiment*, 18–29; ibid., *Puritanism*, 2–3; ibid., *First Founders*, 3–7; Hall, *Worlds of Wonder*, 4–5, and ibid., *A Reforming People*, 194.

3. Fischer, *Albion's Seed*, 46–49.

4. Dunn, *Great Rising*, 136–37, 140.

5. On the population of Chelmsford in the early seventeenth century, see Jones, *Chelmsford*, 19; and Grieve, *Sleepers*, 2:3. On the Chequer, see Jones, *Chelmsford*, 22–26; and Grieve, *Sleepers*, 1:161, 169.

controversial speaker. As Lecturer at Chelmsford, he belonged to a wide-spread network whose purpose was to give public voice to the Puritan perspective. Using language suited to the community and its Puritan segment in particular, he frequently incorporated mercantile idioms into his sermons. For instance, in the final paragraph of "The Poor Doubting Christian" from 1629, he offered this analogy:

> When men use to make a purchase they will reckon up all and say, "There is so much wood, worth so much, and so much stock, worth so much;" and then they offer for the whole, answerable to all the parcels. So there is item for an heavenly mind, that is worth thousands, and item for an humble heart, that is worth millions.[6]

While Hooker's preaching reflected Chelmsford's commercial tradition, it also brought "flocks and tumults" to the market, which, as one scholar remarked, was "no small achievement during a severe depression." Years later, a colleague in New England would characterize Hooker as "a Man of a Cholerick Disposition, and . . . a Mighty Vigour and Fervor of Spirit," but with strong self-control, "as a Man has of a Mastiff Dog in a Chain." Area clergy were split into supporters and opponents of his ministry. Even though Hooker's position as Lecturer was funded privately and therefore was not dependent on ecclesiastical endorsement or support, when dueling petitions about him came to the attention of William Laud, the bishop of London, Hooker retreated in 1629 to a farm called "Cuckoos" a couple of miles away at Little Baddow. There he established a school and continued to preach and teach in pointed and provocative ways with the assistance of John Eliot, a recent Cambridge graduate who was just twenty-four years old. In time, Eliot became one of the most prominent ministers in Massachusetts. When Laud eventually threatened to censure Hooker he fled to Holland in 1630. Eliot left for Massachusetts in 1631. By 1633 Hooker, too, was on his way to New England.[7]

The Reformation movement also flourished in the Pynchons' ancestral village of Writtle. The population there seems to have been strongly divided in what was at one time a "nest of recusancy" dominated by the Petre family,

6. "The Poor Doubting Christian Drawn Unto Christ" in Williams, *Thomas Hooker*, 186. See also ibid., 152–86. On Hooker, see *ODNB*, 27:978–82.

7. The observation on "flocks and tumults" is from the London Public Record Office, quoted in Hunt, *Puritan Moment*, 198–99. The assessment of Hooker's character comes from Henry Whitfield of Guilford, Connecticut, and is reported in Mather, *Magnalia Christi Americana*, 3:64. On John Eliot, see *ODNB*, 18:63–65.

who were secretly Roman Catholics.[8] Even after the Puritan ascendency had reached its peak and failed, and a king regained the throne, the parish did battle with its long-term establishment rector. The Rev. John South spent his career from 1624 to 1663 serving the Writtle and nearby Roxwell churches. He stuck with the parish through the cataclysmic upheavals of the seventeenth century. But towards the end of his ministry he was obliged to turn to the bishop of Winchester for the £100 he expected annually. The people of Writtle and Roxwell refused to pay—though not because they could not afford to. A memorandum from his final year as rector read,

> hee intends hee saith to leave Writtle & deliver the Lease into our hands, to dispose of the Vicaridge unto whom wee please & to betake himselfe unto Pepper in Oxonshire ffor his now Parishioners at Writtle (as Mris Pynchon saies) doe not like his Preaching complaineing of his low voice, etc. They are most of them, they say, Presbyterians & against common prayer & therefore abide him not . . .[9]

Roxwell was probably the site of the Pynchon family's historic home, and home to quite a few other Puritans as well. Richard Younge of Roxwell (active 1636–1673) was a staunch Puritan and the author of dozens of tracts. In a preface composed for a collection of Younge's pamphlets, the well-known Puritan Richard Baxter (1615–1691) called him "an ancient and faithfull Servant of Christ [who] hath enriched this Nation with many of his Labours." An elegant dwelling called "Blackwalle," not far east of the Roxwell Church, continued to remain in Pynchon hands; a drawing of it, captioned with the name "Pinchon," appeared on a 1635 map of the area. Frances Rose-Troup identified more than a dozen people connected to this village, who were either investors in the Massachusetts Bay Company or participants in the Winthrop fleet or both, as "The Roxwell Group." Some had participated in earlier efforts to colonize New England.[10]

8. Hankins, "Papists, Power, and Puritans," 689–717.

9. "Copy of Notes of Progress of Warden Woodward of New College, Oxford," ERO, T/A 92/2, 12. South came to Writtle in 1624 and is listed in Platt, *All Saints Writtle*, 53. On Writtle and recusancy, see Hunt, *Puritan Moment*, 90, 146.

10. For Baxter's assessment of Richard Younge, see his preface to Younge, *A Christian Library*. Younge's biography is in *ODNB*, 60:956–57. The map showing the Pynchon property is "The plott of the Manor of Skreens of Teyhalle and of the farmes and lands vnto them same belonging," ERO, D/DGe P3. According to Rose-Troup, *Bay Company*, 162, those with identifiable connections to Roxwell, in addition to the Pynchons, included John, Kellam and Samuel Browne, Francis Flyer, Daniel and Anne Hodson, Thomas

The Winthrop fleet was a massive trans-oceanic undertaking. It was named after a principal in the Bay Company and chief organizer of the expedition, John Winthrop (1678–1649).[11] The fleet was tasked with supplementing the meager Puritan colony that had been planted two years before in Salem, Massachusetts. All told, about seven hundred immigrants were on board the seven passenger vessels in the flotilla. Since they could not be resupplied from England for a long while, an additional four ships carried stores they would need to become established in the New World, livestock they hoped to propagate, and their personal belongings.

The journey was slated to begin on March 29, 1630 from the port of Yarmouth on the Isle of Wight, but the ships got hung up at Cowes when the wind blew in the wrong direction. They finally took to the seas on April 8. A few slight mishaps occurred along the way. A dramatic pirate scare occurred at dawn on the second day, when eight unfamiliar ships appeared astern. Fearing just such an encounter, the captain had tested the "landmen's" marksmanship with muskets two days before the fleet left port. Now twenty-five passengers were enlisted to defend the ship alongside the sailors. The captain worried that the sails astern might be Spanish privateers from Dunkirk, so he made preparations for a fight. Hammocks were unhooked and stored, flammable material thrown overboard, and the *Arbella*'s guns were manned. Firearms were distributed to the men as the women and children were sent below decks. Then Capt. Lowe boldly brought the ship about to meet their pursuers head-on. But it turned out to be a false alarm; it was merely a convoy of friendly vessels bound for Canada. The only shots fired were friendly salutes, much to the relief of all. At another point in the journey, the *Ambrose* and the *Jewel* nearly collided when they stopped two suspicious ships, which proved to be a friendly Dutch man-of-war and the Brazilian cargo ship she had captured, both of them bound for the Netherlands. Another accident occurred when shrouds on the *Ambrose* broke one midnight, requiring emergency repairs. On Thursday, May 13, the *Ambrose*'s fore-topsail split under the force of heavy winds. And two of their cows died.

Even so, with the exception of some rough spring weather, the trip was comparatively uneventful. The voyage was made more pleasant by the sight of whales sporting and spouting alongside the ships as they cut through the waves, birds flying and floating on the water two hundred leagues from

and Margaret Waldegrave as well as their daughter Jemima and her husband, Sir Herbert Pelham, and Samuel and William Vassall.

11. For more on Winthrop, see Bremer, *John Winthrop*, and *ODNB*, 59:802–806.

any land, and even a swallow that landed on the ship ninety leagues south-west of the Scilly Isles. A couple of births occurred during the crossing. But several persons died; at least two on the *Ambrose*, while the *Talbot* lost a distressing fourteen.

The crossing offered unexpected observations and discoveries to any who were curious. The weather was colder than expected; the voyagers experienced mixed snow and rain as late as May 25. John Winthrop noted that it did not matter much from which direction the wind blew—it was always cold, and he advised any who planned to follow to bring plenty of warm clothing. Landlubbers found that being on such an unfamiliar expanse of open water played games with the senses. In Winthrop's observations, the mid-Atlantic "sun did not give so much heat as in England." He was disappointed that the eclipse of May 31, which was total at Land's End in Cornwall, was not at all visible from the western Atlantic. He thought the North Star was closer to the horizon than he expected. He was also tricked by an illusion that has fooled many: he thought the moon seemed smaller under a sky that touched the horizons in every direction.

Still, crossing the Atlantic was not so lonely as one might think. Winthrop spotted at least seven vessels in the course of the journey between the Lizard promontory near Land's End and the Isles of Shoals, New Hampshire. By early June, the flotilla's ships began arriving one by one in Salem harbor. The *Arbella* reached port on Saturday, June 12. When the leaders and their wives went ashore that afternoon for a celebratory meal with the Salem colonists, some of the women were so glad to be back on solid ground they did not return with their husbands to the ship that night. The *Ambrose* anchored on the thirteenth after sixty-six days at sea. By July 6, the entire fleet had crossed the Atlantic.[12]

But the impetus that motivated William and Ann Pynchon and their family to climb aboard the *Ambrose* in the first place to risk the difficult journey to the New World had its origins in a visionary plan that had been many years in the making. That vision took shape in a company that turned it into a venture. And the Bay Company's grand project captured the Pynchons' commitment and enthusiasm, enlisting their energies and inviting them on a journey between the old world and the new.

---

12. For details about the Winthrop flotilla, see Banks, *Winthrop Fleet*. A good supplement may be found at: Anne Stevens, 2012, "Pilgrim Ship Lists Early 1600's," http://www.packrat-pro.com/ships/shiplist.htm. The voyage is recounted by Winthrop, *Journal*, 1–34; and ibid., *History*, 1:1–31. The mid-ocean meal is mentioned in ibid., 1:15. Data on the solar eclipse may be found in Darren, "Millennium of British Solar Eclipses," 89–90.

2

A Royal Charter and Squantum Neck

NINE A.M., TUESDAY, AUGUST 29, 1629. A General Court of the Massachusetts Bay Company was called to order at the London home of Thomas Goffe, who often played host to the frequent Company meetings.[1] The agenda that morning raised a crucial and potentially far-reaching question: Should the Company physically take the royal Charter to America, and govern their new enterprise from there?

Twenty-seven partners of the Company had assembled the day before to prepare for a thorough discussion and debate. Two teams appointed the previous afternoon to present the arguments on either side had been caucusing since seven a.m. Sir Richard Saltonstall, Isaac Johnson, and Capt. John Venn took the pro position; Nathaniel Wright, Thomas Adams, and Theophilus Eaton argued against.[2]

William Pynchon had been part of the "Governor and Company of the Massachusetts Bay in New England" from its very beginnings. He was named repeatedly in the Company charter that Charles I issued on March 18, 1628.[3] The Bay Company was a joint stock corporation on the model of many others of the era. His Majesty's government granted multiple "patents" to investors, called "adventurers," to expedite the colonization of lands in North America.

1. On Goffe, see Rose-Troup, *Bay Company*, 143. At the time he owned, by himself or with others, the celebrated *Mayflower*, the ship of Pilgrim fame.

2. Not surprisingly, Wright, Adams, and Eaton did not join the Winthrop emigration. Eaton did emigrate in 1637 and served as the first Governor of New Haven.

3. The text of the charter is in Shurtleff, *MBCR*, 1:3–19. For provisions referenced in this paragraph, see ibid., 4 (boundaries), 10–11 (officers), 16–17 (making and enforcing laws), and 11 (Great and General Courts).

Because the earliest explorers could not give clear, consistent reports of the New World's geography, claims often overlapped, which led to much disputation and negotiation. Under the aegis of the Council for New England, headquartered at Plymouth, England, the king granted the Massachusetts Bay Company all lands between two outer bounds: from three miles north of the Merrimack River to three miles south of the Charles River. The charter further provided for everything the Company needed to function legally, including two officers—Governor and Deputy Governor—and a Board of Directors comprised of eighteen Assistants, one of whom was Pynchon. The charter gave the Company authority to replace retiring officers and raise up new ones by election from the freemen, as well as power to "make, ordeine, and establishe all manner of wholesome and reasonable orders, lawes, statutes, and ordinances, direccions, and instruccions not contrarie to the lawes of this our realme of England," and to "have full and absolute power and authoritie to correct, punishe, pardon, governe, and rule all" under their jurisdiction. It required quarterly general meetings called "Greate and Generall Courts." It specified quorums for conducting business.

Of course, the Company would have to pay a price for these corporate privileges. Remembering Spain's very successful and exploitative gold rush among the Indians of central and south America in the previous century, the king expected to receive 20 percent of all gold and silver the colonists could mine, an expectation that would prove fruitless. In addition, a 5 percent duty on imports and exports would be imposed after seven tax-free years.[4]

Though the Bay Company may not have been expected to amount to much at its inception, when Puritans began to buy up stock, and therefore control of the corporation, it became the premier sponsor of their emigration to New England. Pynchon played an active role. Minutes taken at Company meetings recorded his name repeatedly. From May 1629 onwards, he participated in most of the preparatory sessions during the critical year for launching the Company's expedition of 1630. At the request of fellow "Roxwell Group" Puritans (the Browne brothers, John and Samuel) he took their side when John Endecott sent them back from Salem for being "fractious." Their offense had been agitating for the use of the *Book of Common Prayer*.[5]

But Pynchon was also among the provocateurs on the Company's board; he sought to goad the Bay Company into action. With eleven others,

---

4. See the charter's taxation stipulations in Shurtleff, *MBCR*, 1:9, 14–15.

5. The Browne brothers requested that Pynchon and William Vassall, also from "The Roxwell Group," defend them. Their complaint turned into a demand for compensation from the Company (McIntyre, *William Pynchon*, 7; Shurtleff, *MBCR*, 1:51–54, 60, 69).

including "Roxwell Group" members Kellam Browne (John and Samuel's brother) and William Vassall (1592–ca. 1656), Pynchon signed the Cambridge Agreement of August 26, 1629. The signatories promised one another

> to embarke for the said plantacion by the first of march next . . . to inhabite and continue in New England. Provided alwayes that before the last of September next the whole governement together with the Patent for the said plantacion bee first by an order of Court legally transferred and established to remayne with us and others which shall inhabite upon the said plantacion.[6]

This declaration effectively set an ultimatum for the Company, and made the August 29 meeting necessary.

It may have been assumed in some quarters that such a motion was illegal. Did not the charter require the Company to maintain a London headquarters? This supposition apparently prompted a legal challenge launched years later, in 1637, by a *Quo Warranto* ("by what warrant?") which charged the Bay Company with violating its charter in a number of ways. The chief complaint Great Britain's Attorney General John Banks lodged at that time claimed that the Company had overstepped its bounds by taking on governmental functions. Indeed, concern over the independent direction of their Puritan colony led the Lords Commissioners for Foreign Plantations to write to Winthrop on April 4, 1638, ordering him to send the charter back. But the *Quo Warranto* contained no direct challenge to transporting the document to Massachusetts, and Winthrop kept it in Massachusetts. Actually, nothing in the charter itself prevented the Company from moving its operations across the Atlantic, and much required it. The Charter clearly permitted and even specified many powers related to governing the Company's enterprises by empowering it to enact legislation and "rule all."[7]

6. The relevant section of the Cambridge Agreement reads in its entirety: "It is fully and faithfully agreed amongst us, and every of us doth hereby freely and sincerely promise and bynd himselfe in the word of a Christian and in the presence of God who is the searcher of all hearts, that we will so really endevour the prosecucion of his worke, as by Gods assistaunce we will be ready in our persons, and with such of our severall familyes as are to go with us and such provisions as we are able conveniently to furnish ourselves withall, to embarke for the said plantacion by the first of march next, at such port or ports of this land as shall be agreed upon by the Company, to the end to passe the Seas (under Gods protection) to inhabite and continue in New England. Provided alwayes that before the last of September next the whole governement together with the Patent for the said plantacion bee first by an order of Court legally transferred and established to remayne with us and others which shall inhabite upon the said plantacion" (Forbes, *WP*, 1:152).

7. Karr, "Missing Clause," 89–107, especially 95–96. For the text of "A Quo Warranto brought against the Company of the Massachusetts Bay by Sir John Banks

Now, following the Company's lengthy debate as they met in London three days later, Deputy Governor Goffe called the question: "As many of you as desire to have the patent and the government of the plantation to be transferred to New England, so as it may be done legally, hold up your hands: So many as will not, hold up your hands."[8]

The motion carried.

From that significant turning point, Pynchon took several steps to make ready for a new life in the New World. Right after the critical meetings at Cambridge and at the Goffe house in London, Pynchon deposited £25 with the Company. This modest outlay may have been a second installment, but according to the Company treasurer's receipt, the investment guaranteed Pynchon "a division of lands and an adventure of Stock."

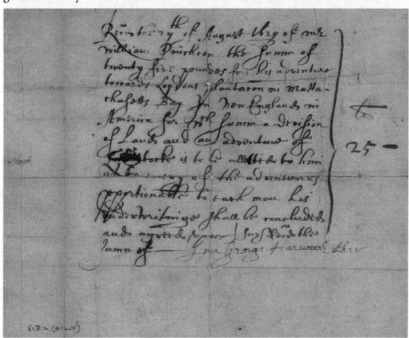

Massachusetts Bay Company stock certificate, August 29, 1629

The Company asked him to take on the task of procuring munitions on their shopping list. To add to the five cannons already on hand, Pynchon was charged with buying one hundred swords, ninety muskets and other personal arms, a whole-culvering (a type of cannon capable of firing

---

Attorney-General," see Hutchinson, *Collection*, 101–103.

8. Shurtleff, *MBCR*, 1:51.

a forty-to sixty-pound shot), a couple of smaller, more portable cannons known as drakes, and a lot of powder and shot to go with them. His budget was £500.[9]

But he and Ann had to take an even more demanding personal step to get ready to emigrate: they divested themselves of their holdings in Springfield.

The Pynchon family had long lived in the vicinity of Chelmsford. Pynchons had owned farmlands in the area of Writtle since the late 1400s. William Pynchon's great-grandfather William (1513–1552) may have been an innkeeper in Writtle. His grandfather John (1534–1573) owned land west of Writtle at Cooks Mill Green, on the western edge of Chelmsford at Wick Street, and properties further afield, including at Bradwell-on-Sea. His father, also named John (1564–1619), inherited the holdings in Cooks Mill Green and Wick Street.

But beginning in 1595, John expanded in other directions. Over time, he acquired additional properties as far to the east of Chelmsford as Danbury. When he died at the age of forty-six in late 1619, these holdings included lands and tenements in the family's traditional area of Writtle as well as a farm in Springfield.[10]

John Pynchon bought the Springfield lands, named "Barneswell Fields" and "Barneswell Moors," a mile or so to the east of Chelmsford from Robert and Martha Pease on February 1, 1597. The symbolic recorded cost, which was not necessarily the actual price, was £80. The very name "Barneswell," as well as a 1617 map that shows the location of "Mistress Pinchons field," suggests that the Pynchon property was within Sir Thomas Mildmay's Springfield Barnes manor.[11]

9. The receipt for Pynchon's investment is found in Massachusetts Historical Society, "Pincheon Papers," 228, and is also reproduced in Adams, *Founding*, 128. The original is held at the Massachusetts Historical Society. Munitions requirements are listed in Shurtleff, *MBCR*, 1:26, 62.

10. Genealogical data on the Pynchons may be found in Waters, *Gleanings*, 2:845–67. John Pynchon's will is in ibid., 854–55. It makes no mention of his sixty acres in Danbury.

11. The record of John Pynchon's purchase of the Springfield property is in Waters, *Gleanings*, 2:863. Scarcely half a year after the purchase John had to deal with a crime on his property when Robert Roylann, a laborer from Maldon, broke into the Pynchons' yard on June 18, 1597, and stole a ram worth 5s. The miscreant was found guilty at Brentwood on June 30, 1597 ("Calendar of Essex Assize Records," ERO, T/A 418/64/54). The "Mistress Pincheon" field is shown in "A new and perfect platt of the mannors of

Field near Pease Hall, Springfield Barnes Manor

The Mildmay story bears mention here because it illustrates the burst of social mobility and change that occurred in the sixteenth century. The Mildmays were particularly successful entrepreneurs who came from Essex's rapidly emerging middle class. Sir Thomas' grandfather Thomas (1515–ca. 1566) operated a stall at the Chelmsford market, and a very successful one at that; with his earnings he bought one of the grandest houses in town from the one-time lord chancellor, Sir Richard Rich.[12] But the fortunes of his de-

Springfielde Hall and Dukes," ERO, D/DGe P2/1.

12. For more on Rich, see *ODNB*, 46:680–83.

scendants were in great part due to the dissolution of monastery lands from 1536 to 1541, when King Henry VIII confiscated Roman Catholic Church properties. Thomas the merchant's son, also Thomas, Esq., was among other things an auditor with the Court of Augmentations, the agency that dealt with properties formerly belonging to religious houses. In 1540 he purchased the manor of Moulsham, directly across the river from Chelmsford. In 1563 he bought the manor of Chelmsford itself, called Bishop's Hall. Thomas' younger brother, Sir Walter (1523–1589), was prominent in his own right. In addition to being a founder of Emmanuel College at Cambridge, Sir Walter joined Thomas in managing royal properties. With his ability to adapt nimbly to changing circumstances, he had a distinguished career that remarkably spanned the reigns of Henry VIII, Edward VI, Mary, and Elizabeth I. A third sibling, William (1516–1570), clearly benefited from his brothers' important connections. When the Cistercians' Coggeshall Abbey fell into bankruptcy in 1538 in the course of Reformation, Edward VI eventually gave its properties near Chelmsford to William Mildmay, making him lord of Springfield Barnes Manor. This William was father of Sir Thomas (1539–1612). Thus, the Mildmays moved from operating a market stall in Chelmsford, to counselors of kings, to lords of the manor and knights of the realm.[13]

Sir Thomas himself created connections in another direction when he married Alice Winthrop, the aunt of John Winthrop. Sir Thomas and Alice had attended a celebratory banquet when the future Governor of Massachusetts dropped out of Cambridge at the age of seventeen to marry Mary Foorth (or Forth) in 1605. The Mildmay and Winthrop families had one other close link as well: as Thomas married Alice, late in life his widowed father, William, married Alice's widowed mother, Agnes.

The Mildmay and Pynchon families also had much in common. They represented two patterns of socially upward aspiration in the sixteenth century. The Mildmays' path was by urban investment, the Pynchons' by agricultural expansion. Business, rather than marriage, shaped the links between the two families over the generations. Like William's grandfather John, Sir Thomas' uncle (who shared with him the Mildmay family's favorite first name, Thomas) was also a justice of the peace. In 1570, the two of them together fined the vicar of Witham 3s. 4d. "for instigating the servant to Edward Dawny to leave his service." And in 1597, the year of John Pynchon's purchase of the Springfield farm, Sir Thomas Mildmay of Springfield

13. For more on the Mildmays, see Grieve, *Sleepers*, 2:1–4

Barnes had John witness a document related to Mildmay's purchase of the Chequer Inn in Chelmsford.[14]

The Pynchon lands in Springfield Barnes consisted of flat fields that sloped very gently down to the banks of the River Chelmer. This was the estate William inherited when he reached the age of twenty-one in the year following his father's death. The property included a house and farm buildings, a garden and orchard, twenty-six acres of land, plus a ten-acre pasture. From his mother's brother, Thomas Brett, William inherited properties to the north of Chelmsford in Broomfield in late 1616. He also inherited properties his father had leased as "copyholder," and did fealty for those lands to Sir John Tyrell, the lord of the Springfield Dukes manor, in 1622.[15]

Pynchon's Appearance at Springfield Dukes Manorial Court, 1622.
Reproduced by courtesy of the Essex Record Office, Chelmsford, United Kingdom.

Farm life demanded that William Pynchon acquire a variety of practical skills. He even picked up some rudiments of medicine along the way.

14. Emmison, *Elizabethan Life*, 3:172. Winthrop, *Life and Letters*, 58–59. The September 1597 document conveying the "Chequer" to Thomas Mildmay of Barnes and witnessed by John Pynchon is found in the ERO, Conveyance (Bargain and Sale enrolled) D/DP/O30/9–10 September, 1597.

15. The inheritance from the brother of Pynchon's mother is recorded in Dean, *Register*, 48:251–52. For his Barneswell lands, see "Manorial Court Roll for Springfield Dukes, Essex, 1603–1625," ERO, D/DGe M100; and also Smith, *Colonial Justice*, 70; hereafter cited as Smith, *CR*. A translation of Pynchon's manorial Court appearance is found in my Appendix 2.

Years later, he prescribed a plain diet for Ann Hopkins of Hartford in New England, plus an "attenuating drink" of a thin milk posset flavored with sugar and saffron. To treat a "hot subtell vapor which hath taken possession of [the] brain," he favored lettuce over "nosing powder tobacco," which he found "to violent." When Edward Hopkins thanked him for advice concerning his wife's illness, Pynchon responded, "my iudgment in phisike is but smale, what experience I have I brought with me out of England."[16]

But in January 1630, Pynchon's farming career came to an end when he and Ann transferred their Springfield lands. The buyer of his home, barns, and orchard—the property he held by freehold—was Thomas Hone, who may have been a relative. The record suggests that the Pynchons took a loss on the value of the property, since the £60 sale price was £20 less than the purchase. But they needed all the money they could raise quickly to migrate to New England and to finance a new start there. Their rented "copyhold" lands were transferred to William Bentoll, yeoman, probably at the same time.[17]

In cutting ties with Springfield in such an absolute way, the Pynchons ended a deep relationship with their community. William Pynchon had served as churchwarden of All Saints', the Springfield parish, from 1619 to 1620 and again in 1624. In that capacity, he was a chief lay officer responsible for order and well-being in that part of Chelmsford. A painted wooden board preserved in the belfry records that "William Pinchion" and John Stansted, the two churchwardens in 1624, played a part in enclosing the belfry and altering the stairs to the fourteenth-century Norman tower, as well as adding new pews and rearranging the chancel around a new communion table. A legacy of £40 from Roberte Robinson made these improvements possible. Though the words on a stone plaque on the south side of the church tower were engraved some years before Pynchon was born, they could have applied to him as well: "Prayse God for al the good benefectors."[18]

16. Ford, "Letters of William Pynchon," 55–56. Pynchon's recipe for sugar infused with saffron was "to every ounce of sugar good 3 grains of saffron made into fine powder," to be used "eather in posset drink or in warmed bere" (ibid.).

17. The record of William Pynchon's sale of the Springfield property is in Waters, *Gleanings*, 2:863. The relationship of William Pynchon's first cousin, Jane, to the Hone family may be found in Burt, *Cornet Joseph Parsons*, 93. The acquisition of the rented lands is recorded as: "Item. I give unto Edward Bentoll my sonn all that my house & lands in Springfield which I lately purchased of William Pinchon gentleman upon condition that my said sonn Edward shall surrender & make Mary Bentoll my daughter" ("Will of William Bentall of Springfield, yeoman," ERO, D/ABW 50/45).

18. See Paynter, *Short History*, 13; and Shadrack, *Historical Notes*, 14–15. My thanks

All Saints' Church, Springfield, England

Pynchon's terms as churchwarden offered a valuable, if unintention-
al, apprenticeship for roles he would be called upon to play later in life.
Numerous infractions of one sort or another always required resolution.
Reports from his terms of service also reveal that Puritan goals motivated
the Springfield parish's leadership. Throughout the Elizabethan era, since
the queen's accession in 1572, stricter observance of Sunday as the Lord's
day (as well as the end of saints' days celebrations) was on the reformers'
agenda.[19] Local authorities were keen to enforce Sabbath-keeping laws, and
Pynchon was particularly concerned about this. The 1620 report detailed
"[t]he great disorders of certain alehouse-keepers in Springfield":

> Benjamin Davis (husbandman), being unlicensed, had company
> in his house in the time of divine service on 29 November and at
> other times. Peter Buckely (husbandman), unlicensed, had com-
> pany in his house at cards in the time of divine service likewise.
> Margaret Marshall (widow), unlicensed, had company in her
> house on Sunday before St. Andrew, there was drinking all the

---

to the Reverend Raymond John Brown, Rector, for making it possible to visit the church
and see the painted board.

19. Hill, *Society and Puritanism*, 160–61.

time of service and sermon in the afternoon, and so likewise there was company on the Sunday before St. Thomas's day. Witness, Fra. Smyth, but for the two foremost William Pynchon does justify, being churchwarden and having a constable.[20]

Other Sabbath disruptions also attracted the wardens' attention: "Thomas Herridge, carrier, of Chelmsford comes into our town with his carriage on the Sabbath days and often times in time of divine service and sermon-time." The creaking and clanking of his cart would have disturbed the intended reverential quiet of the day.[21]

The 1625 report by Springfield parish authorities, including the churchwardens, revealed a wide range of issues confronting the parish. Questions of community order, unemployment, inadequate housing and overcrowding, and drunkenness and brawling were all matters demanding the authorities' attention. During their time in office, Pynchon and his fellow warden (John Stansted again) had to deal with five men and one woman who lived in the parish but lacked incomes because they were out of work. In other segments of the report, the wardens cited Henry Field "for annoying the highway by casting a ditch a year hence and leaving the soil there to the offence of all passengers, 20 loads." Shortly before Christmas, on December 15, William Betts of Boreham came "drunk into the house of Benjamin Davis," the Sabbath-breaker of four years previous, and "did there profanely swear two several oaths and being then reproved for it by William Bradley constable, did scandalously revile him by many evil names and speeches, offering to strike him with danger of his life, had he not been by others there present hindered." Peter Buckely was still "victualling without licence." But most scandalous of all, "Matthew Newell doth victual in the parish without licence and further doth harbour in his house four men as sojourners who are very inhumanely and brutishly lodged in the same chamber where he and his wife do lie, there being no partition in the said chamber, to the great offence of the whole parish."[22]

The officials' reports offered ample evidence of social fractures in Essex society in the early 1600s. In the heady enthusiasm of the voyage to the New World, the émigrés may have cherished a hope that vices such as these had been left behind once and for all in old England—but subsequent events would clearly prove otherwise.

20. "Presentment by the Grand Jury, January 14, 1620," ERO, Q/SR 227/13

21. Ibid.

22. "Presentment by the constables, overseers church wardens and surveyors of Springfield," ERO, Epiphany 1625, Q/SR 247/48A.

Within a very brief while after arriving at Salem, many of the newcomers journeyed south seeking potential sites to settle, and the Pynchons went with them. The explorers concentrated their investigations on the heart of Massachusetts Bay, on the hills, headlands, marshes, and inlets at the mouths of the Charles and Mystic and Neponset Rivers—areas that were to become Charlestown, Boston, Dorchester, and Roxbury. The Pynchons settled in Dorchester, which then included land around the southern end of the part of Boston Harbor now known as Dorchester Bay. Pynchon built a house and barn on the south side of the Neponset River in what is now Quincy. His holdings consisted of forty acres of upland, forty of marsh, and twenty acres on a headland that extends into the harbor known as Squantum Neck.[23]

Marsh on the Neponset River, Dorchester (Quincy)

But shortly after their arrival—it may have been on August 30, 1630—in circumstances no longer known, Ann died. William was left to raise their four children, who ranged in age from the young teenaged Anna to their only son, five-year-old John.[24]

23. City of Boston, *Dorchester Town Records*, 7.

24. The date of Ann's death comes from Betty Tikker Davis, July 11, 2000, "Nicholas Pynchon & Seven Generations," http://genforum.genealogy.com/pynchon/messages/1.html.

The widower responded to this tragedy in keeping with expectations of the era: he remarried. His new wife, Frances Sanford, was herself a widow twice over, and the mother of Henry Smith, who was twenty years old at the time. The two of them had been among the 140 passengers of the so-called "Dorchester Company." This tightly-knit group had crossed to America on the *Mary and John*, arriving on March 20, just a few days before the Winthrop flotilla left the Isle of Wight. The Dorchester colonists had all been recruited, encouraged, and to some extent subsidized, through the efforts of Rev. John White (1575–1648), rector of Trinity Church in Dorchester.[25] White himself never came to America, but he remained an indefatigable supporter of emigration to Massachusetts. Sixty or seventy passengers on the *Mary and John*, including Frances and Henry, came from the Dorset towns of Bridport, Thorncombe, and Dorchester in southwestern England. The company was well-organized, with a strong *esprit de corps*. They gathered as a church before leaving England and brought their own leadership with them: the Revs. Thomas Maverick and John Warham, as well as lay leaders Roger Ludlow and Edward Rossiter.[26] Frances had been a stalwart member of that church, and her new husband, William, was also a trusted friend of the Dorchester Company. When White needed an agent to recover monies due him in 1631, he used the good offices of William Pynchon to collect an outstanding sum of £15 2s. to reimburse him for supplies White had shipped to the late Edward Rossiter.[27]

Soon, however, the newly blended Pynchon-Sanford-Smith family left the past behind yet again and made a fresh start together by moving a few miles northwest to Roxbury. Pynchon acquired acreage there from Chickataubut, sachem of the Massachuset tribe. This leader was actually a Dorchester neighbor whose headquarters were very close to Squantum Neck on Moswetuset Hummock. Chickataubut was a skilled politician; he became involved in many interactions with the vast wave of English immigrants to New England, beginning with the Pilgrims. While he always adamantly defended Indian rights, he also did his best to get along with the newcomers.[28] The transfer of property from Chickataubut to Pynchon

25. On the Rev. John White, see *ODNB* 58:594–96.

26. For the *Mary and John* passenger list, see Mary and John Clearing House, 2013, www.maryandjohn1630.com.

27. White's bill is detailed in Ford, "Supplies for Massachusetts Bay, 1631–1632," 343–47. Pynchon had met White at numerous meetings of the Massachusetts Bay Company in London in 1629.

28. For the life and exploits of Chickataubut, see Drake, *Book of the Indians*, 2:43–44.

may have been the first of what would turn out to be many transactions Pynchon carried out with Native people.

Squantum Neck, Dorchester (Quincy)

Once settled in Roxbury, Pynchon played important roles in shaping the new community. In 1632 he joined the Rev. Thomas Weld and Hooker's old associate in Chelmsford, the Rev. John Eliot, in organizing

---

The boundaries of Pynchon's new property proved to be uncertain, however, and had to be verified (with the help of the sachem's Native colleagues) in July 1635, after Chickataubut's death (Shurtleff, *MBCR*, 1:151–52).

the First Church of Roxbury. The two clergymen became Pastor and Teacher (or associate minister) respectively, of the new congregation. Eliot became the better known of the two as the "Apostle of the Indians," translator of the Bible into Algonquian, and an advocate for the Native peoples of Massachusetts. Pynchon's name, plus a description of his exploits, headed the church members' list, followed by the name only of the pastor, "Mr Thomas Weld."[29]

Pynchon's name appeared on other important lists as well. He continued to participate regularly in the Bay Company's monthly government meetings as a member of the Court of Assistants, the Governor's Council. For almost two years, from August 1632 to May 1634, Pynchon served the Massachusetts Bay colony as "Mr Treasurer." In the oath he took when he was sworn in, Pynchon promised to use "all convenient dilligence" in collecting sums due and paying the colony's debts, with the important and practical proviso, "if I shall have it in my hands."[30]

In addition to functioning as treasurer, from time to time the Court assigned Pynchon specific responsibilities. They cast him in the role of armaments expert, not because of any military experience he had, but probably because of his prior assignment to secure munitions in England and his familiarity with such military equipment as culverins, sakers, wadhooks, and bandoleers. On September 25, 1634, the Court asked him to distribute "all such ordinances, goods, & accompts as are nowe sent in the shipp *Griffin*, by Mr Keane, as p[ar]cell of Doctr Wilsons guifte to the plantacon." It took Pynchon almost two years to allocate that bonanza of armaments equitably to the various towns in the Bay by supplementing the weapons the communities already had on hand.[31]

In every respect—as landholder, churchman, Governor's Assistant, and Colony's Treasurer—William Pynchon was firmly integrated into the early Massachusetts enterprise, a leader in the Commonwealth who was clearly respected by his fellow Puritans.

29. Eliot, "Record," 70.

30. Shurtleff, *MBCR*, 1:353.

31. Numerous citations in the first three volumes of *MBCR* give details of Pynchon's public service and the beaver trade. The assignment to deal with new munitions is found in ibid., 1:125, 128. His final report on that assignment, dated September 8, 1636, is in Massachusetts Historical Society, "Pincheon Papers," 228–30.

3

Beaver Pelts and Jaw Harps

TUESDAY, SEPTEMBER 28, 1630. The Bay Company Assistants gathered at the usual hour of 8 a.m. in the governor's dwelling at Charlestown. The "Great House," as it was somewhat grandiloquently called, had been built by an advance party the Company had sent over a year before Winthrop's arrival. It stood on the north bank of the Charles River, on a low-lying neck of land very near the harbor. This capitol *pro tem* of the Massachusetts Bay colony was a primitive structure. It measured sixteen feet by thirty-two, stood two stories high, with four rooms in all, and was clad in plain siding attached to a barn-like post and beam framework. Though lacking a real foundation or cellar, it was anchored in place by heavy uprights set directly into the ground. In spite of this simple setting, Court sessions were treated as occasions of considerable importance. The Court levied fines of a noble (100d.) apiece on William Pynchon, Roger Ludlow, and Edward Rossiter when they all showed up late for a meeting on September 7.[1]

The colony's government convened this morning for its last session in Charlestown; the next month, the Court relocated to Boston. Moving to the other side of the river worked so well that by November 1632, everybody felt Boston was "the fittest place for public meetings of any place in the Bay."

---

1. For details on the Great House, see Thompson, *From Deference to Defiance*, 212. Pre-decimal money in the United Kingdom consisted of a bewildering variety of coins and categories. In Pynchon's era, the basic units and their symbols were these:
pound (£ or *l.*), shilling (s.), and penny (d.).
The values were: 12 pennies = 1 shilling, 20 shillings = 1 pound.
Other terms included the "noble," which equaled 100 pence or 8s. 4d., and the "mark," which came to 160 pence or 13s. 4d. and amounted to 2/3 of a pound.

Not all of the regulars could attend on September 28. Isaac Johnson was absent, probably because the patroness Lady Arbella, his twenty-nine-year-old wife, had died just a month before. Sir Richard Saltonstall, the developer of Watertown, also did not come, but two more than a quorum of seven were present. Those who gathered that morning represented the core leadership of the colony. The ever-serious and usually respected Governor John Winthrop presided, flanked by his collaborator and sometime rival, Deputy Governor Thomas Dudley. Also at the table was the occasionally irascible and often unpredictable Capt. John Endecott of Salem, who had preceded Winthrop as governor but ceded his role to the newcomer now that the full fleet had arrived. The young magistrate, politician, and developer Simon Bradstreet (he was also Thomas Dudley's son-in-law) was in attendance, as well as two who would go on to important roles in other colonies: Roger Ludlow, later a pioneer in the Hartford colony, and William Coddington, who was to join Roger Williams (1606[?]–1683) in founding Rhode Island. Edward Rossiter, the oldest of the Assistants, was attending his last Court meeting before his death that autumn. The indefatigable colony secretary, Increase Nowell, was at the table to take minutes. And William Pynchon completed the assembly.

One item on the agenda offered a preview of numerous future deliberations and decisions that would need to take place as the Massachusetts colony came to grips with a huge question: What should be done about relationships between English colonists and the Natives? It was a concern that loomed large in William Pynchon's life and work. Even at its earliest moments, the Puritan incursion into New England and the resulting clash of cultures introduced alien dynamics to both societies. Neither colonists nor Indians were prepared for these conflicts. For their part, the English hoped to manage intercultural relationships with Indians just as they dealt with relationships in their own communities—through laws and regulations. At this late September meeting, the Court enacted legislation to restrict the use of firearms to settlers only:

> It is ordered, that no person whatsoever shall, either directly or indirectly, employ, or cause to be employed, or to their power permit, any Indian to use any piece upon any occasion or pretence whatsoever, under pain of X£ fine for the first offence, & for the 2 offence to be fined & imprisoned at the discretion of the Court.[2]

2. Shurtleff, *MBCR*, 1:75–76. In the original record, X£ indicates £10. On Boston's status as the favored meeting place, see ibid., 1:101.

This was only the first of many "orders" that dealt with Indian-English relations. Another regulation, for example, addressed the Natives' habit of entering settlers' homes unannounced, which really unnerved the English. The colonists were troubled as well by the Indians' practice of treating domestic swine and cattle as game. The Indians, on the other hand, sought compensation for damage done to their crops by the settlers' livestock. Sexual relations between English and Indians were mentioned as a matter of concern, but never decisively addressed, much less resolved. The giving or selling of alcohol to Native people as well as land sales and purchases involving Indians were also among the intercultural issues the Court faced, but rarely settled, in its first five years.[3]

Even in his earliest weeks and months in New England, Pynchon was no doubt already developing trading contacts with Native peoples. Indian skills and Indian labor were so essential to the development of Massachusetts Bay that some Natives were directly caught up in the colony's economy even from the beginning. The English brought with them a concept of workforce that spanned a wide gamut, from gentleman to husbandman to indentured servant to slave. Early on, the Court required that anyone who had, as they euphemistically phrased it, "received" Indian servants, must release them by May 1, 1631. But actions belied this policy. Another vote permitted the Winthrop family to keep Natives essentially as household slaves, though the word was assiduously avoided.[4]

William Pynchon's own relationship with Indians never involved their enslavement, though slavery was introduced to western Massachusetts after he was no longer there. Nor were Indians brought into Pynchon's community through indentured servitude. Rather, they were employed as subcontractors in the difficult labor of harvesting fur, and were paid at as low a rate as Pynchon could barter. The Court's anti-gun law would be of no help in his commercial efforts. Interestingly, Pynchon was to run afoul of it himself when, in May of 1634, both he and Thomas Mayhew were fined because they hired Indians to go hunting with guns on their behalf.

3. These Indian-English concerns may be found in ibid., 1:89, 96 (entering homes), 87, 88, 143 (killing livestock), 99, 102, 121, 133 (damaged crops), 91, 140 (sexual relations), 106 (alcohol sales), and 112 (land sales and purchases).

4. On the Winthrops as slaveholders, and others who followed them, see Manegold, *Ten Hills Farm*. General Court votes on Indians as "servants" may be found in Shurtleff, *MBCR*, 1:83, 127; the relaxed gun law is detailed in ibid., 1:127.

By September 1634, this blanket restriction was repealed, though Court permission was still required for hiring Natives to hunt with guns.[5]

Pynchon could easily reach the Charlestown Great House, and he could visit sites in Boston even more readily from his home in Roxbury. This settlement was a cluster of buildings at the end of the narrow neck of ground that afforded the only land approach to the Shawmut peninsula, where Boston lay. The location of Pynchon's property in Roxbury is no longer identifiable, but it was near what is now known as Dudley Square Plaza, which remains the site where the First Church in Roxbury has always been located. Here, Pynchon and his family engaged in farming, the indispensable occupation required of every colonist simply to survive. As they cleared land, developed fields, and erected buildings, they faced the multiple challenges of that do-it-yourself era. A smallpox epidemic that broke out in 1633 and spread rampantly across southern New England devastated Native communities from southern Maine to the Connecticut coast. While it virtually destroyed the Connecticut Valley Indian population, the contagion affected few European families. The Pynchons were spared, though a maid in their household, Mary Gamlin, tragically caught the disease and died.[6]

In addition to farming at Roxbury, Pynchon began to exercise his formidable skills as a dealer in furs. Trading with the Indians was a highly competitive business, even though it naturally entailed risks in such an unsettled land.[7] Pynchon came to this enterprise later than others. Not only did he vie with established traders in the Bay colony like John Endecott, the Pilgrims at Plymouth also depended on successful trade in fur to pay off their London creditors, and they operated a widespread rival business. The Plymouth network extended northward to an outpost established at Augusta, Maine, in 1628, eastward to the Penobscot River, and for a while, westward as far as Windsor, on the Connecticut River. Other competition came from the Dutch, who ventured northeast from New Amsterdam to trade at Saybrook, near the mouth of the Connecticut River, and from "Dutch Point," the site of the New Netherland colony's Fort Goede Hoop at what was to become Hartford. The Dutch also had reliable sources for wampum.

5. On Indian slavery in western Massachusetts, see Von Frank, "John Saffin," 269.

6. Eliot, "Record," 77; Thomas, "Maelstrom of Change," 53–54.

7. For the fur trade in early New England, see Phillips, *Fur Trade*, 1:113–45. The role of the fur trade in the development of North America is described in Dolin, *Fur, Fortune, and Empire.*

Every successful trader needed that currency, which was made of shells shaped into beads, because it was favored by Native peoples throughout the east. The Indian wampum factories were closer to New Amsterdam (one was at Cutchogue on Long Island). Meanwhile the French, pushing south from Quebec and the Maritimes in Canada, traded vigorously along the New England coast without the slightest regard for English or Dutch claims to the area.

Long before the Winthrop expedition arrived, the Bay Company had tried to control the fur trade in areas they governed. The Company sold beaver pelts on hand in England in September 1629. The price was 20s. (£1) for every pound of fur. The next month, the Company reserved the beaver trade as its own exclusive monopoly. But like the Pilgrims, the Bay Company faced the problem of recouping their hefty investment costs by trading in furs. They experimented with several varying and sometimes contradictory approaches. Initially they imposed a rather stiff tax of 15d. on every pound of beaver pelts, but that 6.25 percent rate proved impossible. By November 1630 (with operations now relocated to Massachusetts), the usual purchase price of 6s. per pound was repealed, leaving a free market. It became clear, however, that the enterprise needed some form of coordination and collaboration. In June of 1631, the Court encouraged those interested in the fur trade to meet with Endecott in order to allocate the beaver-rich territories amicably among themselves—or face government oversight. The Court went on to outlaw the unauthorized exporting of beaver in March 1632. In June of that year, they reverted to a previously discarded tactic when they imposed a 12d. or 5 percent tax on every pound of beaver fur acquired from the Indians. That, too, proved to be unworkable and was repealed three years later. Clearly, it was difficult to balance tax policy with an effective fur trade industry.

In the meantime, in June 1631 Pynchon skirted the various taxes the colony imposed by offering to pay a total of £25 for all of 1632. His proposal was accepted by the nine other Gentlemen on the Court of Assistants. He later reduced his payment to £20 on the grounds that he had not enjoyed an exclusive license for his community, as he believed the Court intended, and besides, nobody else paid more than £2 4s., scarcely 10 percent of what Pynchon paid. It seems possible, however, if not certain, that Pynchon got the better of the bargain. Accounts that John Pynchon kept in later decades indicate that in the 1650s pelts weighed on average just a little less than one-and-a-half pounds each. The sum William Pynchon paid for his licensing fee would have covered about 275 pelts, and these in turn would have yielded £400 in London at the Bay Company's 1629 wholesale price, which would be a fine profit.[8] Ironically, Pynchon's trading fortune was partially built on what could be considered contraband merchandise; the sale and wearing of "beavr hats" was outlawed in Massachusetts in 1634 as immoderate, ostentatious clothing.[9] Fortunately there were no such restrictions in England.

Business records from Pynchon's earlier years have not survived, but subsequent accounts testify to a substantial traffic in furs, far in excess of 275 pelts annually. In 1654, for example, after the enterprise had matured and John Pynchon was supervising the business, the Pynchon enterprise exported an impressive thirteen hogsheads of furs. They contained 3,572 pounds of beaver pelts, not to mention assorted otters, muskrats, sables, foxes, and raccoons.[10]

Since Pynchon was noted and trusted for his ability to manage money as well as his trading skills, he was invited to bring his financial expertise to public service. Figures from 1643 in the final account of his tenure as treasurer provide a glimpse into the needs and priorities of the colony. During Pynchon's term as treasurer, Massachusetts received £561 19s. 9½d., mostly from tax assessments paid by the various towns, plus some fines and beaver trade taxes. The colony's expenditures, at £560 17s. 8d., nearly equaled its income. Very little of the government's money was spent on human resources. Only four persons, all armed officers, were on the payroll: one salary plus a living allowance was for James Penn, the colony's Marshall, and three generous living arrangements (called "pensions") supported Massachusetts Bay's active professional military commanders, Capts. John Underhill and Daniel Patrick as well as Sgt. Richard Morris. Disbursements also included bounties on wolves; five Indians, among others, collected the

---

8. Deducting his unknown shipping and merchandising costs, his price for a license (£20), and purchase expenses (275 pelts at the former official purchase rate of 6s. per pound would be £123 15s.), Pynchon could have made more than £250.

9. Shurtleff, *MBCR*, 1:126.

10. Figures for the Pynchons' trade in later years are striking. See Judd, "Fur Trade," 217–19; and Phillips, *Fur Trade*, 135. O'Shea, "Puritans and Indians," 70, offers this summary: "The fur trade reached its highest level in 1653, the year after William Pynchon returned to England. The Pynchon account books reveal the dramatic decline of the fur trade after this. From 1651 to 1653, the Pynchons exported an average of 2,800 pounds of beaver pelt per year. Over the next four years Pynchon's son, John, exported an average of only 1,490 pounds per year. Thereafter, the decline continued." Court actions relating to beaver furs are detailed in Shurtleff, *MBCR*, 1:53, 81, 93, 96, and 140.

equivalent of a shilling per wolf killed. And then there were, as always, miscellaneous government payments, most of which could be categorized as defense expenditures. Although the colony's elected officials served without salaries, they could collect for expenses. In this regard, the treasurer paid the largest amount by far to the governor. Winthrop received nearly 60 percent of the total budget, a whopping £328 10s, to reimburse him for outlays on behalf of the Commonwealth.[11]

But Pynchon, the legislator, continued to chafe under regulations. Following his terms in office as Colony Treasurer, he became cranky about the government's taxation policies. Pynchon collected the first colony-wide tax, levied in 1633, which totaled £400. But after he left office, the second tax, in September 1634, was noticeably higher, at £600. Pynchon argued that so far as Roxbury was concerned, the rate was unfair. Roxbury had been assessed £70, second only to Boston, Dorchester, and Newtown (Cambridge), all £80 each. But Pynchon pointed to Roxbury's disadvantage because the soil in what originally—and appropriately— had been called "Rocksbury" was not very fertile. His principled stand cost him £5 when, in March of 1635, the General Court fined him for failing to pay his portion. Perhaps not coincidentally, the Court decided to audit his treasurer accounts shortly after levying this fine. A subsequent review confirmed his faithful stewardship. But Pynchon remained averse to taxes. Since he failed to keep paying for his beaver trading privileges, the Massachusetts General Court was forced to order him to remit what he owed in September 1642 and again one year later.[12]

The opposite of harvesting and exporting furs was importing and selling supplies and finished goods from England. Here Pynchon excelled. He may have partnered from time to time with John Winthrop, as he did in June 1634, when Winthrop helped Pynchon import six chalders of sea coal, about nine-and-a-half tons.[13] Sometimes Pynchon made deals that

11. Pynchon's treasurer accounts are found in Massachusetts Historical Society, "Pincheon Papers," 230–35.

12. On the Roxbury tax, see Shurtleff, MBCR, 1:129, 136. The successful audit is reported in ibid., 1:148. The Court's orders to Pynchon to pay for his beaver license are found in ibid., 2:31, 44.

13. Forbes, WP, 3:169. Winthrop contacted Capt. Thomas Graves on Pynchon's behalf, asking him to bring the coal on his next voyage. Winthrop had just successfully imported twenty chalders, about thirty-one tons, on the Mary and John, as well as window glass, vinegar, frying pans, four millstones, a chest of books, and castile soap. See Ford, "London Port Books," 179, for the manifest of February 17, 1634.

did not work out. In 1632, he traded with Sgt. William Bateman for twelve pairs of stockings that proved to be "badd & moath-eaten;" Pynchon had to take him to court. Still, Pynchon was a born salesman. This becomes clear from a 1636 letter to John Winthrop Jr. (1606–1676), the governor of the Saybrook colony and son of the Bay colony governor. The trader's voice is virtually audible as he hawked the dry goods he imported so profitably, boasting of some 225 yards of tawny, maroon, and liver-colored cloth, "the best that ever came to Quinettecott [Connecticut] . . . all these at 8s. per yard. better cloth by much then any I see here in the Bay." In addition to yard goods, Pynchon's Roxbury storehouse featured cookware, tools, and even toys. His price for a quart pot was 4s., and for a large porringer, 10½d. Small mirrors could be had for 2 1/3d. each. Large hoes went for 2s. Jaw harps (Jew's harps) were a penny apiece. Spoons, awls, you name it—Pynchon had it for sale.[14] At the time, Pynchon was holding a clearance sale in preparation for another move. Perhaps it was his persuasive salesmanship that enticed the younger Winthrop to buy four dozen jaw harps, for which he paid more than twice the London price. But Natives found them intriguing, so probably Winthrop bought them for trading with the Indians.[15]

Yet even as Pynchon's business was flourishing, he began to look in other directions and at other possibilities. His discomfort with some Bay colony economic policies may have been one consideration weighing on his mind. At a time when earlier notions of planned economy inherited from the medieval world still held sway, Pynchon saw a wider relevance of Reformation freedom. Just as surely as Protestant notions applied in political and ecclesiastical spheres, because Reformation practices put more authority in individual hands, those same convictions could also have a powerful impact on economic activity. As a result, Pynchon was a staunch advocate of free trade. He was present when the Massachusetts Court voted to repeal the fixed price for beaver. Years later he wrote to Roger Ludlow, "I cannot see how it can well stand with the public good and the liberty of free men to make a monopole of trade." He pointed out to Ludlow that planned economic control had been proposed but had not worked in the Bay colony. Free trade remained the only realistic policy. "I hope," Pynchon concluded, in one of the few self-reflective comments he ever made, "the Lord in his

14. The bad stockings deal is detailed in Shurtleff, *MBCR*, 1:98. On William Bateman, see Anderson, *Great Migration*, 1:130–31. Pynchon touting yard goods is in Forbes, *WP*, 3:286. Other goods and prices are in Pynchon's bill to Winthrop Jr. in ibid., 3:238.

15. According to the *Booke of Rates* published in 1631 by the London Customs Office, jaw harps cost 5s. per gross in London, or twelve for 5d. (Wright, "*Jews Trumps*," 43).

mercy will keep me from coveting any unlawful gaine: or [consenting to] any man's hindrance where God doth not hinder them."[16]

Furthermore, in addition to the economic policies that Pynchon found so constraining, shifting patterns in the fur trade were also troubling. The eastern seaboard was clearly becoming too crowded for his enterprise. The most accessible stocks of beaver were shrinking rapidly, due in part to Pynchon's own success. Future prospects for hunting and trading along the coast were not bright. For all its possible risks, a move to the frontier, where he would be closer to the inland fur supply, made sense.

Additionally—and this was most important—out on the frontier, Pynchon would be much nearer his fur-trading partners, the Indians.

16. Nichols, "Letter of William Pynchon," 388, quoted in Morison, *Builders*, 354.

4

Canoes and Cotinackeesh

EARLY MAY, 1636. EIGHT explorers nosed their canoes westward into a tribu-
tary of the Connecticut, paddling about half a mile up the treelined river the
Native peoples called Woronoco to the place they called Agawam. A low-
lying meadow there provided an open space on the river's southern bank.
An oxbow of stagnant water defined this field on its landward side, tracing
an ancient bend in the river that dated from when the Woronoco meandered
along a long-forgotten prehistoric bed. On reaching their destination, the
pioneers dragged their crafts up onto the muddy shore, unloaded their gear,
and carted it into the lush, green meadow. They had come to stay.

Mouth of the Agawam (Westfield) River

The English had visited this particular place before. A colonists' building already stood on the meadow. William Pynchon had identified the site the previous fall, when he carried out a preliminary exploration of the area. He was accompanied then by John Cable, John Woodcock, and an Indian interpreter. They had put up some sort of simple structure in the meadow, which the English ever after called "The House Meadow."

Now, they had come back to this field to take the first step towards founding a new plantation. In typical Puritan fashion, they entered a covenant together when, on May 14, 1636, Pynchon and seven others joined in a written agreement to create a new community. Their basic constitution listed thirteen resolutions and regulations, with the initial article acknowledging the bedrock requirement for any Puritan settlement:

> We intend by God's grace as soon as we can with all convenient speed to procure some Godly and faithful minister with whom we purpose to Join in Church Covenant to walk in all the ways of Christ.[1]

Other paragraphs specified that the new settlement would consist of forty families, or fifty at the most, and would include both rich and poor. Each family would have a house lot in "convenient proportion . . . for everyones quality and estate." All would have shares in a pasture area north of the settlement, in the "Long Meadow" to the south, and in either meadow or planting lands in what is now West Springfield and Agawam, the site where the settlers first landed and where cattle and oxen were grazed. Pasturage was particularly important, because "estate is like to be imp'ved in Cattel," as the town record subsequently observed. (The names Longmeadow and Feeding Hills remain attached to the landscape to the present day.) House lots would be laid out along a primitive street that roughly paralleled the river. Everybody would also receive a portion of the low-lying marshlands that ran along the eastern side of this street.

The Springfield covenant was crafted with careful attention to a Puritan core value, the "principle of equity."[2] Real estate taxes were to be levied proportionally. In fact, all was to be done "accordingly to every ones proportion," including taxes on land "aker for aker." Its underlying theme was fairness for all. The covenant's phrasing made it very clear that everyone was supposed to be treated right. That included granting extra acreage to three

1. Burt, *First Century*, 1:156.
2. Hall, *A Reforming People*, 143.

of the founding settlers—namely, Pynchon, his stepson Henry Smith, and Jehu Burr—as a reward for their continuing commitment to the venture "when others fell off for feare of the difficultys." Expenses for establishing the settlement would be born over time by all recruits to the community. Those costs included the price of two small boats known as shallops, which were used for moving to the valley, and a surprisingly inexpensive £6 for the original "House Meadow" shelter. Finally, any trees cut for timber and left on the ground for more than three months would be fair game for anyone. Within two days, they added a rudimentary scheme for dividing property into lots. They also decided on generous minimum sizes for homestead lots. All eight of what Pynchon called the "first subscribers & adventurers for the plantation" signed, two by making their marks.[3]

The community's founding document reveals that Pynchon had already scrapped his original plans. The "House Meadow" building was to have been the beginning of a settlement on the west side of the Connecticut, the "Great River." The fact that it had been inadvertently built on land that flooded in the spring was only part of the problem. Pynchon found that his original choice of a location was "so encumbered with Indians" that a settlement could not be built there. He wrote to Winthrop that he was "compelled to plant on the opposite side to avoid trespassing of them."[4]

The House Meadow, Agawam

3. Details in this paragraph are drawn from Burt, *First Century*, 1:156–160, which provides the texts of both the original May 14, 1636 covenant that created the community, and the addendum of May 16, 1636.

4. Forbes, *WP*, 3:267.

The Agaam[5] Indians were what has come to be called a "segmentary tribe," consisting of several extended families, and numbering around 150 or more. They lived from hunting and fishing, as well as cultivated crops such as maize, squash, and kidney beans, and other foods they gathered. By the time the English arrived in any significant numbers, the Agaam had survived the devastating smallpox epidemic from 1633 to 1634. That tragedy decimated the Connecticut Valley watershed population to a fraction of the perhaps twelve thousand Native people who had previously lived there. While largely independent, the Agaam shared an Algonquian language with other southern New England Indians. They occasionally formed alliances with neighboring communities whenever collaboration was mutually advantageous. This federation, which has sometimes been called the Pocumtuck tribe, occupied lands that spanned from the Connecticut westward into the Berkshires, from northern Connecticut to northern Massachusetts. In addition to the Agaams, residents of a dozen villages comprised this alliance, including those in Woronoco (Westfield), Nonotuck (Northampton), Squakheag (Northfield), and Pocumtuck (Deerfield).[6]

Though the area where Pynchon intended to settle turned out to be directly west of Massachusetts Bay, it had been agreed that this new plantation would fall under the jurisdiction of a new confederation of plantations further down the Connecticut, centered on Hartford. A commission granted on March 3, 1636, by the Massachusetts General Court had retroactively legitimated the expansion to the Connecticut Valley, which had begun in 1635.[7] The Commission's authorization would be valid for one year. Pynchon, Ludlow, and Smith, among others, were given power to function as magistrates during that time, with control over "tradeing, planting, building, lotts, millitarie dissipline, defensive war, (if neede soe require,) as shall best conduce to the publique good."[8] The point about defensive war would turn out to be of significance the following year.

Most of the Connecticut settlers came from two Massachusetts churches that had planned for some time to migrate to the Connecticut

5. Please note that I have spelled the tribe "Agaam," and the place and settlement "Agawam."

6. Thomas, "Bridging the Cultural Gap," 5–21; ibid., "Contrastive Subsistence Strategies," 5–7; ibid., "Maelstrom of Change," 101.

7. The "Commission" is in Shurtleff, *MBCR*, 1:170–71. For brief accounts of the founding of the earliest Connecticut settlements on the River, see Taylor, *Colonial Connecticut*, 6–10; and Jones, *Congregational Commonwealth*, 26–35.

8. Shurtleff, *MBCR*, 1:171.

Valley: the New Town (Cambridge) Church under the leadership of Rev. Thomas Hooker and Rev. Samuel Stone, and the Dorchester Church under the leadership of Rev. John Warham. In addition, nine others came from the Watertown Church under the leadership of John Oldham. They went on to establish towns called, at first, by the same names—though Newtown was soon rechristened Hartford, Dorchester became Windsor, and Watertown, Wethersfield.

The Connecticut River in the Early Seventeenth Century

But the pioneers who joined Pynchon's adventure further upstream were a mixed lot from various places and social backgrounds. John

Woodcock, who had accompanied Pynchon on his exploratory expedition in 1635, was a Roxbury neighbor; he would figure in many legal scrapes with his fellow residents in the magistrate's Court. Jehu Burr, also from Roxbury, was unable to write his name. John Cable came from Watertown, where he was punished in 1631 for teaming up with two others to steal three pigs.[9] Henry Smith, Pynchon's stepson, was also his son-in-law, since Henry and Pynchon's eldest daughter Ann married at some unknown date about this time. Diversity would continue to characterize immigrants to Springfield over the coming years. Some would be recruited from Barnet near London. A surprising number came from the West Country of England and nearby towns in Wales.[10]

Linking the Agawam colony to the Connecticut Valley venture made sense. Certainly, transporting freight was much more practicable via the Connecticut River. Pynchon's move to Agawam meant a sea voyage around Cape Cod and into Long Island Sound, then a journey up the Connecticut. So he rented two boats from John Winthrop Jr. in July 1636. One was the *Batchelor*, while the other was the *Blessing of the Bay*, a thirty-ton bark that had been constructed in Medford as the second seagoing craft ever built in New England. Forty tons of supplies for the new colony were loaded aboard and transported as far as Wethersfield. The cost was £82. Pynchon recorded that the fare for "my Son Smyth and 3 daughters and 1 maid" amounted to £2 10s. The final bill was presented in late September.[11]

———— ⟨◦⟩ ————

In addition to migrating to the Connecticut Valley, the month of July saw another momentous event: the signing of the deed to Agawam and Springfield on July 15, 1636. This contract was made by thirteen individual Indians, who signed by drawing personal symbols such as bows and arrows, and by nine settlers who signed their names or their marks.

9. The Cable case is in Shurtleff, *MBCR*, 1:85.

10. Bailyn, *Barbarous Years*, 421–22, indicates that nearly half the upper Connecticut settlers were from the West Country of England. Of the immigrants who arrived in Springfield between 1638 and 1647, Reice and Blanche Bedortha, Alexander Edwards, Griffith and Sarah Jones, Morgan Jones, Thomas Merrick, Miles Morgan, Hugh and Mary Parsons, Rowland Thomas, and William Vaughan were all of Welsh heritage and from Bristol, England, or nearby southeastern Wales. For indentured servants from Barnet, see Smith, *CR*, 224–26.

11. Green, *Springfield*, 4; Forbes, *WP*, 2:285–286, 314. On the "Blessing of the Bay," see Robinson and Dow, *Sailing Ships of New England*, 11–12.

The payment of eighteen fathoms of wampum and eighteen each of coats, hoes, hatchets, and knives served to confirm it. Interestingly, Pynchon paid more than twice as much for what is now Agawam and West Springfield than he did for the present-day Springfield and Longmeadow. At the time of the purchase, Pynchon's band included eighteen men, several of whom did not stay very long. Eleven years later, he recouped his outlay for the initial purchase through a levy based on acreage. As the largest landowner by far, Pynchon paid £3 5s. 6d., which was basically one-tenth of his total reimbursement of £30.[12]

The Indian deed to Springfield was a remarkable real estate instrument that remains noteworthy for a number of important features. Its provisions were unique at the time and broke new ground for relations with Native peoples. It set a solid standard for clarity, flexibility, and even generosity.

In the first place, Pynchon recognized that Native occupants of the land were its rightful "owners" from an English point of view. He did not accept the so-called *vacuum domicilium* argument—a "nobody lives here" view—namely, that if there were no residents to be seen, the land was up for grabs. The Pilgrim Robert Cushman offered that rationalization in his section of what is called *Mourt's Relation*, on "Reasons and considerations touching the lawfullnesse of removing out of England into the parts of America."[13] In a brief 1629 treatise on "Generall considerations for the plantation in New England," John Winthrop responded in the same way to a question of what right the would-be colonist had to take the Indians' lands:

> This savage people ruleth over many lands without title or property; for they inclose no ground, neither have they cattell to maintayne it, but remove their dwellings as they have occasion, or as they can prevail against their neighbours. And why may not christians have liberty to go and dwell amongst them in their waste lands and woods (leaving them such places as they have manured for their corne) . . .[14]

John Cotton (1585–1652), teaching pastor of the Church of Boston, had expressed the same conviction to the departing Winthrop company back in

12. The original deed with the Indians is reproduced and its text given in Green, *Springfield*, 12–14. Details about the 1647 rate to compensate Pynchon for his purchase of the land are found in Burt, *First Century*, 1:190–91.

13. Bradford, *Iournall*, 68.

14. John Winthrop, "Generall Considerations," in Hutchinson, *Collection*, 30.

England. As the colonists prepared to set sail from the Isle of Wight, Cotton said in his farewell sermon, "God's Promise to His Plantation":

> Where there is a vacant place, there is liberty for the sonnes of Adam or Noah to come and inhabite, though they neither buy it, or ask their leaves . . . it is a Principle in Nature, That in a vacant soyle, hee that taketh possession of it, and bestoweth culture and husbandry upon it, his Right it is.[15]

Pynchon's neighbors in the Connecticut Valley put it even more starkly. The Connecticut General Court spoke of maintaining "our right that God by Conquest hath given to vs."[16]

But Pynchon held a different view. He maintained that a legal purchase agreement had to be made with the Indians. To be sure, this involved introducing and imposing an alien concept of land "ownership" that was not precisely in keeping with Native ways. Still, reaching agreements with indigenous people in such a conscientious way was rarely a consideration with other English settlers.

Moreover, the agreement was careful to guarantee certain rights to the Agaam Indians by providing that

> they shall have and enjoy al that Cotinackeesh, or ground that is now planted; And have liberty to take Fish and Deer, ground nuts, walnuts, akornes, and saschiminesh or a kind of pease, And also if any of our cattle spoile their corne, to pay as it is worth; & that hogs shall not goe on the side of Agawam but in akorne time.[17]

Additionally, the agreement reveals Pynchon's developing respect for Native culture in a number of ways. Indeed, his carefulness in dealing with Indians began at the very outset of his settlement when he abandoned original plans in order to leave the indigenous community intact. The agreement went on to guarantee the local tribe certain privileges. It specified rights they required to continue their way of life, at least in some measure. It acknowledged their hunter-gatherer customs. It also made pointed references to mothers and wives by specifically naming Kewenusk, the mother of the Agaam's chief sachem Cuttonus, and Niarum, the wife of Coes (or Coa). Whether inadvertently or not, Pynchon was showing respect for the matriarchal traditions that were so important to Native peoples.

15. Cotton, *God's Promise*, 4–5.
16. Trumbull, *CCR*, 1:10.
17. Burt, *First Century*, 18. See also Wright, *Indian Deeds*, 12.

Furthermore, by including Algonquian words to clarify precisely what the agreement entailed, the deed indicated Pynchon's appreciation for Indian language. In addition to place names, such as *Masaksick* (long meadow), *Accomsick* (land on the other side of the river), *Usquaiok* (the end of the land), and *Nayasset* (at the corner), the deed mentions *muckeosquittaj* (meadows), *saschiminesh* (peas), *cotinackeesh* (cultivated ground), and *tamaham* (wife). The advantage of including such words was clear: the Indians would recognize some key terms on hearing the document read aloud.[18]

It is important to emphasize that these features of the Springfield deed are subsequently seen only in Pynchon-inspired western Massachusetts Indian deeds in the seventeenth century. Concessions to Native practices and appreciation of their language and customs are simply not a part of other contemporary agreements between colonists and Indians.

A comparison with Indian deeds of other Puritan communities, such as Boston, Salem, and Hartford, makes it very clear that Pynchon's approach was unique. The closest parallel was the March 24, 1638, deed to Providence, Rhode Island, which was drafted less than two years after the Springfield deed. It was a memorandum referring to an earlier (and apparently unwritten) agreement made between Roger Williams and the sachems Canonicus and his nephew Miantinomo. The text simply identified lands the Indians ceded to Williams.[19] When Williams remarked on the pangs of conscience he felt concerning the injustice of the King's patent in "giv[ing] away the Lands and Countries of other men," he mentioned that "some of the Chiefe of New-England" agreed with him; perhaps he meant Pynchon.[20] Plymouth colony did record a "Book of Indian Records for Their Lands," in which the earliest document was dated 1664. It conveyed total ownership to the buyer; there was no mention of price; and there were no stipulations of any rights or privileges or acreages reserved to the Indians. Moreover, there is no deed for Plymouth itself. The earliest Boston deed dates to March 19, 1685, and while it purports to recap an agreement made when Winthrop first arrived, there is no record in Commonwealth sources

18. For the texts of Pynchon deeds, see Wright, *Indian Deeds*. Other Algonquian words found in Pynchon deeds include *wiskheeg*—or perhaps better, *wussuckwheke* (writing)—and *weakshackquock* (candlewood or pitch pine). All spellings are taken from the originals.

19. For the text of the Williams deed, see Bartlett, *Records*, 1:18. The original is preserved in the Rhode Island State Archives.

20. Williams, *Bloody Tenent*, 276–77.

of any earlier document. Like the 1670 "renewal" deed to Hartford, made as a "replacement" of the long-lost 1636 pact with Sunckquasson, or the 1686 deed to Salem, the later texts that do remain are all straightforward property transfers modeled on the English pattern.[21] They seem to have been made—or perhaps better, made up—retroactively. The Puritan colonists generally appear to have considered the King's charter to the Massachusetts Bay Company sufficient warrant to occupy New England properties. Pynchon demanded more.

With the securing of rights to the land and the arrival of settlers and their families, Pynchon was ready to develop his new community. Geology determined the settlement's shape. The plantation on the east side of the Connecticut was laid out along a rise of slightly higher ground that lay between the banks of the river and a hassock-filled marsh, the remnant of an earlier path of the river. The new residents built a string of houses along the west side of a single path, now Main Street. On the east side of the street was a brook or ditch that drained the wet lowlands. Lots were perpendicular to the street and extended eastward from the river in straight lines that crossed the street and continued out into the marsh. Beyond this swampy area, the land rose to a sandy pine barren, which was unsuitable for agricultural development. There was a footpath along the river with stiles over the fences to provide access across property lines. A sawmill and a bridge for reaching it were built at the southern end of the settlement on Mill River, near where it emptied into the Connecticut.

With plantation operations taking place on both sides of the Great River, there had to be means for constant transportation back and forth. Even though round-bottomed dugout canoes were inherently unstable, they were the preferred craft. Almost from the beginning, large birch trees, which could be turned into canoes, were highly prized and legally controlled by the community's laws. Regulations permitted residents to cut "canoe trees" on common land, but only for their own use; and canoes could not be sold out of the community until they were at least five years old. Later, the plantation's permission was required even to do that.

21. For Plymouth, see Pulsifer, *Records*, 12:225–44. On the Boston deed, see Jennings, *Invasion*, 138. The Hartford Renewal Deed is given in Goodwin, *Descendants of Thomas Olcott*, 62–63. For other jurisdictions, see Bangs, *Indian Deeds*; and Perley, *Indian Land Titles*.

But while the river served as a thoroughfare, it also posed dangers. Abraham Munden and William Jess were lost when their canoe, loaded with corn and other goods, capsized in the rain-swollen river at Enfield Falls on October 29, 1645, the day when a fierce northeast storm battered Boston. Towards the end of May 1640, a boy from the Pynchon household, whose name remains unknown, was tending cows by the river when he climbed into a birch canoe, only to have the vessel keel over and drown him.[22]

22. On canoe trees, see Burt, *First Century*, 1:164, 167. On the fatal canoe accidents, see the letters from William Pynchon (Forbes, *WP*, 5:50) and George Moxon (Forbes, *WP*, 4:254). The victims' names are listed in Burt, *First Century*, 42.

5

Pequots and Provocations

MONDAY, MAY 1, 1637. Fifteen solemn men gathered around a table in Hartford. It was by far the largest attendance yet at the embryonic Connecticut General Court.

The Connecticut Valley colony's capitol town was located on a rise beyond a low-lying meadow on the west bank of the Great River. The Dutch had earlier used this exact spot for their trading post. It could be approached from a boat landing where brush had been cleared from the muddy bank of the river. From there, a path led across a grassy space and directly up to Meeting House Yard. A village had developed quickly around this relatively flat, open area since the arrival of the first pioneers just one year before. The houses of Edward Hopkins and John Haynes faced the Yard side by side on its western border. For all but one of the next sixteen years, the two would serve alternating one-year terms as governor. A temporary square meeting house stood in the Yard's southeast corner. Nearby stood the homes of Thomas Hooker and Samuel Stone, respectively the Pastor and the Teacher of the Hartford Church, just down Meeting House Alley, which led off the Yard to the south, parallel to what is now Prospect Street. Together, the two clergy served a settlement of a hundred people or so.[1]

While the colony had made it through the first winter, fear and anxiousness filled the air, and the delegates had nothing to celebrate. Danger threatened. The leadership faced a grim task. Roger Ludlow of Windsor presided as the magistrates and town representatives passed a fateful motion, "that there shall be an offensive war against the Pequoitt, and that

---

1. Walker, *First Church in Hartford*, 88.

there shall be 90 men levied out of the 3 Plantations, Hartford, Wethersfield & Windsor." Other votes in support of the expected combat followed this decision. In addition to ninety recruits, the Court elicited armaments and provisions from the various towns: 180 bushels of corn, which the authorities hoped would be already baked into biscuits, plus quantities of suet, pork, fish, rice, beans, and plenty of butter. Hartford was expected to provide four bushels of oatmeal and two of salt. Windsor was to come up with thirty pounds of rice and four cheeses. Wethersfield was to produce one bushel of Indian (kidney) beans. And there was to be supplied as well a hogshead of good quality beer for the use of the captain and any who might fall sick, with a couple of gallons of sack sherry on the side.[2]

The delegates also voted to impress, for military purposes, a shallop belonging to William Pynchon, and that infuriated him. Pynchon did not believe the hostilities were in his plantation's interest. Agawam was not even represented at this council of war, so it had no hand in developing what the Connecticut Court kept calling, somewhat quaintly, "this design against our enemies the Pequots."[3] Indeed, Agawam was not formally asked to send soldiers. Their upstream location was recognized as vulnerable, and the community's small population made its position precarious. But things were tense in Connecticut, too. Roger Ludlow wrote to Pynchon in mid-May, shortly after the conflict began, "I think of your condition, that, if the case be never so dangerous, we can neither help you, nor you us. . . . it is our great grief we cannot [send any to help], for our plantations are so gleaned by that small fleet we sent out, that those that remain are not able to supply our watches, which are day and night."[4]

The entire tragic episode that followed offers ample evidence of the vast gulf of misunderstanding and competition for resources that marred relations between English settlers and Native peoples. All involved were entangled in a dangerous mix of questionable motives and mistaken perceptions. Presumptions of divine right to the land, mismatched preconceptions, devious dealing, too easy resort to violence, and a mélange of prejudices and mistrusts all played a part in the conflict. The Native practice of individual retaliation to right any wrongs clashed with the English insistence on corporate responsibility, in which the entire community was necessarily involved. Puritan policy legitimated only "defensive war, (if

2. Trumbull, *CCR*, 1:9–10.

3. Ibid., 1:11.

4. Massachusetts Historical Society, "Pincheon Papers," 235.

neede soe require)," as the Massachusetts Bay "commission" to the settlers explicitly stated in the spring of 1636. Fighting with the Indians should be undertaken only reluctantly, for self-protection. But that did not prevent needless provocations to justify military interventions.[5]

A series of loosely connected events led up to the hostilities. In 1634, Indians mounted an assault on Capt. John Stone's trading bark near the mouth of the Connecticut River, probably to avenge the death of a sachem at the hands of the Dutch; the raid resulted in the murders of the captain and crew. The attackers acknowledged their responsibility, but they probably thought Stone was Dutch. Then early in 1636, William Hammond was killed on Long Island when his bark foundered in the course of a trading voyage to Virginia. A story circulated that Pequots were to blame, but Pynchon was not convinced. He wrote to Governor Winthrop, "I . . . think it a pore shift for the Indians of long Island to lay all the fault vppon a Pequat sachem." Indeed, the Pequot grand sachem Sassacus sent word in May that he had a couple of horses for the English and that he wanted to trade for goods with Pynchon's storeroom manager, Stephen Winthrop, at Fort Saybrook. The sachem was interested in trucking cloth, a thick wool fabric for coats, and various tools.[6]

But then in August 1636, Wethersfield's John Oldham was murdered during a trading trip to Block Island. Oldham was probably killed by eastern Niantics affiliated with the Narragansetts.

Though Oldham was widely considered a rogue, the Bay colony responded to his death with alarm. Massachusetts strengthened its alliance with the Narragansetts, who were centered to the east, largely in what is now Rhode Island, and who were nearly always at odds with the Pequots. By mid-April 1637, the Massachusetts General Court sent an expeditionary force of its own soldiers under Col. Israel Stoughton to implement some form of retribution. They were joined by a band of Narragansett warriors. Hunger as well as fear may have prompted this reaction. A devastating hurricane had swept across eastern Connecticut and Rhode Island, Plymouth colony, and Massachusetts Bay in mid-August 1635, demolishing crops

5. Shurtleff, *MBCR*, 1:171. For the Pequot War, see Vaughan, *New England Frontier*, 122–54; Jennings, *Invasion*, 202–27; a reassessment of Jennings' study by Katz, "Pequot War Reconsidered," 111–35; and another reconsideration by Cave, *Pequot War*. See also Cave, "Who Killed John Stone?" 509–21; and Grandjean, "New World Tempests," 75–100. On the Pequot War in general, see also Winthrop, *History*, 1:265–81; ibid., *Journal*, 212–29; and O'Shea, "Puritans and Indians," 65–67.

6. Forbes, *WP*, 3:267; Gardener and Carlton, *Relation*, 7–8.

and damaging buildings all along the way. That, on top of a large influx of hungry English immigrants in 1634, put a real strain on available food supplies and on the precarious transportation system provided by a very few coastwise traders. Stone and Oldham were crucial in the fragile trading network connecting Massachusetts and Connecticut.[7]

Some military posturing followed the rise of tensions between colonists and Pequots, including various forms of pressure the Natives put on Fort Saybrook. There was one relatively harmless standoff, which consisted mostly of taunts from the Indians and bravado by the English. Wishing, apparently, to verify a dark rumor they had heard, the Indians shouted, "Do you kill women and children?" A nervous Lion Gardiner, the commandant of the Saybrook stockade, was in no position to make policy. He yelled back, "You will see that hereafter." Other confrontations occurred; one skirmish early in 1637 claimed the lives of four Saybrook soldiers. By the spring of 1637, both Massachusetts and the upriver Connecticut plantations sent troops to strengthen the Saybrook installation.

Then an unexpected incident caused the conflict to flare up with a fresh, lethal intensity. Settlers at Wethersfield ejected the sachem Sowheag (sometimes called Sequin) from his lands, perhaps because they felt he had settled too close to their own dwellings. The sachem forged an alliance between his Wangunk Indians and the Pequots, and on April 23, 1637, they mounted a counter attack. This assault ended in the deaths of six English men and three women who were working in a field during spring planting, as well as the capture of two girls. The Natives also killed a number of those awkward, meddlesome, alien beasts, the cows. So, shortly after Massachusetts had acted in mid-April, the May 1 meeting of the Connecticut Court seized on the Wethersfield incident as a pretext for taking action. They placed Capt. John Mason in charge of their militia, which was joined by seventy Mohegan allies. Mason was a veteran of the Thirty Years' War (1618–1648) in Europe, having served with the English expeditionary force in the Netherlands during the 1620s. Massachusetts was already up in arms to avenge Oldham's murder at Block Island. The battle was on.

The English soldiers and their Narraganset and Mohegan allies moved toward the centers of the Pequot nation, which were along the Connecticut shore and on either side of the Pequot (or Thames) River. They perpetrated

---

7. Grandjean, "New World Tempests," 80, 82, 85–87. "Plain hunger, greatly exacerbated by the awkward and uncertain communication patterns that made it difficult for the exploding numbers of immigrants to New England to feed themselves, lay at the core of the frenzied English stumble toward war" (Grandjean, "New World Tempests," 78).

a gruesome massacre on the Pequot village near Mystic at dawn on May 26. The settlement stood on a ridge parallel to the west bank of the Mystic River and inside an elongated stockade, roughly oval in shape, on the summit of Fort Hill. Grabbing a firebrand, Capt. Mason shouted "We must burn them!" before throwing the torch onto a wigwam, setting fire to the entire village. Though exact details remain uncertain and are debated to the present day, as many as four hundred men, women, and children died trying to escape the terrible conflagration. Sadly, the Indians' question to Lion Gardner at Saybrook had now received an answer. By any account, it was a shameful disaster. Two of the English were killed, one perhaps by friendly fire. Pequot warriors rushed to Mystic from their fort in nearby Groton, but they arrived too late. Connecticut troops chased after the retreating Indians. A few days later, fresh troops from Massachusetts followed them farther along the shore. On July 14, the warriors were cornered in a swamp at Southport, where they were massacred. Their leaders escaped and headed towards upstate New York.

Pynchon, a staunch opponent of this "design" against the Pequots, did play a part in the hostilities—or rather in ending them. The Mohegans, in league with the Mohawks, intercepted the Pequot leaders as they fled for their lives and killed them all, scalping them at a place Pynchon identified as Paquiany in New York.[8] The Mohawks then delivered the grisly evidence to Pynchon, and pointedly not to the Connecticut authorities. One was the scalp of Sassacus, the sachem who had led the Pequot warriors. Another was his brother's. Pynchon hurriedly led a delegation overland from the Connecticut Valley to present the seven scalps to Winthrop on August 5, 1637. As a result of Pynchon's quick action, the Bay colony government recalled Stoughton before any more blood could be shed, and with that, the ill-conceived and ill-executed "war" and its awful violence came to an end. As one scholar observed, "the Indian wars [in New England] . . . were not crusades or even products of calculated policy, but conglomerations of error–reactive gestures of revenge, the excess of brutal malcontents."[9]

Several historians have placed the bloodshed of the Pequot War in the context of gruesome excesses of the Thirty Years' War. A contemporary observer, Philip Vincent, brought out a brief book very shortly after the war,

8. Green, *Springfield*, 32. The site was a stone gorge in Dover Plains, New York, which is now known as "Dover Stone Church."

9. Delbanco, *Puritan Ordeal*, 96. See also Karr, "Why Should You Be So Furious?" 876–909.

A Trve Relation of the Late Battell. His pioneering efforts at war journalism must have succeeded, since Vincent went on to cover the Thirty Years' War in another publication the next year. In his *Trve Relation*, Vincent tried to make sense of the awful carnage he had witnessed in Connecticut. He put it down to something innate in humankind: "Nature, heavens daughter, and the immediate character of that divine power, as by her light she hath taught us wisedome, for our owne defence, so by her fire she hath made us fierce, injurious, revengefull, and ingenious in the device of meanes for the offence of those we take to be our enemies. This is seene in creatures voide of reason, much more in mankind."[10]

Beyond the bloody results of the hostilities and their devastating impact on the Pequot tribe, the war's tragic legacy included the introduction of a way of fighting that had "no limit of scruple or mercy."[11]

The Pequot conflict was a serious blow to Pynchon's enterprise at a time when his plantation was scarcely a year old. Agawam remained safe, but Connecticut charged the plantation £86 16s. as its share of the costs of the war. Pynchon protested. He had thought, in accord with Roger Ludlow's letter when the war began, that Agawam would be expected only to defend itself. He wrote to Ludlow on January 19, 1638, "I did expect that you would not charge me for the war: . . . [T]his answer as I remember was made that if we would look to ourselves you would expect no more at our hands: . . . Besides I have been rated to [i.e., taxed for] this war in the Bay for my hole estate." It is unknown whether the bill that Connecticut sent in February was eventually, if reluctantly, paid.[12]

◆

The Pequot tragedy was a deeply painful affront to Pynchon because he had always been a proponent of maintaining good relations with Indians and was himself a careful practitioner of that art. Even before embarking on his move to the Connecticut River Valley, Pynchon pressed Winthrop early in 1636 to be very scrupulous to "take careful informations"[13] in a case regard-

---

10. Vincent, *Trve Relation*, B2r, quoted in Kupperman, *Indians and English*, 230–34.

11. Jennings, *Invasion*, 227.

12. Nichols, "Letter of William Pynchon," 387–88. Roxbury's share of two taxations, in August and November of 1637, was £108 8s. out of a total £1400 (Shurtleff, *MBCR*, 1:201, 209). It is unclear what "estate" belonging to Pynchon was taxed in Massachusetts, since at the time his Agawam plantation was aligned with Connecticut.

13. Forbes, *WP*, 3:254.

ing Indians who killed two settlers, so that the Indians as well as colonists would have no doubts whatsoever that justice was done. He based his later counsel of carefulness and moderation on his personal experiences:

> Use dilatory meanes, for I perceive the nature of the Indians is up-pon every little occasion to be much provoked with the desyer of revenge, but if meanes of delay be used but a while the edge of their revengeful desyer will soon be cooled. I perceive they are carefull of this, not to begin first with the English, but they make account, if the English begin first with them, to doe great matters.[14]

> I could not tell how to trust them they are so full of subtle postures: and yet sometimes they tell truth.[15]

> If you doe your businesse by Indians you will find it deerer then to send an Englishman.[16]

> [The Indians'] ordenary manner is, when they would get anything, to give the telling of some pleasing thing.[17]

He urged restraint in all situations, as is evident from these sober and heartfelt words to Winthrop:

> I cannot but admire at the particullorre wisdom and prouidence of god that hath so overruled war as to make it the means of so hope-full an accord between Indians and English: if wars had proceeded as it was like: I apprehend it would have cost the liues of many English as well as Indians, partly by wars and partly by disordered hardship . . . It seemes the Lord did not see sufficient ground as yet to shed so much blood as both sides intended, both of English and Indians.[18]

> You had iust reason to decline the warr which others suggested and thought fit to proced in against the Naricanset [Narragansett]: the distraction of the land and the loss of so many younge men and cheife men will not agree to the cas of war.[19]

14. Ibid., 4:443–444.

15. Ibid., 5:115.

16. Ibid., 4:495.

17. Green, *Springfield*, 32.

18. Forbes, *WP*, 5:95, 115.

19. Ibid., 5:115.

I hope the English will neuer put [the Indians] to the tryall, till
they [the English] be more than a little provoked to it.[20]

Indeed, restraint was such a key component of Pynchon's policy towards
the neighboring Agaam Indians that in late 1652 Thomas Miller was granted a lot for planting crops on the western side of the Connecticut, "by the
higher wigwam," but because he had previously gotten into a scrape with
the Natives, the grant came with the proviso that "hee bee not an occasion
of troble and disturbance to the plantation by any unwise Clashing with
the Indians." If he failed to behave, he would suffer the severe penalty of
forfeiting the property he had just been given.[21]

Pynchon expressed his convictions and his methods in some detail
when he wrote to John Winthrop years later, at a critical moment in 1648.[22]
His letter provides an extensive statement of his perspective. At issue was
the possible arrest of three Indians from Nonatuck (Northampton) who
were suspected of murdering five other Natives in the vicinity of Barre, in
Quaboag territory. One of the Quaboag sachems was allied with the respected Massachuset sachem, Cutshamoquin, who had in turn convinced
the Massachusetts government, through John Eliot in Roxbury, to draw
the English into the matter. Cutshamoquin and Governor Winthrop felt
that this would show the Indians a good example of disinterested English
justice, and Eliot lobbied Pynchon to assist in the manhunt. No doubt Eliot
intended to convince Pynchon to act by relying on his long-term relationship with Pynchon as a former Roxbury resident and member of his congregation. Eliot even cited a biblical text by way of encouraging Pynchon
to provide a stern warning to the Indians: "And those which remain shall
hear, and fear, and shall henceforth commit no more any such evil among
you" (Deuteronomy 19:20).

But Pynchon was cautious. For one thing, unlike most of his contemporaries, he respected the separate status of Native peoples. His views were
sharply at odds with the prevailing attitudes of others in his own era, and
much more closely aligned with the convictions of our own age: he believed

20. Ibid., 4:444.

21. Burt, *First Century*, 1:224. Miller had been found guilty of battery against Nippinsait in June, 1650 (Smith, *CR*, 223).

22. Pynchon's July 5, 1648 letter is transcribed in Temple, *North Brookfield*; quotations cited may be found in ibid., 36–37. It is also reprinted in Winthrop, *History*,
2:467–70. The original is held in the Massachusetts State Archives.

that any who remained outside the jurisdiction of Massachusetts Bay, in their own tribes, belonged to another nation. As he explained to Winthrop,

> I grant they are all within the line of your patent, but yet you cannot say that therefore they are your subject or yet within your Jurisdiction until they have fully subjected themselves to your government (which I know they have not) & until you have bought their land: until this be done they must be esteemed as an Independent free people.[23]

Furthermore, Pynchon was wary of being put in an untenable position between the feuding tribes and the English government. He was a careful observer of inter-tribal relationships, and from his vantage point in the Connecticut Valley, he had much to report to the Bay colony on this important matter. In February 1644, he informed Winthrop that fears that the Mohawks in the Hudson Valley would help Sequassen, the sachem of western Connecticut, were unfounded. He added,

> I do not certainly hear whether they will aid the Naricanset Sachem, but as far as I can understand they reject him also: But whereas you writ that you thought the Naricanset Sachem would be content to sit still: my intelligence from the Indians of the River is otherwise: and they have lately killed a munhegan [Mohegan] woman.[24]

A tangle of intertribal relations between Mohegans-Narragansetts-Niantics was the topic of another letter in September 1645, when Pynchon noted that the Mohegans trusted the sachem of their enemies, the Naragansetts, but were suspicious of the Niantic sachem and expected trouble the next spring.[25] Three years later, Pynchon reported growing pressure from the Mohawks based in New York on the Indians in the Valley. In the 1648 letter he remarked, "the Naunotuk [Northampton] Indians are desperate Spirites, for they have their dependance on the Mowhoaks or maquas who are the Terror of all Indians." Indeed, ever since the Mahicans of eastern New York and western Massachusetts were defeated by the Mohawks in 1628, forcing some to flee to the Connecticut Valley, where they settled

---

23. Temple, *North Brookfield*, 36. Kawashima observes that by this conviction Pynchon "challenged the orthodox view that all accused criminals, including Indians, must be tried at the Court in the area where the crime was committed" (Kawashima, *Puritan Justice*, 231).

24. Forbes, *WP*, 4:443.

25. Ibid., 5:45.

with the Woronocos and Nanotucks, the Valley Indians had been under strong pressure from the Mohawks.[26]

Still, Pynchon did reluctantly agree to do his part to bring the fugitive Indians to justice in 1648, probably out of his innate sense of responsibility to the governor's authority. But he wrote to Winthrop, "I look upon this service in sending them [the Indian suspects] to you as a difficult & troublesome service." Even if the case might be handled more fairly with English involvement, the colonists' intervention would be at odds with Native codes of retributive justice. Pynchon understood the power of kinship in the Native culture. On the advice of the Indians themselves, he determined "not to medle with Wottowon & Reskeshon-ege," two of the suspects, "because they were of Pamshads kindred who is a maqua [Mohawk] Sachim." He maintained that the colonists should not get involved in the Indians' affairs on their own initiative. "[I]t may be of ill Consequence to the English," he said, "that intermeddle in their [the Indians'] matters by a voluntary rather then by a necessary calling."[27] In the end, Pynchon's extreme reluctance persuaded Winthrop to drop the project. Pynchon's guarded view lived on in his son, and John Pynchon echoed it years later when he wrote to John Winthrop Jr. in May 1658, "I wish the English may be silent and meddle less."[28]

Pynchon's letter illustrated as well how he always tried to work carefully with the Indians on their own terms. He had Indian leaders participate in any delicate negotiations or encounters concerning Natives who were wanted by the English for criminal activities. He followed carefully choreographed procedures, partnering with Native leaders but not placing them, or himself, in inextricable positions. For example, sometime around July 20, 1650, Pynchon had his constables arrest and temporarily "bound . . . with their cords" an Indian named Munnuckquats, who was wanted for robbery in Springfield but had fled to Woronoco for refuge. He was accused of stealing Sarah Stebbins' best "red kersy petticote" and a basket of linens. The constables then turned the suspect over to Attumbesund, the sachem of Woronoco. The sachem released him and let him escape, even though he

26. Thomas, "Maelstrom of Change," 45–51.

27. Temple, *North Brookfield*, 37.

28. Bridenbaugh, *Pynchon Papers*, 1:25. The deeds John Pynchon executed or brokered with Native peoples, beginning in 1652 until as late as 1681, show the same attention to the Indians' desires—and sometimes even their language—as are found in the original Springfield deed his father negotiated. See Wright, *Indian Deeds*, 24, 27, 34–35, 38, 52–53, 61, 63, 65, 70, 72, 82, 91, and 95.

came from a distant tribe near New Haven. Pynchon accepted this disappointing outcome. But he expected Attumbesund to make things right by paying five fathoms of wampum when the sachem came to Springfield a couple of days later to see Pynchon about the matter. In so doing, Pynchon adopted a Native tradition for bringing disputes to an end.[29]

The letter to Winthrop also makes it clear that William Pynchon could not have succeeded without considerable help from his Native interpreters. Pynchon seems to have understood the rudiments of his local Indian language, certainly well enough to communicate on daily matters, and he was admired by his fellow English settlers for that ability. But Pynchon mentions in his letter that neither he nor his son could understand the careful negotiations between his translator, Nippinsait, and Quacunquasit, a sachem of Quaboag. Translators were so important that the first to accompany Pynchon was named in the original Springfield deed of July, 1636. He was Ahauton of the Massachuset tribe.[30]

As one commentator has observed, "The manner in which Springfield and its founder William Pynchon related to and viewed its Indian neighbors was very uncommon in Puritan society."[31] Pynchon's relationships with Native peoples appear to have grown out of genuine interest in them. He made it his business to know and understand Indians, and occasionally mentioned individuals he knew by name.[32] He did not disparage Indians with prejudicial words such as "savages" or "heathen."[33] It seems quite reasonable to conclude that Indian–English relationships in early colonial New England could have followed a much more humane and productive course if William Pynchon's principles and practices had prevailed.

29. Smith, *CR*, 223–24; Thomas, "Maelstrom of Change," 153.

30. Temple, *North Brookfield*, 37; Burt, *First Century*, 1:18.

31. O'Shea, "Puritans and Indians," 46.

32. In his October 8, 1644 letter to Stephen Day, he mentioned Ta-mug-gut (Forbes, *WP*, 4:495–96). In his July 5, 1648 letter, Pynchon named no less than nine individuals, all known to him: the prominent Massachuset sachem Cutshamokin, the Quinnipiac sachem Sequassen, his own translator Nippumsait, the Nonotuck sachem Chickwallup, the Quaboag sachem Quacunquasit, Wottowan, Reskeshonege, Pamshad, and Wawhillam (Temple, *North Brookfield*, 35–38). Many others are listed in entries recorded on unnumbered pages at the back of his account book in the Forbes Library, Northampton, Massachusetts.

33. It appears that Pychon did use the term "heathen," but to mean "Gentile," as when he spoke of "heathen Christians" or defined the word to mean "strangers" (Pynchon, *Jewes Synagogue*, 37, 63). His usage was descriptive, not pejorative.

Of course, Pynchon's appreciative attitude was surely affected to a considerable degree by his commercial interests. Indeed, the very exercise of trade created an interdependent Indian-English market, which could stimulate "individuals in both societies to reach an accord on other matters."[34] Pynchon held no exalted or romantic views of those he would have considered his non-Christian neighbors. Though a number of quasi-official statements implied a missionary purpose for the Bay Company's venture to New England, it is unlikely, as one scholar observed, that the colonists "considered missionary work the principal, or even a principal, reason for emigration."[35] No doubt Pynchon shared the passive perspective on mission to the Indians that was articulated in the Bay Company Charter: that the colonists by "their good life and orderlie conversacon maie wynn and incite the natives of country to the knowledg and obedience of the onlie true God and Savior of mankinde." The colonists expected, rather condescendingly, that the sheer virtue of their lives would draw the Natives to Christian faith. That was certainly the view of Springfield's minister, the Rev. George Moxon.[36] It was even the view of Rev. John Eliot before he undertook his famous mission in response to the Massachusetts General Court law of 1646, which urged colonists to "propagate the true religion vnto the Indians." Court-appointed ministers were to explain colony law and preach the gospel at least once a year to those Natives whom they "shall perceve most willing & ready to be instructed by them."[37] But Pynchon sponsored no religious outreach to the Agaam Indians. While Eliot's "Praying Indian" towns in Massachusetts Bay and the Wampanoag mission in Mashpee all had Native participation and even leadership, the only church in Pynchon's community was for English settlers exclusively. Pynchon was basically concerned that hostility between settlers and Indians would be very bad for business.

---

34. Thomas, "Maelstrom of Change," 201. "Where the boundaries of power domains were being contested, and where relative social isolation was maintained, economic exchanges furnished a forum for discussion and a bridge to compromise" (ibid.).

35. Cogley, *John Eliot's Mission*, 2.

36. Shurtleff, *MBCR*, 1:17. Moxon expressed his views in a sermon: "where God hath a people it often falls out that other strangers that live among them receive something of that religion, if not the power of it to their effectual conversion" (John Pynchon, *Notes*, November 4, 1649).

37. Shurtleff, *MBCR*, 3:100. On Eliot and the "affective model" for mission, see Cogley, *John Eliot's Mission*, especially 5–9.

6

Corn and Credibility

WEDNESDAY AFTERNOON, MARCH 21, 1638. "I'll neither make nor meddle."[1] These were the fateful words William Pynchon spoke to Capt. John Mason at some point when they met that day in Agawam.

Mason had come to the plantation to enlist Pynchon's help in buying much-needed corn for Connecticut, since the winter of 1637 to 1638 had been particularly harsh. By the end of January, the snow was waist deep in places. The season took a heavy toll on the cattle at Agawam because of the lack of fodder. This shortage was made worse by the poor quality of hay available at this early point in the settlement's history, before more robust "English grass" could be imported to feed livestock. Pynchon's wife Frances experienced a "dayly grief to see [cattle] in that poore starveing condition for the want of corne." Some settlers were forced to feed their supply of seed to poultry and swine. At times, Pynchon reported, "he hath not had half a bushell of corne in his house for his family & cattell."[2]

The Connecticut Court had foreseen the coming scarcity back in the dark days of winter. On February 22, they voted to prohibit individual trading with the Indians for the corn they urgently needed. They hoped that

1. Green, *Springfield*, 25.

2. See Innes, *Creating the Commonwealth*, 283–84; Pynchon's "Apology" in Green, *Springfield*, 30; and Trumbull, *CCR*, 1:13. Agricultural conditions and practices are described in Thomas, "Contrastive Subsistence Strategies," 2. On the "corn controversy" between the Connecticut authorities and Pynchon, as well as economic and political relations between Springfield and Connecticut in general, see McIntyre, *William Pynchon*, 15–21; Morison, *Builders*, 351–56; Green, *Springfield*, 20–38; and Baldwin, "Secession of Springfield," 12:55–82.

using authorized dealers would prevent competitive bidding, which could destabilize the market by driving up the cost. On March 8, they voted to channel all efforts through Pynchon:

> It is ordered with the consent of Mr. Pincheon that the saide Mr. Pyncheon will deliver att Harteford goods Marchantable Indian Corne att 5.s. per bushell as farr as 500 bushells will goe at, if hee can save by that, for the residue hee is to have 5s. 2d. per bushel . . . In consideracon whereof the[re] is a restrainte of any to goe vpp the River to trade with the Indians for Corne.[3]

But this privilege came with what would turn out to be an important proviso for "dispensing with this order":

> In case of necessity that any family or families do complain of present necessities they are to repair to 3 magistrates which may advise them for the supply, although it be to the dispensing with this order.[4]

In light of subsequent events, it seems unlikely that Pynchon gave his heartfelt agreement to the enterprise. He might have harbored deep misgivings and may have felt pressured into taking on this task, vital as it was felt to be. Pynchon did try—certainly he said he tried—to make a deal. But at that time of year, food was also scarce among the Indians, who depended on corn to stay alive from late September until May.[5] Even the expert trader could not buy at the Court's mandated rates. Within one week, Pynchon sent a messenger to Hartford to report his failure. In its desperation, the Connecticut colony seized on the loophole in its commission to Pynchon and proceeded to "dispens[e] with this order." An unrecorded rump session of the authorities only a week later (so Pynchon concluded) voted to empower Roger Ludlow and Capt. John Mason to trade with the Indians, since Pynchon was "somwhat fearfull of supplying the plantacions."[6] So probably by March 17, Capt. Mason, well-known to the Indians from his violent, bloody role in the Pequot War of the previous summer, set out to go upriver. He was undoubtedly a problematic choice, and maybe the worst possible for such an errand.

---

3. Trumbull, *CCR*, 1:13.
4. Ibid.
5. Thomas, "Maelstrom of Change," 110.
6. Trumbull, *CCR*, 1:16.

It took Mason only three days to discover that he, too, was fated to be unsuccessful in this mission. By March 21, he came to Springfield to consult with Pynchon. Since Pynchon had been replaced in this task, he naturally assumed he had been relieved of all responsibility. But he was willing to confer with Mason, first at his home in the settlement and then at his storehouse across the river. At Pynchon's request, he and Mason were joined at Pynchon's storehouse by two witnesses: the town's new minister, the Rev. George Moxon, and Pynchon's stepson, Henry Smith.

At some point, Pynchon uttered the one phrase that proved decisive. It was the sort of comment that, once spoken, is difficult to take back. "I'll neither make nor meddle" was an old English saying meaning, "I will not do it myself, but I will not stop you."

Mason claimed that Pynchon said this when he first arrived at Pynchon's home with a Connecticut Valley sachem, and that Pynchon was responding to his request for Pynchon's help in assuaging the sachem's fears. Pynchon claimed, however, that he said it later at the storehouse when they were discussing Mason's trading scheme, and Pynchon's two witnesses later supported his account of this exchange. This difference in recollection mattered because of the important fallout from the encounter. Pynchon was unalterably opposed to Mason's plan of giving the Indians a down payment of wampum simply to encourage them to trade. He was convinced, perhaps from personal experience, that it would never work to pay first and deal later. Native peoples did not take that approach seriously.

When the Connecticut Court met two weeks later on April 5, it was not in a pleasant mood. It had to act on relationships with Natives as well as the corn supply. First it voted a perversely worded order, astonishing in its absurd insensitivity, to send six men to the Woronoco Indians "to declare unto them that we have a desire to speak with them, to know the reasons why they said they are afraid of us, and if they will not come to us willingly then to compel them to come by violence."[7]

Then the Court ordered Pynchon to send to William Whiting £40 worth of corn, or the equivalent amount in beaver if he could not provide corn, probably to repay Whiting for supplies Whiting had previously advanced. Next, the Court increased the price for corn to a new high of 5s. 6d. per bushel—but the new price was not to apply to Pynchon, who was held to the original deal.

7. Ibid., 1:17.

Finally, the Court pronounced a devastating judgment. William Pynchon was accused of breaking his word. The Court record states,

> Whereas there was some complaint made against Mr. William Pincheon of Agawam for that, as was conceived, and upon proof appeared, he was not so careful to promote the public good in the trade of Corn as he was bound to doe. It is ordered the said Mr. Pincheon shall with all convenient speed pay as a fine for his so failing 40tie bushels of Indian Corn for the public, & the said Corn to be delivered to the Treasurer to be disposed of as shall be thought meet.[8]

Sometime during the two weeks between March 21 and April 5, Pynchon went to Court in Hartford for a trial of some sort that left no trace in official records. He defended himself with the help of George Moxon and Henry Smith. When Thomas Hooker was brought in for his expert observations, he was reported to have said that "he could not believe but so wise a man as Mr. Pinchon knew how to procure and had such power with the Indians that he might have performed. Else he would not have promised and engaged himself on this manner."[9]

Pynchon was stunned. He had nothing to say. He was done in by his own reluctant agreement to help Connecticut in its dire circumstances. To be charged with dealing unfaithfully and breaking his oath as a magistrate devastated him.

This may not have been the first time Pynchon had to face deep and painful accusations questioning his character, and it was certainly not to be the last. It probably was not the first time he had an unpleasant encounter with Hooker. Still, Pynchon experienced a deeply humiliating moment. He seems to have brooded over the accusations. Just as these charges made others doubt his integrity, they seem to have struck at the heart of his own self-awareness and shaken his own sense of who he was. Charging him with dereliction of duty understandably made Pynchon defensive about himself.

The Rev. Thomas Hooker's subsequent remarks exacerbated the situation. It is not possible to know what part old memories from the years they both lived in Essex might have played in the relationship between Pynchon and Hooker. But Hooker's sharp words in a letter to Winthrop in December 1638 were particularly harsh and hurtful. He implied that Pynchon had

---

8. Ibid., 1:19.

9. Hooker's remarks are reported in a letter from Matthew Mitchell, quoted in Ford, "Letters of William Pynchon," 45.

broken the eighth commandment, the one against stealing. The charge appears to have originated from a misconception about what had happened the previous year, when the Pynchon operation—but not Pynchon himself—had purchased furs sent by Mohawks. The pelts came along with the scalps of the escaping Pequot "War" principals. In yet another example of disastrous cross-cultural misunderstanding, the Connecticut authorities thought the furs were a gift for them. Pynchon pointed out that the pelts and scalps could not be connected; there had not been enough time for that to happen. But those facts did not stop Hooker. It is difficult to miss the sheer meanness in his words, which reveal an unbecoming, graceless anger towards Pynchon:

> If Mr. Pynchon can devise ways to make his oath bind him when
> he will and loosen him when he list: if he can tell how, in faithful-
> ness to engage himself in a civil covenant . . . yet can cast it away
> at his pleasure before he give in sufficient warrant, more than his
> own word and will, he must find a law in Agaam for it; for it is
> written in no law or gospel that ever I read. The want of his help
> troubles me not, nor any man else I can hear of. I do assure you we
> know him from the bottom to the brim and follow him in all his
> proceedings, and trace him in his privy footsteps; only we would
> have him and all the world to understand, he doth not walk in the
> dark to us.[10]

In the complicated cases that ensued, Pynchon became embroiled in a number of legal and quasi-legal challenges. He wrote several self-defense statements, including an "Apollogy" to be shared throughout the colony. Pynchon complained that his accusers did not understand what trading with the Natives required, especially when the colony did not give him a free hand.[11] He protested that Hooker had "delivered his judgment peremptorily, that I had broken my oath, but I being unsatisfied how he could mak his charge good have often called up pon him to make it good and he hath often promised and yet delayed to do it to this day . . . for certain punishment must be grounded upon certain proofe, and not upon surmises or prejudice or the like mistaken grounds."

For Pynchon, much was at stake. As he observed, if Hooker could not prove his allegations, "I am wronged in my Cause and made a grieved

10. Forbes, *WP*, 4:84. For Pynchon's explanation, see Green, *Springfield*, 31–32. Morison, "William Pynchon, the Founder of Springfield," 70, comments on a probable long-standing relationship between Hooker and Pynchon.

11. Valeri, *Heavenly Merchandize*, 47.

magistrate unjustly."[12] He was especially incensed that the desperate Connecticut authorities had expected him to suspend basic English civil rights. He refused to commandeer a neighbor's canoe to transport the Indians' grain. He angrily remarked, "If magistrates in N. E. should *ex officio* practice such a power over mens properties, how long would Tyrany be kept out of our habitations? . . . [T]o lose the liberty of an English subject in N. E. would bring woefull slavery to our posterity."[13] To establish his own innocence, Pynchon proposed using a biblical procedure. "I am ready to take an oath of the Lord hereto, and in cases as materiall as this, where there is but only surmises, and noe proofe, can be had, an oath of the Lord, must determine the cause. Exodus, 22. 10. 11."[14]

Pynchon tried unsuccessfully to fend off a trial initiated by the Windsor Church, where his stepson was considered a member.[15] The church would have justified such a trial on the grounds that Pynchon had been found guilty of a moral failing. When the church did eventually find him guilty over two years later, in September 1640, Pynchon appealed to another jurisdiction. Even though John Eliot attested that Pynchon was "recommended to the church at Windsor" when he moved to the Connecticut Valley, Pynchon felt that he remained a member of the Roxbury congregation, and therefore under its authority. Thus, Pynchon corresponded with and pled his case to the Roxbury Church, which unsurprisingly stood by him.[16] But the controversy had done enormous damage. So far as Connecticut was concerned, Pynchon's reputation was damaged, his character questioned, and his credibility destroyed.

⟨◦⟩

At least one indelible, permanent result emerged from the corn controversy between William Pynchon and the Connecticut authorities. Though the disagreement originated in suspicion and revolved around mistrust between men of conflicting personalities, it eventually led to something much larger that would shape the political life of New England.

12. Ford, "Letters of William Pynchon," 47–48.

13. Ibid.

14. Green, *Springfield*, 32.

15. Windsor Church records do not bear this out; they mention neither Smith nor Pynchon. See the "Matthew Grant Record" in Connecticut Historical Society ("A.C.B."), *Some Early Records*, 7–102.

16. Eliot, "Record," 73 (membership in the Roxbury Church); Ford, "Letters of William Pynchon," 49–51 (correspondence with Roxbury).

Two complementary tendencies towards two different goals were at play in the corn controversy and its aftermath. One was the return of Agawam to Massachusetts' jurisdiction; the other involved creating a closer confederation of the New England colonies. Pynchon supported both. At a meeting on May 29, 1638, Connecticut commissioned Governor Haynes, John Steele, and William Pynchon to work with Massachusetts towards uniting their efforts. Pynchon attended the June 1638 Massachusetts General Court, at which he encouraged this collaboration—and also made known his wish to be part of Massachusetts. Word got around. On November 29, 1638, William Spencer wrote to Pynchon from Hartford to express surprise that Pynchon wanted to be in Massachusetts, since Agawam was "soe far remote" from the Bay. On January 14, 1639 the Connecticut Court adopted "The Fundamental Orders," which created a government for the river towns. This foundational document is generally considered to be the "first constitution in America," the earliest written basis for democratic representative government in what is now the United States. But it did not mention Agawam. Two days later, Deputy Governor Edward Hopkins wrote to Pynchon from his home on Meeting House Yard in Hartford to collect the balance still due on Pynchon's fine. Hopkins pointed out that the Dutch dollar Pynchon had sent him was not really worth the 5s. he claimed—more like 4s. 6d. "at most." Presumably, Pynchon paid the remainder of the debt.[17] In any case, by February 14, Agawam was fully independent.

A combination of hard-headed negotiations and blustering threats ensued even after the *de facto* break. In 1640, Connecticut gave now-Governor Hopkins the right to buy land in Woronoco, which was due west of Agawam and so presumably covered by the Massachusetts charter. Hopkins even built a trading post there. On June 2, 1641, the Massachusetts Bay General Court mentioned free access to the river in their finding, which, not surprisingly, supported Massachusetts' jurisdiction over Springfield.[18] By 1644, the inter-colony confederation that had been so long in the making was in operation, and by 1647, the "Congress of United Colonies" decided in favor of Massachusetts' claim to Woronoco. Connecticut threatened to levy tolls to maintain the fort at the river's mouth in Saybrook; Pynchon refused to pay. He pointed out that he

17. Massachusetts Historical Society, "Winthrop Papers," 266 (Spencer letter); Schechter, *Roots of the Republic*, 24; Jones, *Congregational Commonwealth*, xi, 61–98 ("Fundamentall" orders); Ford, "Letters of William Pynchon," 39 (Hopkins).

18. Shurtleff, *MBCR*, 1:321.

could handily defend his plantation from an attack on the river because no vessels large enough to be a threat could possibly make it up to Agawam. He also noted that trying to levy tolls on Agawam amounted to tacit admission that Pynchon's plantation was actually in Massachusetts, because Connecticut would never exact tolls from their own! Massachusetts countered with a threat to charge citizens of other colonies to maintain defense of all New England through the fortifications in Boston Harbor. At this point Connecticut blinked, and the matter came to an end.

Two years as a dependency of Connecticut had proved to be enough for Pynchon. And Massachusetts, for its part, was generally pleased to welcome him back. The dispute resulted in a reexamination of the boundaries between the Massachusetts Bay and Connecticut Valley colonies. The result was the most far-reaching legacy of William Pynchon in America, and maybe the only enduring one: the community he founded is Springfield, Massachusetts.[19]

19. Interestingly, while it was determined very early that Springfield belonged to Massachusetts, a line that was drawn below Enfield Falls gave Massachusetts a strip of land eight miles wide which is now in Connecticut. A subsequent compromise line in 1713 left Enfield, Suffield, and Woodstock in Massachusetts. The Connecticut General Court asserted its jurisdiction in 1749, but only in 1804 did Massachusetts abandon its claims. See Baldwin, "Secession of Springfield," 81–82.

7

Commerce and Community

THURSDAY, FEBRUARY 14, 1639. The settlement's residents—perhaps thirty-five adults at the time, twenty of them men—gathered in the multi-purpose room of the Pynchons' home. Though the family lived in a simple structure at the corner of what is now Fort and Main Street, it was the grandest house in a not very grand village. The meeting was scheduled for 10:30 a.m. In most Puritan communities, Thursday was the day for the mid-week religious service called a Lecture, and Agawam was no exception. While Lecture sounds like one-way communication, the day also afforded opportunities to transact the public's business. The court in Pynchon's plantation usually met on Thursdays. So did their town meetings, which sometimes took place on the same Thursday as court, though decisions were recorded in different volumes. Citizens were expected to take civic responsibilities very seriously and respond promptly. To assure quick action on matters of public concern, it was decided in May 1645, that including a call for a town meeting among the notices at the end of a Lecture would provide sufficient warning for convening that very same afternoon.[1]

One item on this day's agenda would turn out to be of lasting significance. A formal motion was put to the assembly:

> We the Inhabitants of Agaam upon Quinnettecot taking into consideration the manifold inconveniences that may fall upon us for want of some fit magistracy among us . . . therefore think it meet by a general consent and vote to ordain (till we receive further directions from the General Court in the Massachuset Bay) Mr.

1. Burt, *First Century*, 1:48.

William Pynchon to execute the office of a magistrate in this our plantation of Agaam.[2]

In Bay colony practice, the governor and Court of Assistants invariably appointed magistrates. But in this rare instance, Pynchon recorded a remarkable innovation: the citizens themselves created a magistrate by election. Granted, it could not possibly have been a contested election; there was one candidate only. Yet with that vote, the community, under Pynchon's leadership, took a giant step towards its future. It would be another two years before the name "Springfeild" (to use Pynchon's preferred spelling) would be adopted on April 16, 1640, in honor of his former home village in England. And it was not until June of 1641 that the Massachusetts General Court endorsed Pynchon's authority by giving him "full power and authority to govern the inhabitants at Springfeild" as a magistrate. But the Court's action was considerably after the fact. Pynchon and the people had long since done it themselves.[3]

Pynchon divided his attention largely between the development of Springfield and his trading business. Samuel Eliot Morison remarked that Pynchon managed the plantation with the collaboration of "[h]is son, John, his sons-in-law, Elizur Holyoke and Henry Smith, and his friend the minister," who "formed with him a little aristocracy of wealth, piety, and talents." But Pynchon did take some few steps to initiate participatory government on the local level. In a memorandum written by Pynchon himself, early Springfield records show that by September 26, 1644, the town had chosen a five-man Prudential Committee with a wide range of governing responsibilities. As a combined Board of Selectmen, Public Works, and Education, this new board exercised responsibility over a surprising variety of tasks. The job description in Pynchon's minutes implied that it functioned as the "Whatever Needs to be Done Committee." The committeemen were to arbitrate disputes. They were responsible for unclogging the ditches that drained the swamp. They were in charge of getting rid of wolves as well as educating children. The School Board function accommodated the provisos of a Massachusetts Bay law of 1642, which encouraged universal literacy and apprenticeships in useful crafts. And as if swamps, education, and settling local squabbles were not enough, the Committee was also tasked with building a road across the "muxie meddow" marshland to connect with the Bay Path; in 1645, a

2. Smith, *CR*, 203.

3. Burt, *First Century*, 1:167; Shurtleff, *MBCR*, 1:321–22.

corduroy road consisting of logs laid side by side was set along the present course of State Street.[4]

The Prudential Committee was also responsible for making sure that chimneys were clean and fire was handled safely. The danger from fire remained a constant concern in this settlement of wood-framed and wattle-walled houses capped by thatched roofs. Community regulations required every home to have a ladder of at least fifteen rungs, long enough to reach the roof peak. Also, the Bay colony had strict no-smoking laws. The use of tobacco in public places was first outlawed in 1632, and as of October 1633, constables throughout the Commonwealth were to be on the lookout for such idlers as "common coasters, unprofitable fowlers, & tobacco takers."[5] Smokers were successfully prosecuted in Pynchon's Court.

Pynchon himself never served on the Prudential Committee. In addition to his courtroom duties as magistrate, he seems to have concentrated his public service efforts on acquiring new land and, in collaboration with others, assigning lots for new recruits to the community and dividing available acreage as the plantation developed. The distribution of 673 acres to twenty-one men and their families on April 6, 1643, represented a substantial expansion of the town. Pynchon received a king-sized 128½ of those acres. But even newcomers Alexander Edwards and James Bridgeman, who had arrived in Springfield that very year, were granted eleven acres apiece for planting, as well as lots in the meadowland on the west side of the river. As more land was doled out, the community's agricultural output grew. Springfield became "New England's wheat belt" by the late 1640s. Pynchon's enterprises exported 1,500 bushels in 1652.[6] The plantation continued to allocate its acreage with a measure of conscientiousness and fairness. A town meeting in December 1640 codified the generosity of land distribution that had been evident at the community's beginning. The regulation called for apportioning property on a sliding scale that took individual circumstances into consideration. More land was to be given to those who were thought to require more:

---

4. Morison, "William Pynchon, the Founder of Springfield," 81. For the Prudential Committee, see Burt, *First Century*, 1:175–76. The Massachusetts education law is found in Shurtleff, *MBCR*, 2:6–7.

5. Ibid., 1:101, 109.

6. Bidwell and Falconer, *History of Agriculture*, 12. Thomas, "Maelstrom of Change," 92. George Moxon earned £33 from the 153 bushels he harvested and Pynchon exported— more than half his annual stipend as minister (Bridenbaugh, *Pynchon Papers*, 2:198).

"Single Persons are to have 8 rod in breadth [132 feet], married Persons 10 rod in breadth [165 feet], bigger families 12 rod [198 feet]."[7]

To develop its infrastructure of roads and bridges, Springfield carried out various public works by drafting citizens and their teams of oxen for up to six days per year. Three days' notice was required. Skipping out on this civic duty would lead to a 2s. 6d. fine for truant persons, and a much stiffer 5s. fine per day for oxen. Projects in 1647 included the long-planned "Horse way over the meddow to the Bay path" and a bridge over the Three Corner Meadow brook. But there were also other ways to get things done. Late in 1648, the town permitted nine landowners on the West Springfield side to build a cartway, where they could collect tolls of 4d. per load. Among the investors was one woman, Abigail Burt Ball, the widow of Francis Ball, who had drowned in the river earlier that same year.[8]

While Pynchon wanted a free market for his own trading enterprise, he did not favor a free market for labor. He established fixed wages for most workers in his plantation. This was in keeping with a practice that had been attempted in the Bay colony. The Court had tried to enforce a uniform, colony-wide pay scale in the very first months of its existence in 1630. While this initial arrangement did not prove practicable, the idea was not completely abandoned. Instead, on October 28, 1636, the General Court voted to leave wages to local discretion by authorizing the freemen of each town to set wages and prices. Pynchon's plantation followed this rule. On November 14, 1639, the salaries for farm laborers were set at 2s. per day for most of the year. Others with particular skills were supposed to earn more: carpenters and mowers, for example, got 2s. 6d., which dropped to an even 2s. in the winter, and sawyers were paid on the basis of their output in hundredweight of lumber. The Springfield rates were higher than in the eastern Massachusetts towns.

Then in December 1641, all Springfield salaries were cut; this action also followed the lead of the General Court. What the legislature called "the scarcity of money, & the great abatement in the prices of corn, cattle, and other commodities of the country" had led in the previous June to a vote that strongly encouraged workers to accept lower wages in relation to the falling prices. The government reasoned that in this way it could protect

---

7. Burt, *First Century*, 1:171–73 (land apportionment rules), 71–73 (1643 land allotments).

8. Ibid., 1:193 (drafting laborers and oxen), 196 (cartway). Apparently the new toll road was opposite the foot of State Street (Ball, *Francis Ball's Descendants*, 15–16).

employers from being bankrupted by a financial squeeze over which they had no control. This economic collapse occurred in the wake of the Short Parliament, which met in London from mid-April to early May 1640, when it raised issues of royal threats to individual property rights, refused to vote money for Charles I, and extracted concessions on the part of the king.[9] Thanks to their stand, Puritan prospects in England seemed greatly improved. As a result, emigration from England slowed to a trickle, with the consequent loss of new cash and fresh consumer markets for New England.

Because of this crisis, Springfield's carpenters and mowers were reduced to 2s. per day (20d. in the winter) and laborers were pegged at 20d. (18d. in the winter). This dramatic slash in compensation resulted in 15 to 20 percent less income for the plantation's workers. Town records report that the community instituted this pay reduction "mutually by vote." But even though prices had fallen, cutting wages could not have been a truly popular decision. The earliest pay scales in Springfield seem to have been comparable with current ones in England, though the high costs of living in the colony would have eliminated any apparent advantage. In February 1643, the common laborers' wage was reduced even further, to 16d. for an eight-hour day. One scholar has pointed out that in 1646 there were thirty-nine men in Springfield out of a total population of one hundred. Twenty-two of those men stayed over the ensuing years, and fifteen of those twenty-two derived a substantial portion of their income as employees of William Pynchon, and later of his son, John. Moreover, twelve of the twenty-two longer-term residents would "experience serious indebtedness problems with the Pynchons."[10] Springfield remained very much Mr. Pynchon's company town.

Cash was so scarce in the early days of Massachusetts that not only did wampum pass for money, but so did beaver, corn, and wheat. All were accepted as tax payments at rates set by the General Court. Their official prices fluctuated roughly in relation to availability. Corn, for example, varied from a high of 6s. per bushel in the early years, until March 1636. By that September, it was at 5s., and it dropped to 3½s. per bushel in November 1637 before returning to 5s. by the spring of 1640. On several occasions, however—in the fall of 1631, spring, 1634, and summer, 1637—the value was allowed to float. Sometimes Springfield set its own commodity

9. Scott, *England's Troubles*, 142.

10. Innes, *Labor*, 10–11, 74–75. For the General Court's various maneuvers on wage policy, see Shurtleff, *MBCR*, 1:74, 77, 79, 91, 109, and 183. For Springfield town actions fixing salaries, see Burt, *First Century*, 1:166, 168–69, 171.

prices. In 1645, pork was pegged at 3½d. per pound, and wheat at 3s. 4d. per bushel. The 1646 contract with Francis Ball to build a shop to aid in recruiting a blacksmith called for payment in wheat at 3s. 8d. per bushel. By November 1650, the same commodity was 3s. 6d. (Meanwhile the shop seems to have stood idle until after John Stewart came in 1651).

It took until late 1637 for the General Court to recognize an official rate for wampum: six per penny for payments less than 12d. Values rose in 1640 to four per penny for white, two per penny for blue. Pynchon often made reference to his trade in wampum. He paid close attention to its quality, writing to Stephen Day in 1644, "I had rather haue white wampam then bad blew at 6 a peny." In 1642, the General Court even made Dutch guilders legal tender at 2s. apiece, "considring the oft occasions wee have of trading with the Hollanders."[11]

Although Pynchon, like everybody else, was strapped for cash and frequently resorted to wampum to pay his debts, he clearly continued to prosper. His fur trading ventures were more lucrative than ever, to the point that he "became the greatest fur trader of New England, and, largely through his enterprise, furs became the principal export of Massachusetts Bay."[12] He was so successful that Peter Stuyvesant, Director-General of the New Netherlands colony, complained in 1650 that the fur trade was "much damnified and vndervalued" by Pynchon's overpaying the "natiue barbarians" the outrageous sum of "eleuen gilders . . . for a beauer skine."[13] As beaver became increasingly difficult to find, Pynchon's hunt for furs competed directly with Dutch efforts in New York. Beaver had probably been hunted out of existence near Springfield even before Pynchon arrived in 1636, so his traders were forced to go farther and farther afield.

Pynchon maintained three trading posts on the Connecticut River. One was a room at Fort Saybrook, a locale that was particularly useful for loading and unloading goods from ocean-going vessels.

---

11. Rates for corn are recorded in Shurtleff, *MBCR*, 1:110, 142, 180, 192, 206, 294, among others; wampum exchange rates are listed in ibid., 208, 302, 329. By 1648, wampum beads circulated at eight white per penny, with the blue (or black) at double that rate (ibid., 3:146, 4, pt. 1:36). Details on the blacksmith shop and wheat prices are found in Burt, *First Century*, 1:177, 185, 218. Pynchon's letter to Day is found in Forbes, *WP*, 4:495. On the value of Dutch money, see Shurtleff, *MBCR*, 2:29.

12. Phillips, *Fur Trade*, 134.

13. Hazard, *Historical Collections*, 2:155. At the official Massachusetts rate, eleven guilders amounted to 5s. 6d. I thank Strother E. Roberts for permission to cite his comments on the absence of beaver in Agawam; see Roberts, "Changes in the Water," 37.

A second was the palisaded storehouse in Agawam, where Pynchon traded with both the English colonists and Natives. In his daybook for 1645 to 1650, he and his son, John, recorded the accounts they kept with several Indians. In 1648 and 1649, for instance, Walerimo bought red cotton yard goods, a blue cap, and a couple of blue coats, one long and one short. Pynchon recorded the prices in hands of wampum. She paid the bill in wampum. Coa also ran an account with Pynchon, but paid in corn and one deerskin, which Pynchon valued at 7 hands of wampum. From merchandise he kept on hand in 1644, Pynchon supplied an exploratory mining undertaking in Sturbridge undertaken by Stephen Day of Cambridge, the colony's first printer. Pynchon provided Day with bacon, tobacco, sugar, salt, and ginger (in lieu of the pepper that Day had ordered, but was out of stock at the time). The bill came to 9s., plus 6 pence that Pynchon tacked on to cover the containers as a sort of shipping and handling fee.[14]

Pynchon also did a brisk business out of his storage facility near the falls at Warehouse Point in Enfield, Connecticut. This structure seems to have served as the major depot for his import-export business, and probably the site where pelts were packed in hogsheads for the trip downriver on the way to England. Since Pynchon relied on the Connecticut River as his highway to the sea, the threat from the Connecticut Court to charge tolls to use it became a principal point of contention in the controversy between Connecticut and Massachusetts.

Two of the Pynchon commercial structures were marked on the Jansson-Visscher maps of New Amsterdam and New England. They were first included on a map issued in 1650, shortly before Pynchon moved from the Connecticut Valley, and they continued to be shown as landmarks on this series of hand-colored Dutch maps for more than a century. The Agawam store was labeled "Mr. Pinsers Handel haus." The location of his Enfield structure on the east side of the river, at its highest naturally navigable point, was identified as "Mr. Pinsers;" it was very near the "Cleyne Thal" ("small waterfall").

14. Thomas, "Maelstrom of Change," 187–91, provides details of Pynchon's accounts with Indians; see especially the tables on 189–91. One "hand" of wampum was about twenty-four beads (worth 3d. in 1650); a "fathom" comprised ten hands (worth about 2s. 9d.). For a discussion of supplies available at Pynchon's store, see Forbes, WP, 4:495.

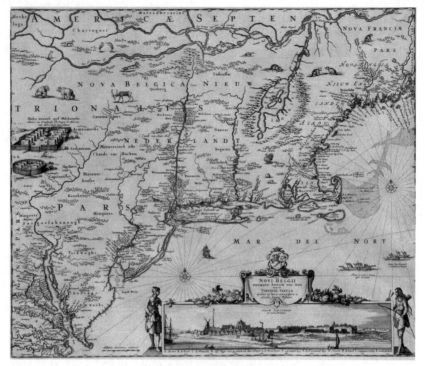

Jansson-Visscher Map, 1655

Not far to the north and east of Pynchon's sites, the map showed the legendary and mythical "Lacus Irocoisiensis," the fabled "Lake of the Iroquois" that lured numerous expeditions in search of the mother lode of furs. This imaginary inland sea would have stretched from Quabbin northward, nestling among the mountains of New Hampshire—what has been called "a beaver El Dorado." If the Jansson-Visscher information about this fantasy resource had been true, Pynchon would have been in a prime position to profit even more handsomely.[15]

As Pynchon's business and plantation grew, so did his family. The last three of his children married in the first half of the 1640s. Mary wed Elizur Holyoke in late November, 1640; Margaret married William Davis, a druggist from Boston, in late October, 1644; and just one year later, his son, John,

15. For information about the Jansson-Visscher maps, which were published in the US before 1923 and are in the public domain, see: http://www.newnetherlandinstitute. org/history-and-heritage/digital-exhibitions/charting-new-netherland-1600/the-maps/ novae-belgiae-angliae-nec-non-parties-virginiae-multis-locis-emendata-1655/. The remark about the "Lake of the Iroquois" is found in Dolin, *Fur, Fortune, and Empire*, 81–82.

married Amy Willis, daughter of the governor of Connecticut from 1642 to 1643. Grandchildren soon followed. Of those who survived infancy, by 1650 Mary and Elizur Holyoke had John (1642), Hannah (1646), Samuel (1647), and Edward (1649). Margaret and William Davis had Thomas (1645) and Benjamin (1649), while Amy and John Pynchon had Joseph (1646) and John (1647). Anna and Henry Smith, married several years earlier, had Anna (ca. 1632), Martha (1641), Mary (1643), Elizabeth (1644), and Rebecca (1649). Excepting for the Davises in Boston, the families lived on adjoining properties. William lived on Fort Street. John and his family were across Main Street from him. The Holyokes lived just to the south of William, and the Smiths in the next lot south of that.[16]

Connecticut River at Warehouse Point

16. "Springfeild Marriages," in Hampshire County, *Register Booke*, 55. For genealogical information regarding the William Davis family, see Whittemore, *Genealogical Guide*, 137. Pynchon family properties are indicated on a map in Demos, *Entertaining Satan*, 282.

8

Three Missing Boards and a Man in White

THURSDAY, DECEMBER 12, 1639. Springfield Court came to order, with the Honorable William Pynchon presiding.

Like all public gatherings at the time, Court sessions convened in the largest room of the Pynchon home. Seated in his magisterial chair, the judge surveyed the scene before him, peering with his intent, hazel eyes. His long, narrow face featured a prominent nose, strong jaw, a mustache across his upper lip, and what is now termed a "chin puff" beard. His reddish-brown hair was closely cropped and just barely visible around the brim of his tightly-fitting skullcap, which he wore as a sign of the magistrate's office. Dressed in a fancy black coat with two rows of metal buttons down the front, with a large white collar lying atop his shoulders, Pynchon was every inch the very picture of authority.[1]

At this late fall session, the Court faced a mystery. What had become of three missing boards?

The conundrum began the previous month. The always-watchful Mr. Pynchon had lodged a suit against Thomas Merrick for failing to return three boards that Pynchon had lent him. Pynchon not only presided over the case; he also won it when the "six good men and true" who sat on the jury that day found for him. At today's session, Pynchon presented another complaint, this time against Thomas Horton for taking certain planks from

---

1. Details of Pynchon's appearance come from a portrait by an unknown artist, the caption of which indicates that it was painted in 1657, when he was sixty-seven years old. The 29½" by 25" painting entitled "Portrait of William Pynchon" is item number 106815 in the Peabody Essex Museum, Salem, Massachusetts.

the piles of lumber at the sawmill on Mill River. But the six men on this jury, including Pynchon's stepson, Henry Smith, and long-time collaborator Jehu Burr, found they could not render a decision. They felt that Horton had to finish the project he was working on before they could tell just how much lumber it consumed.

That case was followed immediately by a second. After his loss to Pynchon in November, Thomas Merrick now sued Thomas Horton for taking the three boards he had borrowed from Pynchon. A related case came up in February of the next year, when Horton countersued Merrick, both for Merrick's taking the planks and, for good measure, a new charge that Merrick had cut down two trees on Horton's property. Since Pynchon did not record the judgment, the mystery remains unsolved. Who ended up with the boards—Merrick, Horton, or somebody else?[2]

These cases provide a glimpse into the nature of life in early Springfield. Pynchon's own home had to double not only as meeting hall, but also as courtroom for the first years of the settlement. The village was still very much under construction. The Pynchon sawmill at the south end of the main street was doing a brisk business. Moreover, so much hand-cutting of beams and boards was going on around town that a regulation had to be passed on March 26, 1640, requiring that roads be kept cleared of "all stubbs, sawpits & timber." Still, the plantation remained quite small. It did not have a meetinghouse for civic gatherings and church worship until 1645, or a courthouse until 1723. The population was so limited that the General Court had repeatedly permitted half-sized juries of only six.[3]

No records remain of Pynchon's earliest years as a magistrate in the Connecticut Valley when he served under the March 1636 Commission from Massachusetts, with the exception of one troubling report. In early March 1637, the Connecticut Court questioned him "aboute imprisoning an Indian at Aggawam, whipping an Indian and freeing of him."[4] This note reported an incident involving a Native who stole cloth from Pynchon's store and was subsequently captured and punished. Pynchon's firm treatment of the crime was not repeated in later cases detailed in the Court

2. Smith, *CR*, 204–206.

3. Burt, *First Century*, 1:166; Shurtleff, *MBCR*, 2:41, 109.

4. Trumbull, *CCR*, 1:13; Green, *Springfield*, 36, cites the April 18, 1639 critique of Pynchon by John Haynes and Thomas Welles. See also Thomas, "Maelstrom of Change," 147–48.

record of his experience at Springfield, which began with his election as magistrate on February 14, 1639.

William Pynchon's judicial administration proved to be strict but fair. He did his best to treat all cases with objectivity. A legal scholar observed that an "outstanding feature [of Pynchon's Court] is the flexibility of administration, both in taking jurisdiction without seeking support in the letter of the laws and in awarding punishment." Such elasticity corresponded to the trend towards innovative legal practices at the time in Massachusetts Bay, which allowed a variety of experiments to solve problems. Such innovations exhibited the "suppleness and adaptability" of Puritan jurisprudence.[5] Pynchon's even-handedness extended to levying a 5s. fine on George Moxon, the minister, for violating a town order against letting oxen roam on the west side of the river where the Indians lived. Moxon and Thomas Cooper owned a team of oxen jointly, but they failed to provide an oxherd to tend to their animals. Though Pynchon later cancelled Moxon and Cooper's fine as part of a wider resolution of the case, they did have to deliver a bushel and a half of wheat to Henry Burt to compensate for damage done to his Agawam crops.

Pynchon ran his Court by rudiments of English law that he adapted creatively to the frontier. Classic English texts informed his magistrate's sessions. One was Sir John Fortescue's volume on constitutional law; another was Michael Dalton's *The Countrey Iustice*.[6]

But the era was also characterized by what one scholar has called an "orgy of code-making" in New England.[7] The very composing of legal codes represented an important innovation in the many-faceted project of law reform the Puritans undertook in the new world. In the twenty years from Plymouth's 1636 code to New Haven's of 1655, each New England colony issued its own law code.

The process of developing new laws for a new continent revealed a variety of approaches. Rhode Island was unique: it based its code of 1647 heavily on the Dalton text, Pynchon's favorite. For a document composed just two years before the execution of Charles I, the code employed royalist language to a surprising extent. It explicitly mentioned the British king,

5. Smith, *CR*, 127; Nelson, "Utopian Legal Order," 192.

6. In Forbes, *WP*, 5:135, Pynchon mentioned his reliance on Sir John Fortescue's *Learned Commendation* and Michael Dalton's *Countrey Iustice*.

7. Warden, "Law Reform," 676. The article addresses the wide range of Puritan legal experiments and innovations in New England.

"who is acknowledged the common Father of the Countrie, in his person, Queene and Children, Authoritie, and Realme which is the common Mother of us all." It also featured frequent references to royal precedents, some dating back to Edward III in the fourteenth century, and cited the monarch's regnal dates—as, for example, "23 Hen. VIII., 1."[8]

By contrast, the 1648 Massachusetts *Book of the General Lawes and Libertyes Concerning the Inhabitants of the Massachusets* never mentioned the king or English courts. It was organized alphabetically by subject as a way of providing easy access, and like all Puritan codes, was informed heavily by biblical notions. The constraints of biblical principles made a very definite impact on the Puritan legal system. On the one hand, punishments for actions identified as crimes in the Bible, like witchcraft, were written into the law. On the other hand, the number of capital crimes was drastically decreased. One could not be executed for stealing a loaf of bread, as was possible in England. Pynchon probably picked up a copy of the comprehensive compilation of Massachusetts statutes and regulations that the Court had enacted since 1630 when he attended the General Court session in Boston in early May. He read it to the gathered inhabitants of Springfield on May 29, 1649.[9]

In its extensive preface, signed by Increase Nowell, the colony's secretary, the *General Lawes* used a nautical simile to underscore that "a Common-wealth without lawes is like a Ship without rigging and steeradge." The full document ran to many pages, so perhaps Pynchon did not read to his inland audience all the maritime details regarding "Ships and Ship Masters," "Wharfage," and "Wrecks of the Sea."

He may not have read the section on "Ana-Baptists," either. Pynchon expressed no more sympathy for those who limited baptism to adults than did the Court when it adopted a stern law against them in 1644. Indeed, Pynchon himself later wrote of "the stumbling blocks of Anabaptistry." The Massachusetts law harshly castigated Anabaptists and their hundred-year-old history, calling them "the Incendiaries of Common-wealths & the Infectors of persons in main matters of Religion, & the Troublers of Churches in most places where they have been." It also charged them with concealing their true purposes "as hereticks use to doe." Worst of all for the General

8. Bartlett, *Records*, 1:160.

9. Smith, *CR*, 219. *The Book of the General Lauues and Libertyes Concerning the Inhabitants of the Massachusets (1648)* can be found at http://puritanism.online.fr/puritanism/sources/lawslibertyes1648.html. The Anabaptist law can also be found in Shurtleff, *MBCR*, 2:85.

Court, Anabaptists denied the legitimacy of the magistrates' "lawfull right or authoritie to make war, or to punish the outward breaches of the first Table [the first five of the Ten Commandments]." Anyone who obstinately held to what the magistrates identified as Anabaptist convictions was to be banished from the colony.

Pynchon most likely did read the fifteen circumstances calling for capital punishment. Each was supported by suitable biblical references against murderers, witches, rapists, disobedient sons, and other undesirables. The extensive sections on "In-keepers, Tippling, Drunkenes" would be relevant. Applicable, too, were the Bill of Rights liberties guaranteed in the very first paragraphs, which provided that "no mans person shal be arrested, restrained, bannished, dismembred nor any wayes punished," though this guarantee was accompanied by a very large loophole: "unles it be by the vertue or equity of some espresse law of the Country warranting the same established by a General Court & sufficiently published." Also pertinent were the regulations about bringing suit in Court, as well as measures concerning burglary and theft, idleness, lying—and even regulations on the quality and price of bread, including the requirement that every baker "sign" his work with his own mark. And Pynchon may well have read the brief reference to monopolies, which placed severe limits on the practice, a law he clearly approved.[10]

The Court record diary Pynchon kept provides a vivid picture of legal challenges he faced and the solutions he found for the cases that came before him. Morison noted that there was "hardly a case which would come before a court of justice today." Yet those were the issues troubling the community, and Pynchon sought to resolve them.[11] Pynchon documented no instances of the problems that plagued the parish in Springfield, England, when Pynchon served as churchwarden. No controversies over public drunkenness, unlicensed taverns, and not even Sabbath-breaking came before Pynchon's Court.[12] Certainly such misdemeanors may have occurred, even in a "godly" Puritan plantation, but Pynchon did not record

10. See *General Lauues and Libertyes*, 5–6 (capital laws), 29–31 ("In-keepers, Tippling, Drunkenes"), 1 (personal liberties and immunities), 3 (bakers).

11. Morison, *Builders*, 360. See also Warden, "Law Reform," 687.

12. Pynchon did record the case of his own indentured servant Samuel Terry, who was caught masturbating just outside the meetinghouse during a sermon in July 1650. Terry elected not to have his case come to trial. Pynchon gave him six lashes as punishment (Smith, *CR*, 224).

them. Still, his experiences as warden at All Saints' had taught him what to look for to keep his community in order.

For a settlement of less than a hundred people, the wheels of justice were kept spinning.[13] Between November 1639 and October 1650, more than thirty residents came before the Court. A few were chronic litigants, including the constable, Thomas Merrick, who seems to have learned just enough about jurisprudence from his law enforcement experience to keep the Court busy. Many cases involved suits over quarrels between individuals at odds with one another. There were some cases of slander. In December 1639, Rev. George Moxon complained against John Woodcock, a Springfield founder and Pynchon's companion on the exploratory expedition in 1635. Moxon charged Woodcock with taking a "false oath" against him; the jury found for Moxon and awarded him a hefty £6 13s. (It probably did not help Woodcock's case that he was also charged with "laughinge in Sermon tyme.") Woodcock in turn sued Henry Gregory for two counts of slander in late September 1640. Those charges were payback for a suit Gregory had brought and won against Woodcock earlier in the month. Legal encounters like these show the degree to which spite and revenge played a major part in many cases. For example, Judith Gregory testified against John Woodcock in yet another Woodcock-Gregory battle in February 1641. She called him a "prating fellow"; Woodcock claimed he heard her swear, "Before God, I could break [your] head." Goody Gregory acknowledged her slip of the tongue, and said that "she hath been much humbled for it," so Pynchon sentenced her to sit in the stocks for three hours if she did not pay a twelvepence fine for uttering her ill-advised oath. In April 1645, John Dibble won his suit against Morgan Jones, who had allegedly threatened to "make an end of his Cow."

Except for the two suits concerning missing boards that Pynchon initiated at the beginning of his magistracy, perhaps to demonstrate how he would administer justice on the frontier, he never brought charges again. Also, nobody in Springfield ever brought charges against him. He seems to have been exempt from the legal hassles the plantation residents inflicted on one another. As the historian Stephen Innes remarked, "because of the

13. Details of the cases mentioned below are found in Morrison, *Builders*, 360–64; and Smith, *CR*, 205–208 (Moxon and Woodcock slander suits), 209–210 (Judith Gregory's oath), 216 (threat against Dibble's cow), 214–15 (pig problems), 215 (Leonard removed as constable), 220–21 (Moxon fined).

strength and scope of patron-client ties in seventeenth-century Springfield, the townsmen challenged one another instead of their social betters."[14]

Occasionally Pynchon had to deal with the difficult task of finding accountable leadership in his frontier community. In February 1644, Deacon Samuel Chapin was made constable, replacing John Leonard, "who was put out of his place as a mark of disfavor for swearing to a lie" in a case that Thomas Merrick had recently brought against Robert Ashley. The dispute concerned an allegedly stolen pig. The saga of that pig continued in subsequent cases. "Hogges and pigges" on the loose were a continuing problem in early Springfield, and swine ownership and control became the subjects of several Court cases. Eventually, in 1647, the community enacted legislation to provide for impounding swine without rings in their noses and yokes around their necks. They even approved a provision for selling confiscated pigs that had damaged crops.[15]

While Pynchon ran an English Court for English people, a number of cases involved relationships between the settlers and Native people. A Massachusetts law of 1647 provided that a couple of magistrates who agree to do so might hold a Court four times a year "concerning the Indians only," and that sachems also could hold Court sessions monthly for "small causes"—which is no doubt exactly what sachems had been doing for eons before the English came. But the magistrate of Springfield did not operate a segregated Court. He clearly intended to administer uniform justice to all parties when both English and Indians were involved. He ordered Francis Ball to pay damages of two hands of wampum for hitting the wife of an Indian named Coes in 1648. (The initial 1636 written agreement with the Agaams names her as Niarum). Ball claimed in his defense that he had struck her lightly with a small stick, which could not have hurt because she was wearing a bearskin coat. But that did not get him off. In another case in 1650, Pynchon sentenced Thomas Miller to fifteen strokes of the lash for striking Pynchon's translator, Nippinsait, with the butt end of his gun. The offender chose to pay four fathoms of wampum instead of taking the whipping. Miller was frequently an inter-cultural troublemaker. When he was granted land in Agawam near the "higher wigwam," he had to be explicitly warned against "any unwise Clashing with the Indians." If he failed to behave, he would suffer the severe penalty of forfeiting that

14. Innes, *Labor*, 150.

15. The April 1, 1647, swine law is found in Burt, *First Century*, 1:191–92.

property.[16] When Secousk, the widow of Kenip, came to Pynchon in June of 1644 and asked him for an adjustment in the price of land Pynchon had purchased from her three years before, "he gave her a childe coate of Redd Cotton" and a glass and a knife, which "fully satisfied" her and her present husband, Janundua. Experience made Pynchon realize that Natives did not consider the sale of their lands to be quite so final as the English assumed. He responded to repeat requests by offering further symbolic gifts, never by confronting those whom he would have considered the land's former owners.[17]

In addition to a degree of fairness, Pynchon's judicial decisions dealing with Native people reveal an extraordinary carefulness. When he sent Constable Thomas Merrick on July 20, 1650, "to make inquiry among our Indians on the other side [of the Connecticut River] what Indian hath broken open Rowland's house," he added a cautionary postscript: "If you find him at Woronoco [Westfield] you may persuade him to come and push him forward to make him come, but in case you cannot make him come by this means, then you shall not use violence but Rather leave him."[18] This restraint was in marked contrast to the reckless Connecticut General Court's order in 1638 "to compel them [Woronoco Indians] to come by violence" to Hartford.[19]

As well as being aware of cultural considerations, Pynchon appears to have been intentionally sensitive to the economic situations of those he sentenced. He adjusted fines to accommodate individual circumstances. When Pynchon sentenced Francis Ball in 1648 to pay two hands of wampum for hitting Coes' wife, he said, "but I also ordered that the boys that scared his cattle . . . to pay [him] 3 hands." (Ball proved obstinate, however, and in a pique of pigheadedness, or racism, he opted for corporal punishment, letting himself be hit two times rather than paying the Indian.) On

---

16. Smith, *Colonial Justice*, 223; Burt, *First Century*, 1:224 (February 10, 1652). Remarks by Henry Morris quoted in Green, *Springfield*, 581, report that Miller was one of only four or five Springfield residents to die in the so-called "King Philip's War" raid on October 5, 1675, when Metacom and his warriors attacked the settlement and burned most of it to the ground. Advanced warning was sent from an Agaam living in Windsor help to prepare the residents and keep them safe.

17. Shurtleff, *MBCR*, 3:105–106 (Indian courts); Smith, *CR*, 217 (assault on Coes' wife), 223 (assault on Nippinsait). The "Redd Coat" transaction is described in Ford, "Letters of William Pynchon," 52. See also O'Shea, "Puritans and Indians," 61.

18. Smith, *CR*, 223.

19. Trumbull, *CCR*, 1:17.

another occasion, Pynchon sharply chastised the widow Horton for naively letting an Indian borrow her late husband's gun early in October 1640. "I told her [to] speedily get it home againe," he said, "or else it would cost her dere for no commonwealth would allow of such a misdemeanor." But the magistrate did not fine her, perhaps because he felt compassion towards her. At the time, Mary Horton was recently widowed; her husband Thomas, one of the original Springfield pioneers, died sometime that spring or summer. The "Widdow Horton" (Pynchon never recorded her first name) was probably not much more than twenty years old; she had in her care at least one young son, Jermy, and was nursing her youngest child. In a distribution of agricultural land that December, the community saw to it that "wid: Horton" received fourteen acres, greater than all other grants, even to those with large families.[20]

In his capacity as magistrate, Pynchon had one other duty as well. He kept in touch with Massachusetts colony authorities as needed. In July of 1646, he wrote an extensive report to Governor Winthrop, warning him about a petty thief who had escaped from Springfield. Daniel Turner had run off one day in spite of the leg restraints that allowed him to work while a prisoner. That night he returned and stole a couple of white blankets, a bed ticking, a pillow, a bag of meal—and a pair of scissors. He was next sighted at Sudbury, "in a white waistcoat and in a white pair of drawers," for he had ingeniously fashioned his new wardrobe from the stolen blankets. Pynchon forewarned Winthrop to be on the lookout, presumably for a man dressed all in white, adding that "if he be not suddenly taken he knows the way so well to play the thief that he will do more Robberies quickly."[21]

20. Smith, *CR*, 208; Burt, *First Century*, 1:167.
21. Forbes, *WP*, 5:90–91.

9

Meetinghouse and Minister

SUNDAY MORNING, OCTOBER 21, 1649. John Matthews had been drumming up and down the street since nine o'clock. His route took him from the minister's house to Rowland Stebbins', which today stretches from Boland Way to Union Street. That was far enough for the families at the southern end of town, where the Bedorthas, the Cooleys, the Lombards, and the Parsons lived, to hear his steady drumbeat. People responded to his rhythmic call to prayer by moving quickly to get to the meeting on time. It would be another year before William Pynchon could buy a church bell. Now it was almost 9:30, when the gathering for Sunday worship was set to begin.

As the Reverend George Moxon climbed the steps to the pulpit, William Pynchon took his place at the front, in a separate seat near Deacons Chapin and Wright. The text on this Lord's day was Psalm 86:11: "Unite my heart to fear thy name."

Moxon proceeded in the usual methodical Puritan way. His sermons typified the "plain style" favored by Puritans: "straightforward scriptural explication that moves directly toward practical application and avoids rhetorical flourish for its own sake."[1] First he stated a doctrine, followed by reasons for this teaching, and finally uses or applications that might be relevant to the people of Springfield. It was all quite logical. His thesis on October 21 was a typical one: "It is and ought to be the serious desire of the godly that their hearts might be united to God and the fear of his name." Moxon's words echoed in the sparsely furnished hall:

1. Neuman, *Jeremiah's Scribes*, 4.

Godly men—yea, all men—meet with many temptations. Everything—yea, every condition—hath its temptations . . . If God should not keep your heart and mine, we are apt to consent unto any temptation. How willing are your hearts to listen and hearken to any temptation? David complied with his temptation to prosperity: "I said in my heart, I shall never be moved." (Psalm 10:6) David complied with his temptation to adversity: "I shall one day perish by the hand of Saul." (I Samuel 27:1) And so with other temptations . . . The longer that the spirit sits [far] from God, the more apt it is to comply with all these temptations.[2]

Next, the preacher called on his people to take stock of their own situations and spiritual practices: "Try," he said, meaning, "Test it out," or "Ask yourself."

And if you question whether your spirit sits thus, loose towards God, try:

First, whether your spirits do not sit loose from God in Ordinances [worship, spiritual practices, and participation in church community life], public or private. Do you never, when you come home, bewail the looseness of your spirits? And your absence from ordinances, especially on the Lectures, is it not much from looseness of spirit? And when you are at ordinances how do you attend upon God? What weakness, distractions may [there be] in your closet services? . . . Second, is there no looseness of spirit in regard to your comfort, food, raiment, children? Being too close with the comforts rather than God in the comforts argues looseness of spirit.[3]

Moxon then offered an answer in response to these questions for examining one's conscience. As a remedy for spiritual laxity, he urged, "Get your heart united to God and the fear of his name." He went on to express some possible hesitations his listeners might raise: "What means should I use? For I find that my heart hath been tied closer to God than now it is." In reply to these imagined questions, Moxon provided what he called "Directions":

1. Find what it was that brought your heart out of frame. How camest thou to looseness of spirit? Find it out. If it be neglect of

2. Pynchon, *Notes*, October 21, 1649.
3. Ibid.

duty or breaking forth of corruption, what ever it be, bewail it and repent of it. Remember from whence thou art fallen, and repent.

2. [I]n the next place, renew thy watch [watchfulness]; neglect of watch hath brought you to this frame and temper; renewing thy watch must bring you out of it. Thou must not now go from day to day without reading; thou must not go from day to day without praying. And desire a blessing of God upon thee; thou must not go from day to day without considering the sins of the day, without meditation, and so forth.

3. Prize and improve the ordinances. Kitchen physic, the country people will say, is good physic. The more skillful will say that there needs to be more wholesome diet to recover the body. [Worship and spiritual practices] and afflictions of God are as kitchen physic.[4]

For early New England Puritans, the church gathering was an indispensable basic unit of society. The Massachusetts Bay churches were virtually all of the "Congregational Way." The colonists gathered self-governing congregations, each of which selected its own leadership, including its ministers. Every church composed its own covenant as a written basis for membership. All were responsible for admitting members and exercising mutual accountability in their shared life as Christians. But because Puritans placed the church at the heart of the entire community, everyone was expected to attend. So neighbors came together in a social setting of all ages and genders to learn personal and public values and exercise incipient democratic principles. It was a place where consciences were shaped and right was distinguished from wrong. Church was therefore vital for the very life of the community, and the only institution that included a wide cross-section of the population.

For those reasons, weekly worship experiences were thought to be essential rather than optional for the community's life. As Pynchon later remarked, "It is a dangerous thing therefore to prefer a mans own private meditations, and speculations, to publicke Ordinances upon the Sabbath."[5]

An extensive sermon based on Scripture provided the core of the Sunday experience. Moxon began his message on Sunday morning, continued with the same theme in the afternoon service, and either expanded on the same verse or simply proceeded to the next verse in the Bible for

4. Ibid.

5. Pynchon's comments on worship in this and the two subsequent paragraphs may be found in Pynchon, *The Time when*, 61, 62 (margin), and 63.

the following week or two. His purpose was to move the congregation. In Pynchon's view, preaching required two kinds of sermons: carrot and stick. The minister should "preach every seventh day upon [humankind's] miserable fall, or else upon the riches of Gods grace."

The service consisted of more than a sermon based on the Bible. It included lengthy prayers, though nothing rote, such as compositions from a prayer book, or even the Lord's Prayer. The assembly also sang psalms. Pynchon might not have enjoyed singing very much, since he once somewhat grudgingly remarked that the "Singing of Psalms also must be added (sometimes at least)." If the congregation on October 21 sang the psalm from which Moxon chose his text, they may have used words from the 1640 *Bay Psalm Book*, the first book printed by Stephen Day of Cambridge—and indeed the first book printed in North America:

> Jehovah, unto mee
>
> o make thy way appeare,
>
> walk in thy truth I will; mine heart
>
> unite thy name to feare.
>
> Withall mine heart I will
>
> o Lord my God thee prayse:
>
> & I will glorify thy name,
>
> for evermore alwayes.

The congregation may have sung it to the lively though now largely forgotten tune, "London."[6]

Meetings for worship as well as governance had been part of life in Agawam-Springfield from the beginning. Late in 1637, the settlement accomplished the first goal stated in its covenant of 1636, "to p'cure some Godly and faithful minister with whom we purpose to Join in Church Covenant," when a congregation was gathered under the ministry of Rev. George Moxon (1602–1687). Moxon was well-trained for his profession; he graduated in 1624 from Sidney Sussex College at Cambridge and was ordained in 1626. He was reputed to be so skilled in language that he could imitate the Latin poetics of Horace. But because he intentionally omitted some ceremonies as curate at St. Helen's in Lancashire, the

---

6. For metrical texts of all the Psalms as sung in New England churches, see Haraszti, *Bay Psalm Book*; and the accompanying volume, ibid., *Enigma of the Bay Psalm Book*. The tune "London," which is of anonymous origin, first appeared in Damon's *The Former Booke* (1591). See Christ-Janer, Hughes, Smith, *American Hymns*, 15, 48.

Bishop of Chester John Bridgeman cited him for non-conformity in 1637. He escaped from Bristol in disguise, and following his crossing to America Pynchon recruited him to serve the Springfield community. A special vote by the Colony's Assistants made Moxon a Bay colony freeman, very likely at Pynchon's behest, as part of the only action it took at its meeting on September 7, 1637.

The plantation built a home for Moxon and his family in the spring of 1638. Town records describe the structure as a wood-framed, thatched-roof house measuring thirty-five by fifteen feet. Stairways led to both the second floor bedrooms and the cellar, the walls of which were planked. Double chimneys heated the four rooms and accommodated a built-in oven. A five-by-seven-foot "porch" extended out from one side to provide space for an entryway at ground level, as well as a small study on the second floor.[7]

For the first few years, meetings for worship were held regularly in Pynchon's home, both the Sunday services and Thursday Lectures. A letter Pynchon wrote to Governor Winthrop in February 1644 reported some success in Moxon's ministry in Springfield: "The Lord has greatly blessed Mr. Moxon's ministry to the conversion of many souls that are lately added to our Church."[8] No doubt the influx of eleven men and their families that Springfield experienced in 1643 affected this growth. Indeed, the newcomers proved to have a tonic effect on the community.

In February 1645, the growing settlement decided to build a proper meetinghouse. Forty rods had been reserved as the meetinghouse "pale" as early as 1639, but in the end, the building and its yard required only six rods, an area about ninety by ninety feet. They raised a simple structure measuring twenty-five feet or more by forty feet, and located it on the south side of the town common. Built on stones for a foundation, with daubed half-timbered walls, it boasted a shingled roof rather than the more prevalent and precarious thatched roofs. Two large windows on each side and smaller windows on each end provided light. There were two turrets, an unusual design for the time. One accommodated a bell, and the other was for the use of the night watch every community was required to provide.[9] The

7. For further information about Moxon, see *ODNB*, 39:601–602. His Springfield house is described in Burt, *First Century*, 1:160. His skill in poetry is reported by Calamy, *An Account*, 128.

8. Pynchon's letter is found in Forbes, *WP*, 4:443. On religious matters in Springfield, see Morison, *Builders*, 346–47.

9. For more on the requirement of a "watch house," see the March 9, 1637 entry in Shurtleff, *MBCR*, 1:190. For another meetinghouse with two turrets, see the 1970 Simsbury,

building's main door was on the south side, facing what is today Elm Street. Another was on the east, facing Main Street. To help with its construction, residents were expected to volunteer as unpaid laborers for up to twenty-eight days each under the direction of Thomas Cooper, who served as the contractor. Much of the work was done in the slack winter days of March. In what must have been a building blitz, citizens erected the structure by March 26, 1645, six months ahead of schedule.

As with many early Springfield projects, the community faced a challenge in financing this construction. By assigning values to various commodities—wheat, peas, and pork—by March 1645, the town raised in-kind contributions amounting to £30 of the £80 total due. The final £40 had to be raised one year later by a tax on "all uplands (meddows excepted) and all livinge stock in town." Since Pynchon was the town's highest rate payer by far, he no doubt covered a substantial share of the cost. But as with the tax to reimburse him for the original purchase, he was careful to insist on community funding for community projects. He even required Springfield to reimburse him £5 for the bell he bought for the meetinghouse.[10]

By the end of 1649, each man's meetinghouse seat on benches on the east end of the building was appointed by the town selectmen and the church deacons "as they in their discretion shall judge most meet." Presumably women and children sat at corresponding locations on the opposite side of the central aisle. By 1662, when the building assumed its final form with a balcony in place on three sides, it could accommodate 160 adults or more. That same year, the authorities made explicit arrangements for three prominent women: "Goodwife chapin [wife of Deacon Chapin] is to sitt in the Seate along with Mrs. Glover [wife of the minister] and Mrs. Hollyock [Pynchon's son-in-law Elizur Holyoke's second wife, Editha]."[11]

There was a reason for this imposed orderliness. The seating pattern represented a sort of social map of the community. Lists that survive from 1659 and 1662 show that citizens were assigned to the ten rows of benches on the ground floor, and when those filled as the town's population grew, to the balcony benches as well. In the earliest days, a person's placement depended not so much on wealth as on seniority and prestige in the

---

Connecticut, tercentenary reproduction at Simsbury Historical Society, "Meeting House, 1970: Simsbury," http://www.simsburyhistory.org/buildings/meetingHouse.html.

10. On the first meetinghouse, see Green, *Springfield*, 75–76; and Burt, *First Century*, 1:176–77, 184–85, 218 (reimbursement for the bell).

11. Burt, *First Century*, 1:330.

community. Generally, selectmen sat at the front. But Rowland Stebbins also sat in the first row, and so did George Colton. Neither was a selectman. Because Stebbins and his family came to Springfield at the beginning of a major influx in 1639, they enjoyed some seniority. Colton came only in 1646, but he was involved in many town committees, and as a public-spirited citizen, he would be charged with helping the poor when he eventually did serve as a selectman. In the second row was Richard Sikes, a member of the town's first Prudential Committee in 1644. Selectman Jonathan Burt had to be content with a place in the fourth row—though his father, Henry, who served on the first Prudential Committee, sat up front next to the deacons. Both Burts arrived in 1640.[12]

The 1659 list placed Peter Swinck in the back corner, in a seat in the tenth row. He sat next to Edward Foster, who may have arrived the same year he did, and on the same bench as Deacon Chapin's seventeen-year-old son, Japhet. Swinck was an indentured servant to John Pynchon, and an African. He may have come to Springfield as early as 1650. In 1662, he was granted a lot on the west side of the river as encouragement to stay in the community after his time of service was over. Among other skills, Swinck was a cooper; he made forty-gallon barrels for the resin trade John Pynchon developed as a way to profit from the pitch pines growing in the sandy soil east of Springfield. Swinck received a further thirty acres in 1666 and fourteen more over the next six years, all near Westfield Street and Block Brook in what is now the Tatham section of West Springfield, where he lived with his wife, Maria(h).[13]

To be sure, some meetinghouse seats were assigned on a purely pragmatic basis. The "younger persons that wants yeares" were first seated in the back row by the stairs (on the other side of the front door from Swinck and his seatmates). A subsequent generation in 1665 would oblige "al youths or boys under the age of twelve years of age," if they chose not to sit with their families, to "sit on that seat under the deacons seat." That would put them up front, where the deacons could keep a close watch on them. When

12. Arrangements for seating are found in ibid., 1:198, 126–29. Dates when settlers arrived in Springfield are listed in ibid., 41–45.

13. Swinck's origins and age remain unknown. Because of his infirmity, in later years he received support as a town charge. Peter died in 1699; his widow died in 1708 (Carvalho, *Black Families*, 122). On Swinck's date of arrival, see Armytage and Tomlinson, *Pynchons of Springfield*, 31. On Swinck's land, see Burt, *First Century*, 1:302, 358, 373, 402. Details concerning twenty-four barrels ordered from Swinck are listed in Bridenbaugh, *Pynchon Papers*, 2:240–41.

others who were older also took to sitting there, in what had come to be called the "Guard Seat," it became clear that the old orderliness was endangered. It may be that among them were some who broke meetinghouse windows while playing in the yard the previous winter, leading to a town bylaw that fined parents whenever their children were caught in that area behaving in a way that might damage the windowpanes.[14]

Clearly, some younger Springfield residents no longer accepted being assigned, and that led to a strict and lengthy town ordinance complete with fines for persons who sat "with a high hand" in the wrong seats. Their real offence was snubbing the authorities who presumed to "order" single-handedly the whole community, and particularly its younger members. The new generation seems to have turned restless following the William Pynchon era.

A series of sermon notes made by William's fifteen-year-old son, John, capture Moxon's preaching in 1640. John transcribed what he heard in a "short-writing" code of his own invention. John's notes reveal that Moxon did not preach the stereotypical parody of hellfire-and-brimstone Puritan sermons. Instead, Moxon stressed the gracious forgiveness of God. For five successive Sundays in 1640, beginning February 16, his sermon text was 2 Thessalonians 2:16–17: "Now the Lord Jesus Christ himself . . . comfort your hearts, and establish you in every good word and work." He chose just as positive and encouraging texts for other Sundays. On January 26, and again on February 2, he preached on 1 Peter 5:7: "[Cast] all your care upon him, for he careth for you," saying that God's mercies are "not lik summer rivers that com a shour of rain & therefore in a draught [are] drawn dry butt God's more lik the sea." He added,

> And where it is said, "The eyes of the Lord run to and fro" [2 Chronicles 16:9], now to what end is it? Why do the Lord's eyes "run to and fro"? To spy out our faults? No, to have his eyes providentially over us, to exercise his goodness and to supply our wants, and not to behold all our faults; not only as a bystander to look on things, but "the eyes of the Lord run to and fro" to order the affairs of the world so as to help all in their need that cast their care on him.[15]

14. Burt, *First Century*, 1:330, 429, 343–45, 314.

15. I have transcribed the quotations given here, found in Moxon's February 2, 1640 sermon, from the original notes taken by John Pynchon, possibly as a homework assignment of sorts. The document is preserved at the Springfield History Library and Archives of the Lyman and Merrie Wood Museum of Springfield History under "John Pynchon Sermon Notes," Springfield–ESM-05–06–02.

Moxon commonly concluded his sermons with a series of applications, and even when his message called for repentance, he invariably included a comment "for the comfort and consolation of all the godly." He obviously intended to encourage the struggling community in the most constructive ways possible.[16]

Committed Puritan that he was, Pynchon worshipped elsewhere when he was not in Springfield. He once remarked of Rev. John Warham of Windsor that he had "herd him many Sermons." Sometime earlier in 1649, he was at the Windsor Church when Warham had critiqued a brand-new book by thirty-four-year-old Richard Baxter called *Aphorismes of Justification*. On this occasion, the veteran preacher had taken on an innovative Puritan of the next generation and charged him with believing in "justification by works"—namely, that people are reconciled to God by doing good deeds. This was a heavy accusation; Protestants strongly rejected that notion even as they debated whether faith itself might be a kind of works as a human action. Wareham thought that was Baxter's erroneous position. Pynchon disagreed, and commented to friends (but apparently not to Warham himself) that Warham had misinterpreted what the young theologian was saying. "[H]e is a most pretious godly man," Pynchon remarked of Wareham, "though in this particulars to[o] much transported with passionate Zeal."[17]

Moxon was not the only speaker at Sunday worship in the Springfield church. On occasion, Deacon Samuel Wright and Pynchon's stepson and son-in-law, Henry Smith, offered lay sermons. And during Moxon's absence one Sunday in the summer of 1649, William Pynchon himself stepped into the pulpit.

Pynchon's text for both the morning and afternoon services on August 19 was the Beatitudes in Christ's "Sermon on the Mount" (Matthew 5:1–12). Notes taken at the time, again by John Pynchon, give a good idea of the message. His points were traditional: Pynchon identified the "marks" of a "blessed soul" in a conventional way. He emphasized values that characterize a compliant, obedient citizen of the community. The blessed are the poor in spirit who come begging to Christ. They mourn their sins. They are meek towards others, exercising control over anger and any desire

16. Moxon also stressed the power of forgiveness in his February 9, 1640 sermon on Psalm 32:5, "I acknowledged my sin unto thee, and mine iniquity have I not hid. I said, I will confess my transgressions unto the Lord; and thou forgavest the iniquity of my sin."

17. Keeble and Nuttall, *Calendar*, 1:179–80 no. 244.

for revenge. They are also meek towards God as they submit their lives to Christ, "yielding inward spiritual obedience to the will of God." In fact, their eagerness to do what God wants is so strong that they hunger and thirst after a right relationship with God. A passionate hunger is a powerful motive, said Pynchon:

> O what will hunger and thirst cause a man to do! To jeopard his life! The appetite of hunger and thirst has a strange, violent passion. It will make men break through stone walls. So when the soul apprehends that nothing will save its life but righteousness, now it falls a hungering and thirsting after righteousness.

In a paragraph near the end of the afternoon portion of his sermon, Pynchon dealt with a weighty theme, the "righteousness that will save the soul." He used language that confused even his son, whose repetitious notes suggest he misheard some of the phrases. Applying the terminology of Aristotelian logic, Pynchon maintained that the act of atonement involved the entire Trinity. "The formal finishing completing cause of a sinner's righteousness," he said, is the Father's free grace in giving a Mediator, Jesus Christ, accepting Christ's sacrifice, and freely forgiving. "If the fathers attonemt be procured this is the upshot of all: & there can be nothing more."[18]

These words and ideas were very much on Pynchon's mind at the time. He would have occasion to use them again.

18. John Pynchon, *Notes*, sermon of August 19, 1649, "Mr Wm Pynchon in Mr Moxons absence." The paragraph in question may be transcribed as follows:

> But it is a right[eousness] conferred upon us
> by all ye psons of ye Trinity
> 1. ye first pt of a sinners right is gods
> free grace in giving ye mediator
> to be ye procuring cause of o[u]r attonement
> 2. Je Cht himse ye sacrifice of his blood
> being ye procuring cause of the ffathers
> attonemt: 5. Romans. 9
> 3^d. pt of a sinners Justification whereby a
> sinner is made right[eous] is by ye working
> of ye holy ghost: working faith in ye soule
> I Corinthians. 6. 11
> 4. ye formall finishing compleating cause
> of [ye fathers] a sinners right[eousness] is ye fa-
> thers attonemt: & If ye fathers
> attonemt be procured this is ye upshot
> of all: & there can be nothing more
> & wt ever right[eousness] you obtaine besides
> this will never sattisfie you:

10

Dogs and Witches

TUESDAY, MARCH 18, 1651. Constable Thomas Merrick brought the prisoner in shackles into Pynchon's home for a second hearing. A parade of witnesses had testified against him in the waning days of winter. Eleven depositions from February 21 through March 18, 1651, reported strange phenomena, which all the deponents linked to the person of Hugh Parsons. Now William Pynchon guided a direct examination of the accused:

> Pynchon to Hugh Parsons: Not long since she [Mary Parsons, your wife] saith that you said to her if ever any trouble do come unto me it will be by your means and that you would be the means to hang me.
>
> Hugh Parsons: I might say so because she is the worst enemy that I have considering the relation that is between us: and if anybody bespeak evil of me she will speak as ill and as much as anybody else.[1]

Pynchon faced a daunting challenge, his most difficult case as a magistrate: suspicions of witchcraft had broken out in Springfield, Massachusetts.[2]

---

1. Hall, *Witch-Hunting*, 41.

2. Ibid., 29–60, provides transcriptions of original documents of the especially tragic case of Hugh and Mary Parsons. Pynchon's extensive notes for use in any subsequent trials can readily be recast to reproduce the courtroom conversation, virtually verbatim. I have retained punctuation, but adapted pronouns for a more conversational flow. Demos, *Entertaining Satan*, places aspects of the case in sociological frameworks.

Stephen Innes has suggested that in the Parsons witchcraft episode Springfield residents saw an uncomfortable "parody of Springfield's self-image: acquisitiveness became greed, individualism became vengefulness, deviance became diabolical."[3] Certainly Springfield was designed to provide opportunities for economic success. Even the preaching of George Moxon legitimated economic gain. "In matters of the world," he said, "in getting or keeping, we cannot expect them without diligence; but the diligent hand makes rich even in worldly matters." Innes concludes that the people of Springfield may have "deflected their dissatisfactions with William Pynchon onto Parsons."[4] He has speculated that rather than directing their discontent at the robust economic success of Springfield's patron and expressing their anger at their own indebtedness to him, they took out their frustration on a more vulnerable embodiment of "extreme economic individualism," the local brickmaker. Some contemporary comments do support this portrayal of Parsons. Both a next-door neighbor and a man who had lived in the Parsons' home thought he was "eager after the world."[5] His wife later remarked that Hugh wanted her to take a job nursing Pynchon's grandchildren, the sick daughters of Henry and Ann Smith, "for lucre and gain, one may well know his reason." She then added a typically self-deprecating remark, "but . . . doth anyone think me a fit nurse for them?"[6]

Parsons was among the skilled laborers in Springfield; he owned thirty-seven-and-a-half acres of land in 1647, just one year after he arrived in the plantation. But that much property placed him near the middle of the range of the forty-two Springfield landowners, not towards the top. Twenty-three had more property than Parsons; eighteen had less. It is not clear that the laconic, morose, contentious, and sometimes reluctant laborer could be perceived as a stand-in for Pynchon.[7]

Whether or not Parsons was largely a scapegoat, by the time the case came up, Pynchon's role in Massachusetts had come into serious question, and as later events revealed, he surely had much weightier things on his mind. Still, Pynchon dutifully took down a whole rash of affidavits by the Parsons' neighbors. A witness' recollection years later suggested that

3. Innes, *Labor*, 137.

4. Pynchon, *Notes*, June 3, 1649; Innes, *Labor*, 137.

5. Testimony of Benjamin Cooley and Anthony Dorchester, quoted in Hall, *Witch-Hunting*, 46.

6. Ibid., 47.

7. Burt, *First Century*, 1:190–91.

Pynchon was nonplussed by witchcraft testimony some brought to him. He was heard to "wonder" at one of the occurrences submitted as evidence for culpability, "but said he could not tell what to say to it."[8]

The testifiers reported a jumble of happenstances. They offered little "spectral evidence" of the kind that was to play such a damaging role in the accusations and trials at Salem in 1692. They said nothing about signing the devil's book. Only Mary Parsons mentioned satanic possession and shape-shifting into cats one night in Rowland Stebbins' lot, but that testimony came late in the process as she began to imagine herself as a witch. In the practical atmosphere of Springfield, it was more the case that strange things were happening. Kitchen knives had been going missing from Griffin Jones' table when needed, then reappearing later. George and Hannah Langdon's puddings oddly and neatly sliced in two when the bags in which they had been cooked were opened—not once, but twice. A trowel was gone from where it had been left just outside John Lombard's door, only to reappear on the lintel three days later. The milk from Sarah Edwards' cow was said to turn yellow and then change to other odd colors at each milking for a week. The sound of a saw being sharpened was heard under cover of darkness, and on a Sabbath, no less, according to Benjamin Munn. And people were seeing things. Weird lights lit the night in Jonathan Taylor's bedroom, while a phantom dog terrified the two-year-old son of Blanche and Reice Bedortha—sometimes he thought he saw it under the stool, sometimes under the cradle.

But at this second hearing, the most powerful testimony against Hugh Parsons came from his wife. Mary Parsons tried to present herself as an anti-witch Christian. Quite possibly she enhanced her testimony with invented piety, since her husband could not recall any of her alleged conversations and pleadings with him about witchcraft. In any case, Hugh Parsons' silence made an already remote man seem even more distant. Mary's words sealed his fate:

> Mary Parsons: One reason why I have suspected my husband to be a witch is because almost all that he sells to anybody doth not prosper: I am sorry . . . for that poor man Thomas Miller, for two days after my husband and he had bargained for a piece of ground Thomas Miller had that mischance of that cut in his leg.

> Mary Parsons then spoke directly to Hugh: One reason why I do suspect you to be a witch is because you cannot abide that anything

8. Testimony of William Branch, quoted in ibid., 103.

should be spoken against witches . . . You told me that you were at a neighbor's house a little before lecture when they were speaking of [a couple named Carrington from Windsor, Connecticut], that were now apprehended for witches . . . [W]hen you came home and spake these speeches to me I said to you I hope that God will find out all such wicked persons and purge New England of all witches ere it be long[.] To this . . . you gave [me] a naughty look but never a word.

Mary added, speaking to Pynchon: I have often entreated him to confess whether he were a witch or no, I told him that if he would acknowledge it I would beg the prayers of God's people on my knees for him, and that we are not our own, we are bought with a price, and that God would redeem from the power of Satan, &c.

Pynchon to Hugh Parsons: Had your wife spoken anything to you at any time to confess witchcraft[?]

Hugh Parsons: Not anything to me about witchcraft that I remember.

Mary Parsons: [D]id not I speak of it to you upon the death of my child: did not I tell you then that I had jealousies that you had bewitched your own child to death[?]

(Hugh said nothing.)

Pynchon to Mary Parsons: Did ever you know your husband [to] do anything beyond the power of nature[?]

Mary Parsons: On[e] a time my husband sent me to Jonathan Taylor to get him to work on the morrow: and as I returned home in the twilight I saw a thing like a great nasty dog by the path side[.] I suspected it was done by witchcraft from my husband[;] he sent me out . . . because usually he doth such things himself.[9]

Hugh and Mary Parsons' story began in 1645. Mary Lewis had led a difficult life. Originally married to a Roman Catholic who abandoned her, she left England for Massachusetts and eventually came to Springfield. After seven years of separation from Lewis, she sought permission to marry Hugh Parsons. Like Mary, he had also arrived recently in Springfield, where he worked as a sawyer and bricklayer. Unlike others who were caught up in witchcraft hysterias in early New England, he was not economically disadvantaged. One scholar points out that the crafts Parsons practiced placed

9. Ibid., 33, 41–42, 46.

him "roughly with in the middle ranks of colonial society," which made him uniquely prosperous among those accused of witchcraft in the earlier decades of the seventeenth century.[10]

Pynchon must have sensed some reason for concern about the marriage, for he wrote to Winthrop about Mary's circumstances a couple of times in June and September of 1645. He provided Winthrop with the facts as he understood them, including corroborating testimony of a Springfield resident who had actually known Mary back in Wales. Alexander Edwards substantiated Mary's report of mistreatment at the hands of her husband, her efforts to locate him, and her attendance at the Puritan ministry of the Rev. William Wroth, which spanned the border at both Llanvaches, Wales, and across the Severn at Bristol, England. Still, Pynchon may have wondered about the appropriateness of her remarriage.[11] Winthrop and other authorities approved, so Pynchon granted permission. The couple married on October 27, 1645.

The specter of witchcraft came onto the Springfield scene almost four years later in 1649 when Mary, obliquely at first and then directly, charged the widow Marshfield with witch-like behavior. Mary was pregnant at the time, and she claimed that Goody Marshfield envied every woman who had a child because Marshfield's own daughter had none. Pynchon ordered Mary to be "well whipped" unless she could pay the widow £3 for the slander. (Hugh paid the damages in Indian corn the following winter). Unsupportable witchcraft accusations were dangerous to the community and to anyone who made them. Mary's child was born in October, but lived only a year. Hugh showed little emotion when the child died. He said that "he was loath to express any sorrow before his wife, because of the weak condition that she was in at that time."[12] Was his apparent indifference simply Puritan stoicism? Or something more sinister?

Then things got worse. In late October 1650, the Parsons had a second son who died on March 1, 1651, at the age of four months. Suspicions of witchcraft against Hugh Parsons arose throughout the community. All the various pieces of evidence seemed to point in his direction. For example, the Moxons' daughters, Martha and Rebecca, suffered from "fits" at the very time Parsons was disputing with George Moxon about chimney work the

10. Weisman, *Witchcraft*, 78–79.

11. Clapp and Dorchester Antiquarian and Historical Society, *History*, 75–77; Forbes, *WP*, 5:45.

12. Smith, *CR*, 220; Hall, *Witch-Hunting*, 42.

brickmaker was supposed to do for him.[13] Neighbors noticed that Parsons was often nearby when the strange things they detailed in their affidavits took place. And Mary Parsons directly accused her husband of witchcraft. As the scholar Jane Kamensky remarked, Hugh Parsons exhibited what would have been seen under community norms of the time as "distinctly unmanly willingness to endure [his wife's] unwomanly tongue."[14] Indeed, George Colton testified that he had heard Mary Parsons speak "very harsh things against him before his face: and if he had been innocent he would have blamed her for her speeches for she spake such things against him as are not ordinary for persons to speak one of another and yet he being present said nothing for himself in way of blaming anything that she had spoken against him."[15]

Hugh Parsons' conduct simply added to the suspicion. He was given to peculiar responses and incautious statements. He constantly threatened that payments others had collected from him would do them no good. He kept saying things like "I shall remember you when you little think on it," and "I will be even with him." When confronted by allegations, he tended to be taciturn, either out of fear or sullenness. He froze whenever talk turned to witchcraft. Was this behavior simply caution in the face of possible hysteria? Fear about the direction the conversation was taking? Or guilt?

Innes has pointed out that the thirty-five persons who came forward to testify against Parsons represented a considerable percentage of the population: "Parsons apparently had managed to alienate most of his fellow villagers."[16] Several of the most vocal deponents in the witchcraft case against the Parsons were relative newcomers to the community. The Marshfields, Anthony Dorchester, Jonathan Taylor, Thomas and Sara Miller, and Benjamin Munn had arrived in Springfield only in 1648; they seem to have brought a measure of social disruption with them. The widow Marshfield in particular aggravated fears about witchcraft when she taught Mary Parsons how to detect witches.[17] The community was changing in other ways as Scottish immigrants began to arrive and exert new influences

13. Ibid., 37–38. The work seems to have been completed and paid for by William Pynchon out of credit extended to Moxon at the Pynchon store. The bill came to £6 18s 4d, which was 18s less than the original estimate; see William and John Pynchon, "Account Book," manuscript volume, Forbes Library, Northampton, Massachusetts, 209.

14. Kamensky, *Governing the Tongue*, 158.

15. Quoted in Hall, *Witch-Hunting*, 43.

16. Innes, *Labor*, 137.

17. Pynchon, *CR*, 219.

on Springfield. The first, John Stewart, had been deported to New England by Cromwell after the Battle of Dunbar in September 1650, where he
had fought on the side of Charles II. As Innes remarked, these newcomers'
"personal commitment to [English] Puritan norms was minimal."[18] Then,
too, the dynamics which have been documented in other early New England witch hunt episodes may have been at work in the Parsons case. Surely
individual animosities directed at difficult people played a part. So, too,
did the social tensions between landowners like Pynchon and independent
craftsmen like Parsons. Individuals seen as threats to shared and expected
social norms, including gender norms, were easy targets. The marginaliza-
tion of women was a factor in the community's dynamics, as was concern
for personal and communal survival in the face of scarcity. As events would
sadly show, the Parsons case was an early episode in a story that would
be reenacted elsewhere in later decades during times of social instability.
The most notable occurred at Salem, where panic over witchcraft broke
out in 1692 for other reasons than in Springfield—and with far more tragic
consequences.[19]

Following the two examinations Pynchon held on March 1 and 18,
1651, Parsons was "attached upon suspicion of witchcraft" and the case was
transferred to Boston. Since the charges could potentially result in a capital
trial, the matter was beyond the jurisdiction of a local magistrate's Court,
probably much to Pynchon's relief.

Mary later remarked bitterly of her husband, "if that dumb dog could
but have spoken it would have been better with me then it is: but . . . if I
might but speak with him before Mr. Pynchon face to face I would make
that dumb dog to speak." From mid-March on, there was such concern for
Mary that she was put under a protective custody of sorts, with villagers appointed to watch her at all times. It was obvious something was wrong with
her, but the cause was not clear.[20] Sufficient charges were lodged against
her during the first week of April 1651 to warrant a trial in Boston the very

18. Innes, *Labor*, 143; Burt, *First Century*, 64–65.

19. Of the many studies based on the carefully documented episodes of witchcraft
in New England, see in particular the pioneering analyses of Paul S. Boyer and Stephen
Nissenbaum, *Salem Possessed: The Social Origins of Witchcraft*, and Carol F. Karlson, *The
Devil in the Shape of a Woman: Witchcraft in Colonial New England*.

20. Drake anachronistically blames Pynchon for failing to recognize mental illness:
"Had not the Brains of Magistrate and People been turning Somersets, nearly as much
so as those of the Accused, she would have been treated as one entirely bereft of Reason."
(Drake, *Annals*, 245).

next month. In spite of some unguarded comments she had made about possibly being a witch herself (remarks she quickly qualified by saying, "but . . . why do I say so, I have no skill in witchery") she was acquitted of the charge on May 22.[21] But Mary was a hurt, fragile person. She was deeply distraught following the recent death of her second child, and in her anxiety-wracked condition she confessed to causing the child's death. On the basis of her confession, she was convicted of murder. It is likely she died in prison shortly thereafter, since there is no record that she was hanged.

In the end, a jury convicted Hugh Parsons of witchcraft in May 1652. But the verdict was reviewed by the Assistants, who sent it to the General Court because most of the testimony was not by eyewitnesses, but consisted only of Pynchon's written depositions—and besides, Mary had already confessed. When the full Court voted for exoneration, Hugh became a free man on June 1.[22] Understandably, he never returned to Springfield. Rumors at the time had it that he went first to Narragansett, then to Long Island.

The Pynchon Court record book reports the 1649 spat about witchcraft between Mary Parsons and the widow Marshfield, but it makes no mention of the Hugh Parsons case. Indeed, the book's annals break off on October 25, 1650, when William Pynchon reported the payment of 20s. worth of new clothing to Samuel Terry. Those provisions were to start him on his way as an apprentice with the linen weaver Benjamin Cooley. The notes do not pick up again until more than two years later, on November 22, 1652, when a new administration consisting of John Pynchon, Elizur Holyoke, and Samuel Chapin took the oath as magistrates. That gap is wholly due to critical events at the mid-October 1650 session of the General Court in Boston and the traumatic aftermath that followed.

21. For Mary under watch and her comments on "dumb dog" and "skill in witchery," see Hall, *Witch-Hunting*, 48, 49, 51.

22. Final disposition of the cases are recorded in Shurtleff, *MBCR*, 3:229 (Mary), and 273 (Hugh).

11

A Doctrine Cleared and a Book Burned

WEDNESDAY, OCTOBER 16, 1650. As luck would have it—or not—the Great and General Court was in session for its fall term when *The Meritorious Price* arrived in Massachusetts. It took no more than a glance at the cover for the authorities to know this unexpected volume, sent straight from London, would be trouble. It practically begged to be banned.

Nobody knows why William Pynchon wrote the first book banned and burned in Boston. Perplexity about his motives may have resulted from his public profile in earliest Massachusetts. In spite of an extensive written legacy that includes books, letters, and his Springfield Court records, Pynchon remains a figure in the shadows. Unlike other Puritan leaders (John Winthrop Sr., for example), he left no personal spiritual reflections or autobiographical memoirs. He stayed at the edge of the Commonwealth and its government and rarely expressed anything other than agreement with fellow leaders. In fact, his inclination to agree to take on difficult tasks created a large problem for him in the Connecticut corn controversy of 1638. It is therefore not surprising that there were no prior indications in any New England chatter that *The Meritorious Price*, with its distinctly contrarian claims about the atonement of Christ, was in the works.

So it was that Pynchon's colleagues on the Court of Assistants and the Deputies representing the towns voted a "protestation" of it.

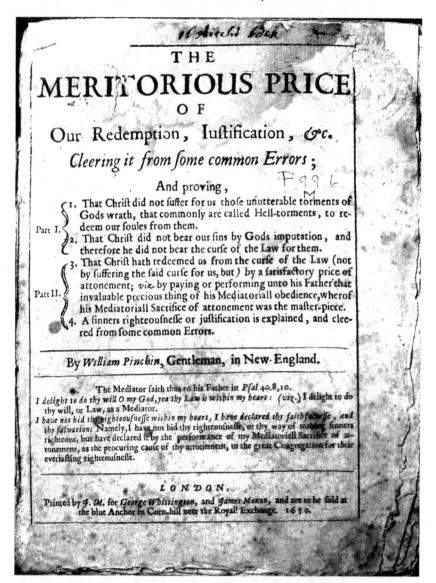

Title Page of *The Meritorious Price*, 1650.[1]

Their condemnation was decisive. They found Pynchon's assertions to be "false, eronyous, & heriticall."[2] They further urged:

1. Taken from the copy in the Congregational Library, Boston, Massachusetts.

2. Records of the Pynchon case are found in Shurtleff, *MBCR*, 3:215–16, 229, 239, 248, and 257, with an alternative account in ibid., 4 pt. 1:29–30, 48–49, and 72. See also

1. that a protest be drawn up "that this Court is so far from approving the same as that they do utterly dislike it & detest it as erroneous & dangerous;"

2. that "one of the reverend elders" write an answer for Pynchon to consider (they soon chose John Norton, the Teacher of the Ipswich Church);

3. that Pynchon be summoned to appear at the next Court to answer for his book; and

4. "That the said book now brought over be burnt by the executioner (or such other as shall be appointed thereunto, provided the party appointed be willing,) & that in the market place in Boston, on the morrow, immediately after the lecture."[3]

They also voted the sum of £20 to pay Norton for the rebuttal on behalf of the Colony.

A letter from several prominent Bay clergy hinted at who may have been behind this action. The signers included John Cotton and John Wilson of Boston, Richard Mather of Dorchester, and Zechariah Symmes of Charlestown. All four had been heavily involved in the Antinomian controversy of 1636 to 1638. That spirited dispute with Anne Hutchinson (1591–1643) and her followers became a symbol for any perceived threat to the Massachusetts experiment. Mrs. Hutchinson had hosted gatherings of as many as eighty persons in her home to discuss sermons. She believed that personal revelations, "the immediate witness of the spirit," enabled her to understand the biblical book of the Apocalypse properly. She may also have maintained that of all the ministers in the colony, only John Cotton preached a covenant of free grace, with no good works required, and that all other clergy "were not able ministers of the New Testament." The authorities became so afraid of the challenge Hutchinson and her followers posed to both clergy and lay authorities that they confiscated guns and other arms and ammunition from seventy-five men. The memory of that watershed moment, like a nightmare vividly remembered, may have aggravated the ministers' concern in Pynchon's case.[4] In any event, the clergy

---

McIntyre, *William Pynchon*, 33; and Morison, *Builders*, 369–75. See Appendix 3 for the full text of the General Court's "Declaration & Protestation."

3. Shurtleff, *MBCR*, 3:215.

4. For more about Mrs. Hutchinson, see *ODNB* 29:5–6. On the Antinomian controversy, see Hall, *Antinomian Controversy*. See also Hall, *Puritans in the New World*,

letter explained that the Court rushed to judgment so word could be sent to England via a ship that was just about to sail from Boston. Pynchon was not even present at the time; his signature on Springfield Court records places him in the Connecticut River Valley on the previous day.[5]

One well-known voice questioned the Court's action less than a week later. Roger Williams wrote a letter from Rhode Island that John Winthrop Jr. received on October 23:

> He [Hugh Caulkin, deputy from Gloucester] tells me of a booke lately come over in mr. Pynchons name, wherein is Some Derogation to the blood of Christ. The booke was therefore burnt in the market place at Boston, and mr. Pynchon to be cited to the Court: If it come to your hand I may hope to see it: however the most High and only wise will by this Case discover what Libertie Conscience hath in this land.[6]

Williams' ironic taunt about liberty of conscience was a mocking reminder of his own treatment at the hands of the Massachusetts government. The Winthrop administration had expelled Williams from Massachusetts in 1636, though over the succeeding years the governor saw to it that the two remained on speaking terms. Occasional correspondence between the two lasted until Williams received a Royal Charter for Rhode Island. Now, a year after Winthrop Sr.'s death, Williams continued to stay in touch with Winthrop's son. He seemed to have had no doubt that copies of the proscribed volume were available in spite of its blatantly public condemnation.

Pynchon's own immediate reaction to his colleagues' censure was not recorded, but the Court's "Protestation" had introduced a chilling term: "heresy." The visceral impact of that word is tremendous. Heretics are so near, and yet so far. They share much with their accusers. But however slight it may seem, the heretics' divergence makes it difficult to be sure of them. It is impossible to know precisely what they mean by their use of the very same words. They have chosen a different way of talking and believing; that is what "heresy" means at its root—to choose. Because heretics

---

219; and also Morgan, "Case against Anne Hutchinson," 635–49, for an analysis of what was at stake in that controversy. The Court's order confiscating weapons is found in ibid., 1:211–12.

5. See Burt, *First Century*, 1:122. For the letter from John Cotton and John Wilson of Boston, Richard Mather of Dorchester, Zechariah Symmes of Charlestown, and William Thompson of Braintree, see the final pages of John Norton's *A Discussion*. The evidence that Pynchon was in Springfield at the time is taken from Smith, *CR*, 227.

6. Forbes, *WP*, 6:76. For a biography of Williams, see *ODNB*, 59:293–97.

opt to distance themselves from the usual definitions of customary words as well as the generally shared convictions and ordinary sentiments of the prevalent community, heretics cannot be counted on. In such a situation, what was the meaning of the "fellowshippe of the Govornor of the Matthew: Baye in New England" to which Pynchon had sworn his oath as an Assistant many years ago?[7]

The Court's vote also implied a symbolic destruction of Pynchon himself. In an act of sheer humiliation, his book was burned by the executioner.

It turned out that unbeknownst to almost everybody, Pynchon had been reflecting theologically on the theme of his treatise for quite a while. As Pynchon later remembered it, he had intended as early as 1630 to "publish something on that subject when I should get tyme."[8] Pynchon named his original inspiration for *The Meritorious Price* on an introductory page of his essay. "This Argument," he said, "was thus framed by M. Henry Smith a godly Preacher, neer thirty yeers since, in my presence." Considering the publication date, Pynchon's epiphany must have occurred around 1619. As Pynchon remembered it, Smith held that "Christ hath not suffered the infinite wrath of God for our redemption." Smith took it for granted that "every article of our faith is set down in the Scripture, and whatever is not proved by Scripture I am not bound to believe." On that basis, he felt free to dispense with any doctrines that stress the centrality of Christ's sufferings in the process of redemption. The claim that Christ suffered the infinite wrath of God is one such unfounded assumption. Smith believed that all the Bible texts ordinarily used to prove that Christ had suffered the torments of hell do not actually require such an interpretation. That includes the key verse of Isaiah 53:6: "and the Lord hath laid on him the iniquity of us all." Smith claimed that inferences about God's wrath were smuggled into the orthodox interpretation without warrant. The proposition that "[h]e that had the iniquity of us all laid upon him, did suffer the infinite wrath of God, . . . must be well proved before I can assent to the Conclusion."[9]

There is no historical trace of a contemporary "Henry Smith," and in fact, Pynchon's later writings corrected this to "Robert Smith." A graduate of Trinity College, Cambridge, Smith served from 1605 at Holy Trinity

---

7. Shurtleff, *MBCR*, 1:350.

8. See de Jong's obvious understatement: "It is not clear what made Pynchon enter the arena of theological debate" (de Jong, "Christ's Descent," 131). For Pynchon's intention to publish, see Keeble and Nuttall, *Calendar*, 1:179 no. 244.

9. Pynchon, *MP*, A4v.

Minories on a lane off off Minories Street near the Tower of London. Because that church was exempt from the bishop's control and therefore to some extent self-governing, it had hosted gatherings of more deeply committed reform-minded believers since at least the 1560s. In fact, the godly who frequented Holy Trinity Minories were probably the earliest objects of the epithet "Puritans." The church remained a premier Puritan pulpit for decades.[10]

The Court ordered Pynchon to respond at its next session, which was slated to take place in the spring. The scanty Springfield town records for 1650 and 1651 make only a passing reference to William Pynchon. His magistrate's Court record is silent. Only the witchcraft depositions for the Parsons' case of February and March 1651 give any hint of Pynchon's activities that winter and spring. But on May 8, 1651, right after the Court convened for its regular spring session in Boston, Pynchon came before his fellow Assistants and the deputies from the surrounding towns to acknowledge that the book was indeed his.

10. de Jong, "Christ's Descent," 134, 152. Pynchon's mistaken first name may have occurred through a mix-up with the name of his own son-in-law. On "Puritan," see Collinson, *Elizabethan Puritan Movement*, 86–87.

12

Discussions in Divinity

THURSDAY EVENING, MAY 8, 1651. Responding to an invitation by the General Court, four men gathered for a solemn task. Earlier that day, "out of their tender respect to him" the Court had suggested that William Pynchon confer with any ministers of his choosing. He picked three clergy present that day. John Norton (1606–1663), the "reverend elder" chosen to write the General Court's response, was a 1627 graduate of Peterhouse, Cambridge, and as an author with several volumes to his credit, was an obvious choice to speak for the Massachusetts Court.[1] Norton had been parsing and critiquing Pynchon's book over the previous half-year and now presented Pynchon with his response. Edward Norris II was Teacher of the church in Salem. John Cotton served the church in Boston. Of the three, only Cotton was a local resident. His home on the slopes of Beacon Hill overlooked the harbor and the town, a scattering of spare, unpainted wooden structures—homes for the citizens and sheds for their animals. Cotton's house would have offered a private place for a delicate conversation. A path from the waterfront led past the marketplace, where Pynchon's book had been burned the previous year, and the Meetinghouse where the Court met, and directly up the hill along what is now Court Street to Cotton's property near the present John Adams Courthouse.

1. For more on Norton, see *ONDB*, 41:175–77. His Latin defense of congregational polity, *Responsio ad Totam Quæstionum Syllogen à clarissimo Viro Domino Guilielmo Apollonio*, was published in London in 1648. It was translated by Douglas Horton and published as *The Answer to the Whole Set of Questions*.

At question this night was the theme of Pynchon's book: the atoning work of Christ. The mystery of salvation intrigued Pynchon. How could Christ's suffering save? What unique role did Christ play in connecting people of faith with the forgiving love of God? What was there about Christ that energized the forgiving, empowering love of God? A classic theological answer maintained that Christ redeemed humankind by making amends for the offence of sin. God accepted the "satisfaction" Christ accomplished by his vicarious death on the cross, through which Christ paid the penalty God justly expected from fallen mankind.[2] The doctrine of the atonement was a live issue in sixteenth- and seventeenth-century theology. Many theologians of the era delved into the fine points of the matter. The kind of suffering and its extent, what part of Christ's person was involved—these were real issues for an age where suffering and torture were commonplace. They were also questions that interested Pynchon.

The three consultants were tasked with retrieving Pynchon from errors the Court had detected in his condemned book. Pynchon made a terrible mistake, said John Cotton as they met together, in "extenuating the bitterness of the soul sufferings of Christ . . . as if such pangs were incompatible to Christ's pure and innocent nature and life."

"I see that I have not spoken in my book so fully of the price and merit of Christ's sufferings as I should have done," Pynchon admitted.

"Unless the whole guilt of our sins be imputed to [Christ]," said Cotton, "and his perfect obedience to the Law [imputed] to us, we shall fall short, both of the matter and the form of our justification." Cotton felt that the very heaviness of Christ's suffering revealed the depth of God's grace. "The more bitter the cup was which Christ drank for us," he added, "the deeper was the guilt of our sin, and the greater was the measure of his love towards us."

"Imputation," John Norton patiently explained, "is the actual and effectual application of the righteousness of Christ unto a believer. Imputing and believing are as giving and receiving."[3]

---

2. The traditional view of the atonement in western European originated with Anselm of Canterbury (ca. 1033–1109) (O'Collins and Farrugia, *Concise Dictionary*, 214).

3. John Cotton, "To the Judicious Christian Reader," in Norton, *Orthodox Evangelist*, A4v; Shurtleff, *MBCR*, 4 pt. 1:48; Norton, *Discussion*, 245, 226. In addition to Cotton's comment, in 1652, the Reverand Richard Mather (1596–1669), pastor of the Dorchester Church, editor-in-chief of the *Bay Psalm Book*, and participant in all the early Massachusetts theological and political controversies, addressed the meaning of "imputation" in his *Summe of Certain Sermons*, which strongly affirmed the notion that

And Pynchon seemed to listen.

The Meritorious Price is written in the form of an imaginary conversation between a Tradesman and a Divine. The Tradesman provides the orthodox voice, while the Divine offers Pynchon's own views. There is no give-and-take between them; the Tradesman concedes to the Divine, never the other way around. The volume is heavy on the Scriptures. Much of it involves serial interpretations of biblical passages, as Pynchon sought to explain texts that were usually thought to prove that Christ experienced "the Wrath of God for our Redemption."[4]

The learned clergy meeting with Pynchon would have recognized most of the sources he relied upon. In addition to the Scriptures, Pynchon drew heavily on volumes by thirty-three authorities whom he had carefully cited, some from secondary quotations. He referred to two volumes by Roman Catholic authors, but most of his books were written by Reformed and Puritan theologians.

One resource he did not name was the Jesuit scholar Konrad Kircher's 1607 *Concordantiae veteris Testamenti.*[5] Pynchon studied biblical texts eagerly and took an academic approach using a variety of Puritan biblical commentaries. He was very interested in Jewish practices and interpretations and the light they could shed on Scripture texts. He was fascinated by the words of the original languages. By using Kircher's two-volume dictionary, even without an effective working knowledge of Hebrew, Pynchon could read back from Latin definitions of the semantic roots, and so find where individual Hebrew words were used in the original.[6]

Only two of his sources were unavailable in English, and all except one existed in editions published before Pynchon left England in 1630.[7]

Pynchon (whom he did not name) had so vehemently attacked.

4. The texts that became central to Pynchon's argument included Genesis 2:17; Isaiah 53:4, 5, 6; 2 Corinthians 5:21; Matthew 26:37; Hebrews 5:7; Psalm 22; and Galatians 3:13.

5. Pynchon's copy of Konrad Kircher's *Concordantiae Veteris Testamenti* is held by the Andover-Harvard Theological Library in Cambridge, Massachusetts. It contains notes by William Pynchon and was signed by his grandson, Joseph, and given to Harvard by his great-great-grandson, William, between 1764 and 1766.

6. McIntyre, *William Pynchon,* 33, concluded that Pynchon had not read the Bible in its original tongues, which is preferable to the unsupported claims by others that Pynchon "had mastered Greek, Latin and Hebrew" (Burt, *First Century,* 80; Smith, *CR,* 26; de Jong, "Christ's Descent," 131). Winship noted that Pynchon "made it clear repeatedly in later publications that his forays into Greek and Hebrew were made only through a dictionary" (Winship, "Contesting Control," 810 n. 38).

7. For a list of books and authors Pynchon mentioned in *MP,* see Appendix 4.

Kircher's *Concordantiae* and a translation of the Scriptures from Syriac and Hebrew by Emmanuele Tremellio (1510–1580), an Italian Jewish convert to Christian faith, both required knowledge of Latin. Pynchon took material from respected heavy-hitters like Geneva reformer John Calvin (1509–1564), the Puritan professor in exile in Holland, William Ames (1576–1633), and the expatriate Congregational pastor and scholar, Henry Ainsworth (1571–1622), also in the Netherlands. With Ainsworth, he even carried on a private correspondence.

In addressing his topic, Pynchon was nothing if not methodical. As the General Court found to its dismay, he had neatly outlined the four points of his thesis on the title page. His first point protected Christ from suffering at God's hands:

> I. That Christ did not suffer for us those unutterable torments of God's wrath, that commonly are called Hell-torments, to redeem our souls from them.

At the core of Pynchon's theology is his concept of Mediator: Jesus Christ as a buffer between God the Father and humankind. Proceeding from his idealistic understanding of Christ, Pynchon did his very best to shield the uniqueness of Christ as a person and to secure Christ's role as Redeemer. His Christ is timeless and protected and pristine. Pynchon claimed that since Christ, as "second Adam," is utterly unique, he is incapable of undergoing the kinds of suffering ordinary humans might experience. He is, in effect, genetically different from other human beings. Christ cannot be "one of the fallen sons of Adams posterity; for he was conceived by the Holy Ghost, and not by natural generation."[8]

Pynchon argued that Christ did really suffer. But he suffered at the hands of human beings only, and never God. Also, Christ really died, as both malefactor in the eyes of the Romans and as Mediator in the sight of God. But like an invincible video game character, Christ could not be killed by his oppressors. His death occurred because he voluntarily gave up his life by "the separation of his soul from his body . . . by his own active power." Jesus could not be killed "till [he] himselfe pleased to actuate his own death, by the joynt concurrence of both his [divine and human] natures."[9] His

8. Pynchon, *MP*, 5.

9. Ibid., 64.

body as "the Holy Habitation of the Godhead" was not corrupted in death. Pynchon claimed that Christ's descent into hell mentioned in the Apostles' Creed actually meant to the "place of Joy," to "paradise" in Hades.

Pynchon got this notion, and several other exegetical novelties, from a reinterpretation by Hugh Broughton (1549–1612), a lively, controversial, colorful scholar of rabbinic literature and a major influence on Pynchon. Broughton had attained fame for his chronological analysis of the Bible in *A Concent of Scripture* (1588).[10] He achieved public notoriety as well when the dramatist Ben Jonson (1572–1637) pointedly satirized Broughton in his 1610 play, *The Alchemist*, a parody that placed typical Broughton terms and convoluted concepts on the lips of a character who had fallen into a "fit," rambling on about calling "the Rabbines, and the heathen Greekes . . . to come from Salem, and from Athens, and teach the people of great Britaine."[11] Broughton summed up his thesis in the title of a tract he wrote in 1605: *Positions of the VVord Hades: That it is the generall place of Soules: and holdeth as vvell the Godly which are in Paradise, as the vvicked that are in Tartarus.* (Pynchon offered an unwittingly humorous illustration of this point, also borrowed from Broughton: "Hades" includes both a place for the bad and a place for the good, "as great Britain doth comprehend England and Scotland.") Pynchon was convinced that Christ could not possibly have suffered the separation from God's favor and the painful sensations of everlasting fire and brimstone that constitute the real torments of hell.[12] He never wavered from that conviction.

The role Broughton played in Pynchon's thinking was so extensive that some details about him are warranted here. Even though Broughton remained very much in the public eye, Pynchon probably became acquainted with him through shared Puritan circles, and it may be that in his youth Pynchon carried on a personal correspondence with him. It is difficult to say when or even if the two ever met. Excepting for brief trips home to England—one in 1603, when Pynchon was thirteen—Broughton lived on the continent from 1592 until nine months before his death on August 4, 1612, when Pynchon was twenty-two.

---

10. For more on Broughton, see *ODNB*, 7:984–87.

11. Jonson, *Alchemist*, 4.5.446–85, especially ibid., 4.5.457–60. References are to act, scene, and line.

12. Pynchon, *MP*, 10–11, 74. The Great Britain-Scotland-England analogy comes from Broughton, *Two little workes*, unnumbered page 7.

Broughton graduated from Magdalene College at Cambridge, where Sir Walter Mildmay of Chelmsford sponsored him as a lecturer in Greek. He was an accomplished scholar of rabbinic literature and the prolific and sometimes acerbic author of numerous volumes—most of them pamphlets, really—as well as many scribal publications (handwritten documents that were circulated) on a variety of scriptural themes. Broughton believed that "[w]ithout knowledge of Rabbins [rabbis] & Heathen Greeks, none can be a fit Bishop to expound soundly the Ebrew and the Greek Testament." Knowing that "[t]he Ebrew tongue is full of equivocations," he was eager to explicate and explain the ambiguities of the language.[13] Fascinated by the Apocalypse, devoted to biblical chronologies and genealogies, conversant with ancient Greek parallels to biblical accounts, a master of abbreviation by initials (the Queen was "Q," "your majesty" was "your M.," King Edward VI was "K. Ed. 6.," and he himself was "Br."), Broughton brought a certain panache to biblical studies. He cut an impressive figure. Though he was said to be "waspish and cantankerous in controversy" and given to "intemperate outbursts," he was practically adored by his pupils as "a jovial dinner companion and a loyal friend." In the first decades of the 1600s, Broughton struggled mightily, though unsuccessfully, to secure funding for a Hebrew language and rabbinic studies department at Cambridge. Such a campaign may seem quite atypical in the early seventeenth century, but one motive was his desire to create a center where Christians could be trained to confound rabbis in debate. He felt that Jews rejected the gospel message because of loose ends and nagging discrepancies in the usual Bible translations. In Broughton's view, even very small inconsistencies gave ammunition to those looking for reasons to reject the truth of the Scriptures. He reached that conclusion based on his own public disputations and private conversations with leaders of various Jewish communities on the continent early in his career.[14] Broughton was particularly bothered by differences in biblical chronologies. While he was definitely Puritan in his theology, and derided bishops as "buy-shopps," and was very frequently at odds with the

13. Broughton, *Position*, 8; ibid., *Principal Positions*, 9.

14. Those rabbis included Rabbi Elias of Frankfurt, Rabbi Wolf of Hanover, Rabbi David Farar of Amsterdam, and even Rabbi Abraham Ruben of Thrace, who wrote from Constantinople in 1598 and came to England to inquire about becoming a Christian. Farar and Ruben are mentioned in the extended title of Broughton's 1608 booklet, *Ovr Lordes Famile*. See also Broughton, *Require of Agreement*, and ibid., *Aduertisement of Corruption*, F2r.

Archbishop of Canterbury, Broughton remained an advocate of the episcopal polity of the Church of England.

Broughton addressed a wide range of biblical subjects in his extensive output. Original translations of Daniel, Ecclesiastes, Lamentations, and Job are among his large legacy of writings. His work on Daniel in particular resulted in two longer volumes and multiple paragraphs in shorter studies. In spite of his admitted mastery of Hebrew, Broughton tended towards unconventional interpretations of the original text. He focused closely and exclusively on specific words of the original Hebrew, and it may have been this fastidious attention to detail that Pynchon found attractive. Broughton's phrasings could be quite eccentric. For instance, in his hands, Job 4:17 became pretentious and quaint:

> Can the sorrowful-man be holden just before the Puissant:
> can the human-wight be cleare before him that was his maker[?][15]

Broughton had a generous appreciation of himself and his own intellectual contributions. He was the kind of scholar who frustrated the more mainstream academicians, and in spite of his admitted linguistic expertise, Broughton was not invited to join the fifty-four experts commissioned by King James to create a fresh translation of the Bible because he was difficult to work with. He considered this slight to his reputation a bitter blow. In response, in 1611 he panned the newly available King James Version of the Bible in a brief pamphlet addressed to the king entitled *A Censure of the late translation for our Churches*. He was particularly galled by chronological inconsistencies in the new version—and, incidentally, in every Bible before or since. Regarding the Authorized Version, Broughton remarked, "I had rather be rent in pieces by wilde horses, then any such translation by my consent should bee vrged vpon poore Churches."[16]

In any case, Broughton made an overwhelming impact on Pynchon, who owned at least twenty of Broughton's nearly fifty books, booklets, and scribal publications. He cited or alluded to nine of them in *The Meritorious Price*, always with unquestioning agreement.

Like the vast majority of Puritans, Pynchon did not interpret the Bible with word-for-word literalism. He explicitly identified some of the interpretive tools he used throughout his writings, including figures of speech such as synecdoche (a part used for the whole) and metonymy (one noun

15. Ibid., *Iob: To the King*, 52.
16. Ibid., *Censure*, 1.

used to symbolize another, such as "sin" for "sin offering"). These linguistic devices gave him substantial wiggle room. But Pynchon could be highly selective in how he applied figures of speech. He tended to take literally what others considered metaphoric while taking as symbolic what others considered absolutely literal. Also, he interpreted certain verses as if some of the words in Scripture were in scare quotes. Pynchon understood Psalm 69:5, for example, which he placed on Christ's lips, as "O God, thou knowest my 'foolishness,' and my 'guiltinesses' are not hid from thee"—as if "foolishness" and "guilt" were false charges raised by Christ's adversaries.[17]

Nearly a dozen times, Pynchon pointed to what he considered "gross absurdities" and "woeful inferences" that emerge from the traditional doctrinal claims as he understood them. A series of rhetorical questions at the end of his first section reflect the contradictions inherent in the language surrounding Jesus' divine, yet human nature:

> Did Christ inflict the torments of hell upon his own human nature? Was his Divine nature angry with his human nature? Or did his Divine nature forsake his human nature in anger? as it must Have done if he had suffered the torments of hell: . . . These and such like gross absurdities the common Doctrine of imputation will often fall into.[18]

Pynchon's second assertion is equally crucial for his argument. He had no use for that "common Doctrine of imputation":

> II. That Christ did not bear our sins by God's imputation, and therefore he did not bear the curse of the Law for them.

For Pynchon, there could be no "imputation" or transfer of guilt from the party responsible to somebody else. There could certainly be no imputation of humankind's sin to Christ. That would result in a "Catch-22." If God had "imputed" our sins to Christ, he would be blemished and no longer qualified to be the "immaculate Lamb of God," and in that case, Christ "could not have been a fit person in Gods esteem to do the office of a Mediator for our Redemption."[19]

Therefore, said Pynchon, the innocent Christ could not have suffered punishment for the sins of others. That would never be allowed in the Springfield magistrate's Court, and it certainly should not be the way God

17. Pynchon, *MP*, 26.

18. Ibid., 79.

19. Ibid., 14.

operates. What the classic analyst of early New England theology called Pynchon's "plain common-sense" approach to theological questions is evident at this point. Pynchon simply followed Ezekiel 18:20: "The soul that sinneth, it shall die. The son shall not bear the iniquity of the father, neither shall the father bear the iniquity of the son." Indeed, "God cannot inflict the torments of hell upon an innocent, to redeem a guilty person," remarked Pynchon.[20] It was a position he maintained steadfastly and repeated adamantly in later writings.

For his third point, Pynchon focused on what he felt was Christ's real accomplishment: his "Mediatorial Sacrifice of Atonement."

> III. That Christ hath redeemed us from the curse of the Law (not by suffering the said curse for us, but) by a satisfactory price of atonement; viz. by paying or performing unto his Father that invaluable precious thing of his Mediatorial obedience, whereof his Mediatorial Sacrifice of atonement was the master-piece.

Pynchon conceded that Christ intentionally conformed to the pattern for sacrifices specified in the Hebrew Scriptures (Leviticus 3–7). But Christ's obedience to the moral law in the course of his life had nothing to do with redemption. Christ's blameless life was not required for redemption. Pynchon maintained that Christ's obedience to the Torah, the Law of the Hebrew Scriptures, "was but the work of his flesh or of his human nature" and as such was not sufficient to redeem anybody. Moreover, Pynchon was clear that Christ saves only the elect. In a kind of reverse synecdoche, with the whole standing for only a part, he argued that "the sins of the world," which the Lamb of God takes away according to John 1:19, refers to "the World of Believers only."[21]

Just as there can be no transfers or imputation of guilt, there can be none of merit either. Christ's obedience cannot be credited to mankind's account, because Christ cannot do for us what we must do for ourselves. Pynchon's perspective is totally individualistic at this point: "For the legal promise of Eternal life is not made over to us upon condition of Christ's personal performance, but upon condition of our own personal performance."[22]

Under his final heading, Pynchon replied to the arguments of John Forbes in *A Treatise Tending to the Clearing of Ivstification* (1616). Forbes

20. Foster, *Genetic History*, 20; Pynchon, *MP*, 81.

21. Pynchon, *MP*, 108, 89.

22. Ibid., 95, 107.

served as the widely respected pastor of the Merchant Adventurers' Church in Middleburg, the Netherlands, from 1608 till 1633. In that capacity, he was closely linked to many who were household names in the Puritan world. The exiles Hugh Broughton (Pynchon's favorite scholar), John Norton (Pynchon's nemesis), and John Robinson (the Pilgrims' pastor) all served as his associates. Yet Pynchon criticized Forbes' reasoning:

> IV. A sinners righteousness or justification is explained, and cleared from some common Errors.

Forbes maintained that Christ's "passive obedience" in suffering as a human being to the point of death on the cross was sufficient to redeem God's people. God simply credited Christ's obedience to believers. But, argued Pynchon, Christ's divine nature was part of the equation. His humanity and divinity "were united as one in the making of his Mediatorial sacrifice."[23]

Forbes also claimed that just as all humankind shares a kinship with Adam, so all of Adam's heirs also share a kinship with Christ. Pynchon maintained, however, that humans have what might now be called a chromosomal connection with Adam, but not with Christ. Because of Christ's obedience, those who believe in him, and thereafter are connected to Christ by the grace of faith, are forgiven and then adopted by the Father, "which is the highest degree of happiness that ever any poor sinner can think on."[24]

In his summation on one of the last pages of *The Meritorious Price*, Pynchon resorted to age-old Aristotelian terminology as he distinguished the various "causes" at work in Christ's atonement. Pynchon must have been satisfied with this summary of his view, which he had included in his August 19, 1649, sermon at Springfield in nearly identical language:

> The Fathers Atonement or reconciliation is the top mercy of all mercyes that makes a poor sinner happy.
>
> But the truth is, a sinners Atonement must be considered as it is the work of all the Trinity.
>
> 1. The Father must be considered both as the efficient and as the formal cause of a sinners Atonement.
>
> 2. The Mediator must be considered as the only meritorious procuring cause of the Fathers Atonement Romans. 5.10

---

23. Ibid., 138.
24. Ibid., 148.

3. The holy Ghost must be considered as the principal instrumentall cause of the Fathers Atonement, by working in sinners the grace of faith by which sinners are inabled to apprehend and receive the Fathers Atonement, for their ful redemption, Iustification and Adoption; which spirituall blessings they so receive into their souls as soon as ever they do believe in Christ.[25]

The manuscript Norton handed to Pynchon in the course of conversations between himself, Cotton, Norris, and Pynchon was his response to *The Meritorious Price*. It became the basis for a volume he eventually produced in 1653, *A Discussion of that Great Point in Divinity, the Sufferings of Christ*. In his critique, Norton used a surprisingly simple technique, so deftly that it seems Pynchon never knew what hit him.

Norton's tool was Ramistic logic.[26] Developed by Pierre de la Ramée (1515–1572), the system featured divisibility: everything is composed of two parts. As Walter Ong, SJ, has suggested, the effect is a yielding of more components "through a series of successive openings, like a Chinese puzzle."[27] At the time, the Ramist scheme seemed to be an exciting breakthrough from the traditional Aristotelian logic that Pynchon used, and it became exceedingly popular among Puritan clergy. It could be argued, however, that while the Ramist method provided a certain clarity, its starkly drawn bifurcations also contributed to the unquestioning self-confidence and high-relief contrasts found in Puritanism, and may well have contributed to the lack of malleability in Puritan thought—something must be either one thing or another. At a distance, the method's uniqueness disappears, and within a relatively brief time the Ramist innovation itself and the certainty it engendered faded into oblivion.[28]

On the basis of Ramistic logic, Norton framed a series of eight "Propositions," four "Questions," and five "Distinctions." These all supported his orthodox interpretations: Christ's obedience to God's will entailed

---

25. Ibid., 158 (misnumbered as second 152).

26. For a thorough study, see Ong, *Ramus*.

27. Ong, *Ramus*, 200.

28. The Ramist breakdown of theology is found in Ames, *Marrow*, 72–73. See also Roberts-Miller, *Voices in the Wilderness*, 45–50, 62: "Perhaps due to Ramistic dichotomies, many Puritan theories assume a binary opposition in terms of the positions available," such as elect versus the damned, order versus sin, etc.

suffering, and indeed required it, and as a result of Christ's sufferings God credited grace to believers. Christ's suffering was in accord with the principles of justice God established and continues to exercise in dealing with humankind: "The Decree being passed [Genesis 2:17], and the word gone out of his mouth, God cannot deny himself."[29]

Norton echoed the General Court's charge against Pynchon, concluding that much of what Pynchon wrote in *The Meritorious Price* was "false, eronyous, & heriticall." Norton defined heresy as "a Fundamental Error, that is, such as he that knowingly liveth and dieth therein cannot be saved."[30] But he attributed Pynchon's confusion to his lack of familiarity with logical and theological process. He remained hopeful that something good could come of it:

> That the Authour of this Treatise may arise not only out of those absurdities, but also out of those heresies into which the Dialogue sheweth him to be fallen, is and shall be our praiers, and the rather are we encouraged that God will have mercy upon him herein, because we hope he did it ignorantly and through an erring conscience.[31]

Norton expressed a measure of esteem and appreciation for Pynchon personally in addition to his concern for Pynchon's relationship with God and the community. He prayed that the

> good Spirit of Grace . . . Magnifie his compassion in the pardon and recovery of the Authour, a person in many respects to be very much tendered of us; in so saving of him (though as by fire) as that his rising again may be much more advantageous to the truth, comfortable to the people of God, and honourable to himself, then his fall hath been scandalous, grieving or dishonourable.[32]

Instead of blaming Pynchon, Norton held Satan responsible for his "[h]eretical doctrine so directly and deeply destructive to the truth of the Gospel, and salvation of man, . . . reserving all charitable thoughts . . . touching the compiler thereof [namely, Pynchon], who (we hope) did it ignorantly." The "Epistle Dedicatory," which Norton addressed "To the much Honoured General Court," largely had to do with the appropriateness of

29. Norton, *Discussion*, 10.
30. Ibid., A1v; see also ibid., 267.
31. Ibid., 124.
32. Ibid., 269.

magistrates intervening and the need for them to act "to procure that the people may live a life in all godliness and honesty."[33] While the personal error of heresy was an awful thing, just as awful was its discordant impact on the community.

In spite of his graciousness towards Pynchon, Norton claimed that Pynchon had committed a fundamental error that resulted in Pynchon's confusion about the full scope of Christ's obedience as Mediator. For Norton, the role Christ plays is a gritty one. He actually suffered the worst that could ever happen to a human being. And others do share in Christ's achievement as he fulfilled God's law. God has to expect some satisfaction of the penalty that must be paid for disobedience, as any judge (such as Pynchon!) should certainly know.

Norton's cleverness is most visible in the "Distinctions" he drew between terms that may seem similar but which, he maintained, are distinct in absolutely crucial ways. For example, imputation for committing sin is not the same as for the guilt of sin; that is, Christ was willing to do the time even though he did not do the crime. Likewise, thinking of hell as a particular place is not the same as understanding that it is an unlocalized condition.[34] Norton also criticized Pynchon's theology for the crucial defect of separating aspects of Christ which necessarily belonged together. He believed Pynchon had separated soul from body and human from divine. Norton wove this charge throughout his criticism.

Norton's *Discussion* ends by triumphantly pointing out that "The Dialogue containeth three heresies." It denies that Christ may in any way be credited with taking on the cost for human sin. It denies that Christ obeyed the law as "God-man Mediatour" in order to obtain a secure status for humankind before God. And it denies the attribution of Christ's obedience to human beings in order to set them right with God. As Norton concluded,

> The first holdeth us in all our sin, and continueth the full wrath of God abiding upon us.
> The second takes away our Saviour.
> The third takes away our righteousness and our justification.
> What need the Enemy of Jesus, grace, and souls adde more?[35]

---

33. Ibid., A3v.
34. Ibid., 9–10.
35. Ibid., 267, 268.

So much for Pynchon. The General Court was satisfied, Norton collected the money for his 270 pages, and it was all over so far as the Bay colony was concerned.

Norton had offered a self-sealed argument in which all was in balance and all was made clear. His dense explanations exemplified a highly complex evolution of Ramistic dualisms. His way of thinking and talking seems to have been designed to keep theology in the hands of technical practitioners. His tone was self-assured and condescending. In this he was much like Pynchon, in that he mirrored Pynchon's own self-certainty.

And Norton had echoed that frightening word, "heresy." Being charged with heresy signals a dangerous deviation from the convictions everyone is expected to share. The word stung Pynchon; he never recovered from the pain.

On May 9, the morning following his meeting with the clergy, a letter from Pynchon was read into the Court's minutes. Pynchon reported that he had dutifully met with the clergy, as the Court had advised, and that he had tried to explain his position to them more fully, "as to take off the worst construction." Pynchon seems to have been disposed to mollify the Court, if that were possible. He intimated that his thinking had changed on at least one point. He said that he was now "much inclined to think that [Christ's] sufferinges were appoynted by God for a further end, namely, as the due punishment of our sins by way of satisfaction to divine justice for mans redemption." This vaguely-framed statement, tantamount to acknowledging the imputation of humankind's sin to Christ, could be interpreted as a substantial concession. And the Court was pleased with this response.[36]

But it was not fooled. The authorities wanted much more detail. While expressing satisfaction with Pynchon's efforts to respond so far, they ordered him to be personally present at the fall sessions to "give all due satisfaction."

"All due satisfaction," however, would necessarily require a larger change on Pynchon's part than he was prepared to make. He would need to engage seriously in the wider community's theological conversation, accept the nuances of those who opposed and questioned him, and reframe his position. One historian maintained that in facing the inevitable challenges that serious differences of opinion pose, the goal of Puritans in America was

36. Shurtleff, *MBCR*, 4 pt. 1:48–49, 3:229–30.

to produce "some sort of formula" that would "[harness] the energies of the diverging parties under a single standard."[37] Compromise to achieve common ground was highly valued. But like the self-assured, uncompromising Divine who voiced Pynchon's own point of view in *The Meritorious Price*, Pynchon himself was not ready to negotiate. His dilatory efforts "to take off the worst construction" of his book left too many unanswered questions.

With Pynchon under suspicion, the Court did not reauthorize him to continue in his governmental roles. Right after receiving his half-hearted letter of apology, they voted to make his stepson, Henry Smith, the magistrate for Springfield. The authorities kept expecting accommodation on Pynchon's part. Yet after serving in government in New England for nearly twenty years, Pynchon's name never again appeared on the list of Assistants.

When Pynchon failed to show up on October 14, 1651, the General Court voted that "all patience be exercised" in his case and that he "be enjoined, under the penalty of one hundred pounds to make his personal appearance at & before the next General Court, to give a full answer to satisfaction, (if it may be,) or otherwise to stand to the judgment & censure of the Court."[38]

But Pynchon never attended the Court again.

---

37. "The genius of the American Puritans ordinarily lay in the direction of papering over fundamental division" (Foster, "Challenge of Heresy," 650).

38. Shurtleff, *MBCR*, 3:257.

13

Deeds and Decisions

THURSDAY, DECEMBER 25, 1651. Many of the older residents must have recalled celebrations of this date before they came to the New World. No doubt they remembered yuletide festivities when they were youths in England.

But in Springfield, as in all Puritan communities, where the old holy days were considered a thing of the past, this day was devoted to business. At today's town meeting, the selectmen parceled out land to nine citizens. Three were first-time grants to relative newcomers, Anthony Dorchester, Samuel Wright Jr., and even Thomas Miller, the troubler of the Indians. Other plots went to longer-term residents who needed more land to survive. These inadvertent Christmas gifts were in keeping with an earlier Springfield vote that empowered authorities to distribute excess land "to whom they shall Judge most to be in neede." By actions such as these, Pynchon's community put into practice the New England policy of using the relatively abundant commodity of land to relieve financial distress, and in that way ensuring the viability of families on the economic margins of the community.[1]

The colonists had considerable resources in real estate for developing the community. Pynchon had seen to that. On April 17, 1651, about a month before he attended the Boston Court of Election to answer for his book, Pynchon transferred lands he had bought in 1641 from Nippinsait for Springfield's expansion northward. The brief deed he composed at that

1. Burt, *First Century*, 1:174 discusses property for those in need. See also Warden, "Law Reform," 683.

time placed John Pynchon, Henry Smith, and Elizur Holyoke in charge of distributing the land "by their discretion for Farmes belonging to Springfield at such rates as in their coustome they shall iudge to be Resonable." Over the next few years, the Chicopee properties were indeed distributed, sometimes to long-term residents, but sometimes to newcomers.[2]

Then two weeks before his scheduled appearance at the October 1651 Court to "give a full answer to satisfaction" for his book, William Pynchon made another crucial decision. He transferred the entire 280 or so acres he had acquired as well as all his business interests in Springfield to his son, John, who was then twenty-six years old.[3]

Sometime between September 28, 1651, when he conveyed his property and business to John, and May 27, 1652, when the Court met for its regular spring session, William Pynchon was gone, leaving his frontier trading empire under new management. And because he failed to show up at Court, he skipped out on an unpaid fine of £100 as he headed to a quieter place of retirement.[4]

The situation in Springfield had been slipping during Pynchon's final year. Interestingly, earlier in the decisive year of 1650 the town's circumstances seemed to be improving. On April 22 Pynchon registered legal arrangements with four men from Barnet, near London, who had come as indentured servants to swell the ranks of laborers. But the outlook changed by the end of the year. In the early part of 1651, when he may still have thought he could remain in Massachusetts, Pynchon was preoccupied with the Parsons witchcraft accusations. A February 13 town meeting revealed that things were not getting done. Only three or four persons had paid their part of a special tax to raise £11, with the result that Thomas Stebbins had not been paid for his bell ringing and custodial duties at the meetinghouse. The money contributed was returned to the donors, and John Pynchon advanced Stebbins' salary. He was compensated in turn only a year later. Bounties on wolves had not been paid, and repairs voted on the meetinghouse had not been carried out. William Pynchon was systematically withdrawing from his crucial administrative role in the community. Following his unsuccessful approach at reconciling with the General Court

2. Ford, "Letters of William Pynchon," 52, 54; Burt, *First Century*, 1:223.

3. Burt, *First Century*, 1:86; McIntyre, *William Pynchon*, 35; Morison, *Builders*, 374.

4. Green improbably places Pynchon at Hartford in July of 1652, on the way to England (Green, *Springfield*, 122). For the fine, see Shurtleff, *MBCR*, 3:257.

at its May 1651 meeting, Pynchon became clearly increasingly focused on returning to England.[5]

In all likelihood, Pynchon concluded—and no doubt quite correctly—that he could never successfully defend his theological stance before the political and ecclesiastical officials in Massachusetts. He chose instead a course of least resistance. At over sixty years of age, Pynchon was now in the older generation, and the prospect of retirement under the English Commonwealth may well have appealed to him, as it did to others among his contemporaries.

Pynchon had retained a keen interest in the political environment in England throughout his stay in Massachusetts. He probably shared his constant eagerness for news from England with many of his fellow colonists. In February 1644, he wrote appreciatively of reports he had only recently received of the Solemn League and Covenant negotiated between Parliament and the Presbyterian Scottish commissioners in September 1643. He saw this pact as a crucial turning point. "[I]t is the high way for their deliuerance," he remarked, with strong hopes for the Puritan cause, adding that "I hope it is now the day of Antichrists great overthrow at Armageddon." Four years later he said, "I much longe to heere out of England. I looke vppon that land as in the saddest posture that euer they were for danger of ruine." Indeed, the summer of 1648 had seen contentious struggles between Parliament and King Charles. Parliament forces besieged Pembroke Castle, Colchester, Pontefract, and elsewhere, and Cromwell marched against the Scots.[6]

The political situation in 1650 made return to England an attractive option for those who cherished the Puritan cause. Their movement was thriving in the old country. People were taking matters into their own hands. According to an angry royalist observer, festive bonfires in feisty Chelmsford greeted the news that the House of Commons had voted down episcopacy. He noted that a third of the residents refused to come to the Anglican liturgy, and half would not receive communion kneeling. He added that the town leaders preached a radical message: "That one man should have a Thousand pounds a yeare, and another not one pound . . . hath no ground, neither in Nature nor in Scripture." All this resulted from "the great

5. Smith, *CR*, 224–25 (indentured servants); Burt, *First Century*, 222, 225 (town financial records).

6. Forbes, *WP*, 4:444, 5:271. For chronologies of the pivotal year of 1648, see Kenyon and Ohlmeyer, *Civil Wars*, 375–77; and Ashton, *Counter-Revolution*, 425–29.

increase of Brownists [namely, the Congregationalists/Independents] & Anabaptists at Chelmsford of late yeares."[7] A radically egalitarian ideology was making itself known in Pynchon's old home town.

Meanwhile the decade of the forties had been hard on the colonies. Emigration to New England slowed to a trickle; the flow even reversed at times back across the Atlantic. Though exact figures are difficult to establish, it is likely that at least 1,500 and as many as 3,600 settlers returned to England after 1640, out of a total immigrant population of 13,500 to 17,600. Indeed, "Opportunities abounded for colonists to resume life on the English side of the Atlantic, among old friends and neighbors, and in the context of new Cromwellian ventures."[8] Some of those most eager to return were dissidents uncomfortable with the "New England Way," whether because they preferred episcopacy, or Anabaptism, or some other disapproved theological position. Others had been negatively affected by the economic downturn. Some returned for opportunities they saw in England. A few sought to enlist in the English Commonwealth's army. Others were clergy who felt a calling to support the Reformation in their home country at a time of little growth in New England. Fourteen ministers alone returned to England in the 1640s, and a dozen more either contemplated it or did so in the 1650s. Some key leaders returned. Former governor Sir Henry Vane (1612[?]–1662), who wrote from England to defend Pynchon, had made the trip back somewhat earlier. He came to Boston in 1635 and went back in 1637. Pynchon himself expressed concern in late October 1646 that Herbert Pelham, a member of the Massachusetts Bay Company and the first treasurer of Harvard College, as well as John Haynes, the governor of Connecticut, might return to England. Haynes was Pynchon's—and Hooker's—old neighbor in Chelmsford; Pelham had Roxwell connections. Pynchon felt "the land can ill spare [them] without a shaking ague: the pillars of the land seem to tremble." In the end Pelham returned to England, but Haynes chose to stay.[9] From the Puritan perspective, Cromwell's regime had produced stability in England and Wales. Charles I was executed on January 30, 1649. Scots allied with the uncrowned Charles II were defeated

7. Ryves, *Mercurius Rusticus*, 17, 21–22.

8. Hardman Moore, *Pilgrims*, 53–56, 75.

9. On returning clergy, see Hall, *Faithful Shepherd*, 171. For a biography of Sir Harry Vane, see Adamson and Folland, *Sir Harry Vane*; and *ODNB*, 56:108–121. For Pynchon on Haynes and Pelham, see Forbes, *WP*, 5:115. For further discussion of Pelham, see Wilson and Fiske, *Appleton's Cyclopaedia*; and Rose-Troup, *Bay Company*, 162.

at Dunbar on September 3, 1650, the month before Pynchon's book was condemned. Things were looking up for the Puritan venture.

On September 14, 1652, Springfield citizens were called to a special town meeting to purchase George Moxon's house and lands for the use of any subsequent ministers, since the Moxons also felt the call to return and were about to leave for England, one year after the Pynchons.[10]

The Puritan Commonwealth in Britain was a big tent that stretched to accommodate a wide range of theologies and polities in spite of the fractious infighting that would, in time, became the movement's undoing. Back in England, Pynchon was at liberty to write as he wished.

And write he did.[11]

10. Minutes of the meeting for the purchase of Moxon's property are recorded in Burt, *First Century*, 1:222. Sometime before October 22, 1652, George Moxon bought a pair of chest hinges from John Pynchon, probably to make a container for packing (Bridenbaugh, *Pynchon Papers*, 2:51).

11. Regarding all the books William Pynchon wrote, see Appendix 7.

14

The Pen-Man of Wraysbury

SUNDAY, DECEMBER 17, 1654. The celebrated preacher Richard Baxter took his place at the front of old St. Paul's before the largest congregation he had ever faced. At 586 feet in length, St. Paul's was one of the grandest cathedrals in Christendom; it had stood in its stark Gothic beauty in the heart of London since the thirteenth century. The elongated choir, raised a few steps above the dark, narrow nave, was illuminated by large windows that cast a glow behind the speaker. The lofty nave itself was known as "Paul's Walk" because it afforded room for throngs to promenade daily, catching up on business and the latest gossip.[1]

Baxter was the leading English Puritan minister in the second half of the seventeenth century. He delivered his hour-long message in this cavernous sanctuary by special invitation of the Lord Mayor. Pynchon was in the congregation. At the time he was staying, as he sometimes did, with Thomas Mainwearing, a merchant who traded regularly with the Pynchons, both father and son.[2]

1. Keeble and Nuttall, *Calendar*, 1:161 no. 212. For a contemporary description of this impressive structure, as well as illustrations of its tombs, monuments, and architectural features, most of which were lost in the London fire of 1666, see Dugdale, *St. Pauls Cathedral*. Regarding "Paul's Walk," see Osborne, *Historical Memoires*: "It was the fashion of those times [James I] and did so continue till these [the Commonwealth], for the principal gentry, lords, courtiers, and men of all professions, not merely mechanicks, to meet in St. Paul's church by eleven, and walk in the middle isle till twelve, and after dinner from three to six; during which time some discoursed of business, others of news."

2. Mainwaring, a lay leader of St. Dionis Backchurch parish as well as a participant in the Presbyterian classis, lived not far from the financial district on Cornhill. Pynchon collected his mail from Mainwaring and gave two Fenchurch Street addresses: the

In this "Sermon of Judgment," Baxter invited his hearers to imagine themselves before the bar of final judgment. They would be brought there by Death, "A surly Serjeant, that will have no Nay." But if they were believers, they could count on the Judge's mercy:

> If the God of Love, and Grace, and Truth be Judge, then no man need fear any wrong. No subtilty of the Accuser [either Satan or one's conscience or both], nor darkness of Evidence: no prejudice or partiality, or whatsoever else may be imagined, can there appear to the wrong of your cause. Get a good cause and fear nothing; and if your cause be bad, nothing can deliver you.[3]

Following their return to England, William and Frances Pynchon lived temporarily in Hackney, which was then a suburb of northeast London. Pynchon's brother-in-law Edward Holyoke had relatives there—a sister named Elizabeth, her husband, Col. John Bridges, and their six sons—and Pynchon may have stayed temporarily with them.[4] He spent the late spring of 1652 making arrangements for publishers to re-issue volumes he had previously written.

While in Hackney, Pynchon was apparently looking for a place to retire near London. Strangely, he was not drawn to return to Essex and the Chelmsford roots he and Ann and their children had left to go to New England. Perhaps the noise of radical, egalitarian voices now expressing themselves in his old hometown put him off. In any case, his search ended when, late in 1653, he acquired property in the Thames Valley at Wraysbury. This village, twenty-two miles west of London, is not far downriver from Windsor. The land is low-lying and well-watered by several streams and rivers. Pynchon gained title to Wyrardisbury House from the real estate developer Andrew King and his agent, John Bland. On December 5, Pynchon paid

---

"Crown" and the "Bell." See Keeble and Nuttall, *Calendar,* 1:158–59 no. 206, 179 no. 244. See also Liu, *Puritan London,* 65. For a discussion of Mainwaring as a Pynchon trading partner, see Morison, "William Pynchon, the Founder of Springfield," 90; and Bridenbaugh, *Pynchon Papers,* 2:42–44.

3. Baxter, *Sermon of Iudgement,* 21. See also Keeble and Nuttall, *Calendar,* 1:161 no. 212. Eight years later, in his final volume on *The Covenant of Nature,* Pynchon quoted from this sermon, but from an addendum that was not part of Baxter's original remarks. See Baxter, *Sermon of Iudgement,* 207, quoted in Pynchon, *CN,* 78. On Pynchon's presence, see Keeble and Nuttall, *Calendar,* 1:179 no. 244.

4. For Pynchon's sojourn in Hackney, see Smith, *CR,* 29. In the preface to *Doctrine of Life,* Holyoke dedicated his work to the Bridges and their six "Religious and well deserving sons," writing, "You have a great family."

£145 for the house and its outbuildings, including a dovecote, and perhaps an oast house for curing hops, as well as a garden, an orchard, and three acres of land; his deed was registered in January 1654. Since the Pynchons now occupied manorial lands, the deal included modest biannual rent payments to King.

Wyrardisbury House was a historic property at the eastern end of the village near the main road to the north and east. A later observer remarked that "[t]he rooms [were] small, low, and most inconveniently distributed," though the house's setting would have been embellished by the grand chestnut tree that dominated the yard, as well as the adjoining enclosed garden, which contained a fine fruit-bearing mulberry tree.[5] Next door was the Rectory Farm, which had originally been glebe land, the "Tithe Farm" intended to provide support for clergy of the Wraysbury parish.

Pynchon's new home was not much more than a mile from the north bank of the Thames, just opposite the historic south bank riverside field of Runnymede. In fact, some have claimed that this ancient name applied to both the Wraysbury and Runnymede sides of the river. At Runnymede in 1215, in another, much earlier era when new forms of governance were emerging amid political unrest, the Norman barons compelled King John to affix his seal to the first of several versions of the Magna Carta. This new location close to London in Buckinghamshire made it possible for Pynchon to participate easily in some commercial and religious activities in the city. From 1653 on, Pynchon served as the London connection for the fur trade enterprise, "conducting trade through the family in the traditional medieval manner." He continued to benefit from fur shipments from Springfield that John Pynchon consigned in his name to the merchant William Davis, whose son, also William, was married to Pynchon's daughter Margaret in Boston. In 1657, William Pynchon received a handsome £60, and in 1659, for the last such shipment, £11.[6]

---

5. I am grateful to Mr. Dennis Pitt, Wraysbury historian, for information about Wyrardisbury House and its location. See also Gyll, *Parish of Wraysbury*, 91–92; and Page, *Victoria History*, 3:320–25. Original records of the transaction between Pynchon and King are in the collection of the Library and Archives of the Lyman and Merrie Wood Museum of Springfield History, Springfield, Massachusetts. These include ESM-04-02-03, "Early Deed, Andrew King and William Pynchon, 5 December 1653," and ESM-04-01–09, "Early Manuscripts, Wm. Pynchon, 2 Pieces."

6. McIntyre, quoted in Bridenbaugh, *Pynchon Papers*, 2:41.

Former Grounds of Wyardisbury House, Wraysbury, England

Pynchon's son-in-law Henry Smith arrived in England in October 1652. Smith's wife, Pynchon's eldest daughter, Anne, came late in 1654 with their daughters Martha, Mary, Elizabeth, and Rebecca. Pynchon went to London in mid-December to meet them and bring them to his country home so they could recover from the stressful voyage. But another daughter back in America did not fare so well. Margaret Pynchon Davis died following childbirth in July 1653 at the age of twenty-nine. She left three sons: Thomas, Benjamin, and William Davis, who were six years, two years, and only a few days old when she died.[7]

Pynchon's literary output in those Wraysbury years makes it clear that he must have spent much of his time studying and writing. During the decade of 1652 to 1662, he published five more books and pamphlets. The first three of these volumes, however, were largely written in Massachusetts prior to publication in 1652 and 1654.

The Meritorious Price, Second Edition

A second edition of *The Meritorious Price* was put on sale in 1652 by a London bookseller Pynchon had not dealt with before, but it was essentially identical to the first edition. The new books were assembled from surplus sheets from the original printing and simply issued with a freshly printed title page.[8]

The Jewes Synagogue

Pynchon's next book was a tract of ninety pages, *The Jewes Synagogue: or, a Treatise concerning the ancient Orders and manner of Worship used by the Jewes in their Synagogue-Assemblies*. The title page identified the author as "William Pinchion of Springfeild in N. England." But the volume was addressed "To the Christian Reader in great BRITANY," and had actually been published anonymously on March 14, 1648, under the title *An Endevour After The reconcilement of that long debated and much lamented difference between the godly Presbyterians, and Independents; About Church-government*. It seems never to have come to the notice of anyone in New England, either while Pynchon lived there or afterwards.

---

7. On the arrival of Anne and her daughters in London, see Keeble and Nuttall, *Calendar*, 1:179 no. 244.

8. The only differences were typological variations (and the spelling "Rdemption") on the recomposed and newly printed title page. A copy from this second edition is available at the Folger Shakespeare Library, Washington, DC, http://shakespeare.folger.edu/cgi-bin/Pwebrecon.cgi?BBID=147713.

Principles of polity or church governance comprised one of the hottest topics among Puritans, and it was a major source of divisions among them. That argument troubled Pynchon, so he directed his first book towards the divisions over church structure in England. But the subject was also very much under discussion in New England, where a new document summarizing church order would be approved in Cambridge five months after Pynchon's book was on bookstore shelves in England. Pynchon intended to soften the fierce debate between Presbyterian and Congregational polities in Parliament in the mid-1640s by melding the two into a both/and amalgam. His contribution, in a nutshell, was to split the difference. He proposed that church governance should be based on the example of ancient synagogues: "1. Dependent, when they lived together in the Land of Canaan. 2. Independent when they inhabited in Heathen Countries."[9] This implied that churches should be connected presbyterially, with a central national authority, in England—but governed congregationally in the wilderness of New England. So Independency/Congregationalism represented a fallback position that could be useful for Christians living abroad in dispersion. Pynchon merely stated his thesis, however, and did not expand on it.

Pynchon appropriately renamed this second edition to reflect the bulk of the material the book contained—such topics as the organization of synagogues, elements of ancient worship, the role of the Sanhedrin Courts, excommunication, and the function of magistrates. The title page of *The Jews Synagogue* explained that it was meant to analyze "the ancient Orders and manner of Worship used by the Jewes in their Synagogue-Assemblies," and to ground procedures that truly Christian churches should practice on the basis of those archaic Jewish practices. It was issued on December 31, 1652, by the original publisher, John Bellamy, one of the best-known and most prolific of the Puritan booksellers, who produced numerous works by Independent/Congregational authors.[10]

As with *The Meritorious Price*, Pynchon composed *The Jewes Synagogue* in the form of a dialogue, though in this case the conversation was

9. Pynchon, *An Endevour*, 38.

10. The dated copy of *The Jewes Synagogue* is in the McAlpin collection at the Burke Library at Union Theological Seminary, Columbia University, http://clio.columbia.edu/catalog/5698860. On Bellamy, see Liu, *Puritan London*, 63–64; and Plomer, *Dictionary of the Booksellers*, 20. Bellamy's well-known clients included the Pilgrims' pastor John Robinson, the Pilgrims William Bradford and Edward Winslow, the theologian Henry Ainsworth, Governor John Winthrop, and the New England clergy Thomas Shepard, Thomas Hooker, and John Cotton

between a tutor and student. Pynchon played the part of Teacher to a sometimes wide-eyed and admiring Scholar who at one point exclaims, "Sir, I must confess that your exposition of this verse . . . doth set me at a gaze what to think of other mens Interpretations."[11]

Pynchon's central assumption in this book was that Jesus Christ as the "Angel-Jehovah" "did originally ordain [the Jews' synagogues] as true particular visible churches."[12] He found some slight support for this clearly debatable postulate in Henry Ainsworth's translation of the Psalms, where the scholar sometimes rendered the Hebrew term *qahal*, "assembly," as "churches."[13] The task for Pynchon then became working out the implications for his own contemporary situation.

A Treatise of The Sabbath

Next, Pynchon published *A Treatise of The Sabbath*, which comprised two extended essays with an introductory title page that covered both. The first, entitled *The Time when the First Sabbath was Ordained*, concerned the origins of the Sabbath in the Scriptures. The second, *Holy Time; or, The True Limits of the Lords Day*, dealt with the observance of Sunday. They were printed together in London in 1654, with a shared introductory page as well as separate title pages for each section; they could be produced and marketed either separately or as a single volume.

These twinned tracts were published after Pynchon's return to England, but the issues they addressed were shaped by his experience in Massachusetts. A note in *The Meritorious Price* implies that an early draft of either or both was written before 1649 in Springfield.[14] Pynchon added new material as he honed it in the intervening years. At one point, he inserted a page-long quotation from the fourth volume of John Lightfoot's *The Har-*

11. Pynchon, *JS*, 65.

12. Interestingly, a later Connecticut River Valley author adopted a similar approach. Northampton's Solomon Stoddard (1643–1729) based his 1700 volume regarding *The Doctrine of Instituted Churches* on "the polity of God's church among the ancient Israelites" (Lucas, *Valley of Discord*, 152).

13. Pynchon, *JS*, 1, A2; Ainsworth, "Annotations vpon the Booke of Psalmes," 44 (Psalm 26:12), 102 (PS 68:27) in ibid., *Annotations*.

14. Pynchon referred to it as "my treatise upon the sanctified use of the Sabbath" (Pynchon, *MP*, 153). The two were clearly published simultaneously. A handwritten date on the title page of the British Library copy indicates that they were issued on November 7. Pynchon's *Time when* is 143 pages long, while *Holy Time* is 120.

mony of the Foure Evangelists Among themselves, published in 1650.[15] He also referred briefly to John Norton's recently published official response to *The Meritorious Price*, but it was merely to accuse Norton of a "harsh translation" and to note that "he takes some plain truths for great errors."[16]

Pynchon wrote his Treatise in the wake of a spate of laws passed by the Commonwealth's Court in November 1646 which addressed Puritan concerns about the religious health of the colony. Assumptions that had previously been taken for granted were now finally explicitly detailed. One focus was on integrating Natives more fully into the Commonwealth's regime. Powwows were forbidden, and ministers were encouraged to instruct the Indians in Christian faith and the Puritans' legal system. Ministers and churches were protected from public disparagement. One act passed at that time was the colony's first general heresy law, which, among other things, expressly proscribed anyone's claiming that the Commandment to "Remember the Sabbath" no longer applied. The Court put teeth in this law by voting further that "evry p[er]son shall duely resort & attend [the ministry of the word] respectively, upon the Lords dayes," under penalty of a 5s. fine for each infraction. All the practices these laws fostered or condemned were prized as the warp and woof of Puritan society. But skepticism had emerged in the midst of God's people, coming to light in defiance and cynicism. An anti-blasphemy regulation included in the package of religious laws forbade reproaching "the holy religion of God, as if it were but a politick device to keepe ignorant men in awe."[17]

Pynchon struggled with ways to make the Sabbath workable in New England. He understood and accepted the crucial role of Sabbath for a Christian commonwealth. But he had practical questions: When did the Sabbath start and end? How did the ancient rules apply to modern situations—or at least to Pynchon's own situation?

For Pynchon, as for most others, the historic Jewish Sabbath on Saturday and the Christian "Sabbath" on Sunday differed dramatically because even though Sunday, the Lord's Day, was the successor to the Sabbath, it was properly a "memorial" of Christ's resurrection. That meant the end of ancient Sabbath restrictions. To make the day what it should be required

15. Lightfoot, *Harmony*, 194–96, quoted in Pynchon, *Holy Time*, 91.

16. Pynchon, *Holy Time*, 91–93, 105–106. Pynchon's reference is to Norton, *Discussion*, 160.

17. The laws are found in Shurtleff, *MBCR*, 2:176–80 and 3:98–101. Specific citations in this paragraph are found in ibid., 3:98, 2:178, 177.

everyone to refrain from all work except acts of mercy. Like much of *A Treatise of The Sabbath*, those points were quite conventional.

But Pynchon also favored adaptation. Lighting fires on the Sabbath was expressly forbidden in the Hebrew Scriptures (Exodus 35:3). That would clearly interfere with food preparation among godly people in New England. However, Pynchon concluded that only work-related fires were prohibited. During the Exodus from Egypt, God charged the Israelites to prepare and cook the manna they retrieved from the ground on Friday, the sixth day. Pynchon even imagined a variety of manna recipes:

> They did prepare it (with laborious work) several ways suitable to every ones taste or liking, & therefore they did First grinde it in Mills, or beat it in Morters. Secondly, Then they baked it in Pans, and made Cakes of it. Thirdly, Othersome did boyle it; and thus it was several ways prepared and Cooked (according to everyones taste and liking).

All that work took place on Friday. However, Pynchon added,

> no Christian that is judicious (I think) doth hold it unlawful to temper a Pudding of the Meal that was ground on the sixth day, or to heat a Pye that was made on the sixth day, or to boil a necessary quantity of meat that was killed and quartered on the sixth day, or to use that wood for fire that was carted home, and cut ready for the fire, on the sixth day.[18]

Flexibility solved the problem!

The Time when proceeded to make some unusual claims. One was the unintentionally ironic assertion that "the Hebrew Doctors . . . did appoint a certain distance how far men might travel on the Sabbath day to the Synagogue, and they thought good to restrain it to an English mile." Another claim combined geography with chronology in a way that virtually defies description. Pynchon used a verse from the Bible—Hugh Broughton's translation of Job 26:7, "[God] stretched out the North upon the empty"— to link the "first darkness" of the morning with the north pole, "where the Midnight begins by the Compass-Dyall."[19]

Much more notable, however, was a conviction that is probably unique in all Christian theology. Pynchon believed that God arranged for the Sabbath not during Adam's period of innocence, but after his fall and recovery

---

18. Pynchon, *Time when*, 134–35.

19. Ibid., 141 (English mile), 44–47 (midnight north).

by a new creation. To make this claim, Pynchon had to explain away an inconvenient Bible verse, "And on the seventh day God ended his work which he had made; and he rested on the seventh day from all his work which he had made" (Genesis 2:2). This text clearly states that God constituted the Sabbath at the end of creation week, prior to the story of Adam and Eve and the serpent told in the following chapter. But Pynchon argued that Genesis 2:2–3 is an example of *hysteron proteron*, "the latter before," so those verses about God resting merely serve as a parenthetical announcement of coming events; that is, they interrupt the narrative to offer a preview of where the story will finally end. The account then continues with further details about the sixth day of creation in chapters 2 and 3. Therefore the creation of Adam and Eve, their conversation with the serpent, their eating the forbidden fruit, the arrangement for redemption by a Savior to be born of the woman's seed, and the announcement of that good news to the first couple all happened on the very same (and very busy) sixth and final day of creation. Pynchon remarked, "oftentimes the Pen-men of the holy Scriptures do set that which is after, Before; and so consequently we must by the rule of Chronology place the Institution of the Sabbath after the third Chapter." Pynchon here moved from a possibility (and a very unlikely possibility at that) to a necessity. "Oftentimes" yielded to "must." His writing was increasingly marked by words of logical certainty: "proving," "therefore," "hence it follows," "by necessary consequence," and "must needs."[20]

The second part of this work, *Holy Time; or, The True Limits of the Lords Day*, pinpointed the proper limits of the Christian day of worship.[21] Pynchon dismissed the usual understanding, derived from Leviticus 23:32, that the Jewish Sabbath begins at sundown. He explained that this pattern was only to accommodate ancient purification practices, when "they used to bathe or baptize themselves from their Ceremonial defilement" at the end of the workday at sunset. But ritual considerations were no longer valid for Christians, so the observance of Sunday as the Lord's Day should

---

20. Ibid., 2 (*hysteron proteron*), 33 (Bible Pen-men). Pynchon frequently focused on the chronology of what he took to be the single, fateful, final day of the creation: the extraordinarily long first day of human life. See his earlier musings in Pynchon, *MP*, 122. Among other unique observations he made was that the "cool of the day" when God came to Adam occurred about noon, "for the Evening begins when the Sun begins to decline, and then there doth usually arise a cooling wind (called a Seaturn) which the God of nature hath ordained to cool the air in hot Countries" (Pynchon, *Time when*, 23).

21. A reference to *Holy Time* in Pynchon, *Time when*, 51 suggests that *Holy Time* may have been written first.

continue through what he called the "Natural Day," from midnight to midnight, a full twenty-four hours.

Redefining the beginning of the Sabbath in this way could potentially have had an unexpected economic impact. In order to frame a biblically responsible and religiously observant community in New England, the Massachusetts Bay Company had decided on April 17, 1629, from the comfort of England, that "all that inhabite the plantacon [at Salem, Massachusetts], both for the genall and pticuler imploymts may surcease their labor every Satterday throughout the yeare at 3 of the clock in the afternoon."[22] Quitting work early would give everyone time to prepare for the Lord's Day observance, which (it was assumed) would begin at sundown. For Pynchon, however, "the Evening before the Sabbath . . . was no true part of the Sabbath it self, but in way of preparation onely." On the other hand, "the Sun-set Evening after the Sabbath [Sunday night] was indeed a true part of the Sabbath it self."[23] Delaying the Sabbath's start meant Saturday afternoon would be available for work. Of course, Sunday night would not. But Pynchon's scheme could result in an increase in useable work hours. It must be noted, however, that Pynchon never made use of his argument to call for a change in Bay colony practice, perhaps because his rationale ultimately proved unconvincing to others.

No references in any other authors reflect Pynchon's idiosyncratic views in *The Time when* and *Holy Time*—neither recipes for manna, nor the long sixth day of creation, nor new midnight-to-midnight boundaries for the Sabbath day.

Yet with the publication of his essays on the Sabbath, Pynchon was by no means done. Responses in books by others kept egging him on. Pynchon received an encouraging endorsement from Thomas Clendon (d. 1677), the Puritan era pastor of Allhallow's Barking and a delegate to the Westminster Assembly. In the preface of *Justification Justified* (1653) Clendon praised Pynchon effusively. He called Pynchon "that ancient, pious, & prudent Gentleman" whose *The Meritorious Price* "soberly, judiciously, and clearly explicateth the procuring and formal cause of justification." Pynchon reciprocated Clendon's appreciation by quoting him repeatedly in his later volumes.[24]

---

22. Shurtleff, *MBCR*, 1:395.

23. Pynchon, *Holy Time*, 113.

24. Clendon, preface to *Justification Justified*, 4.

A second response would have been less welcome. Anthony Burgess (d. 1664) included a handful of brief references to *The Meritorious Price* in his 1654 volume, *The True Doctrine of Justification*. Burgess was pointedly critical of Pynchon's "new and wonderfull opinions," but he was less harshly blunt than Norton, and Pynchon (who quoted him in later works) appreciated his graciousness. Yet Burgess responded sharply to Pynchon's unconventional claim that no human being could possibly have had the ability to put Christ to death: "We may not say [Christ] killed himself, or was his own executioner." Burgess felt that Pynchon's novelties should be exposed as unhelpful and should be unequivocally denied.[25]

25. Burgess, *Justification Asserted*, 73, 315–16, 407–408, 425–27.

15

Disputation and Farther Discussion

THURSDAY, APRIL 24, 1655. As the first green leaves emerged on the trees and hedgerows and in the gardens of Buckinghamshire, William Pynchon was poised to strike. His new book was ready to go. Copies appeared on the shelves at the "Sign of the Three Lions" in Cornhill, near the London stock exchange. On this day, he sent a copy to the famous Richard Baxter.

No doubt Pynchon had high hopes for his systematic rebuttal of John Norton's book. He had had Norton's manuscript in hand ever since their meeting in Boston in 1651. It came out in book form in London in 1653. Pynchon had finished his own manuscript in response in 1654, which was at the printer—"R. I.", according to the title page—for six months.[1] Robert Ibbitson was one of the premier typesetters and printers of the era, so maybe the sheer volume of his business slowed things down. But just as likely Pynchon continued to fine-tune his work with additions and amendments and alterations long after submitting it for publication. The finished book was issued under two titles; only the title pages differed. One was *A Farther Discussion of that Great Point in Divinity, the Sufferings of Christ*; the other was *The Meritorious Price of Mans Redemption, or Christs Satisfaction discussed and explained*.[2]

1. Keeble and Nuttall, *Calendar*, 1:179.

2. The second title has caused confusion when commentators have erroneously identified it as a second version of his first book; the text, however, is totally different. For more about Robert Ibbitson, see Plomer, *Dictionary of the Booksellers*, 105–106.

A Farther Discussion

With this new volume Pynchon intended a knockout blow to his adversary. In addition to a hefty 439 pages of text, he included twenty-seven pages of a "Table of the chief Heads," which provided the reader with painstaking instructions to write in more than thirty-five additional marginal notes where they belonged in the book:

> But some of these Heads that have this Mark * are not printed, therefore I desire they may be added by the Readers pen, for the better observation of some Points; and because some of them are too much for the Margin; there set onely the first sentence, and make a reference to the rest in the Table to the same page.[3]

A *Farther Discussion* was dedicated to Oliver St. John (ca. 1598–1673), a Puritan Member of Parliament who served as Chief Justice of the Court of Common Pleas and, after 1651, as Chancellor of the University of Cambridge. Pynchon seems to have found a kindred spirit in the moderate St. John. The author remarked that he was "verily perswaded that your Lordship doth account it your greatest honour to be every way serviceable to God, and his truth, as it is in Jesus." While the formal tone of "The Epistle Dedicatory" suggests that the two were not close friends, the Chief Justice did preside over the proceedings when Pynchon acquired his final home two years earlier in 1653.[4]

Pynchon borrowed Norton's technique: he reprinted his accuser's statements at length and commented on them, often in detail, with much cross-referencing. His extraordinary meticulousness reveals the extent to which his one-sided dispute with Norton had become a fixation in Pynchon's life. His argumentative and condemnatory tone echoed the style of many controversialists of that era. But Pynchon's reaction verged on obsession. He accused Norton of "poysonful assertion[s]." In attacking his attacker, Pynchon took special delight in pointing out various heresies that could be deduced from Norton's views, sometimes in convoluted ways. Hearkening back to an ancient Christian heresy of the later third and early fourth century, he accused Norton of Arian sympathies. He also charged

3. Pynchon, *FD*, c1v.

4. Ibid., B1r. For more about St. John, see *ODNB*, 48:634–640. A "feet of fines" record for Pynchon's acquisition of his Wraysbury property, which names St. John, is preserved at the Springfield History Library and Archives of the Lyman and Merrie Wood Museum of Springfield History, ESM-04-02-03, "Early Deed, Andrew King and William Pynchon, December 5, 1653."

him with the Cathar ("Albanensian") heresy, a sectarian movement of the twelfth to fourteenth centuries. In subsequent writing Pynchon would accuse him of "Socinian poison" and the errors of the "Maniches" and "Arrians." If Pynchon was heretical, it was clear to him that Norton was many times more so.[5]

Although *A Farther Discussion* is sometimes mistaken for a revised edition of *The Meritorious Price*—it was not—much of it simply rehashed Pynchon's prior arguments. He reaffirmed the supernatural perfections of Christ; he felt it would be unseemly and indeed, impossible for Christ to experience any anxiousness or despair, as he felt a note in the Geneva Bible suggested.[6]

In addition, Pynchon expanded on several previously undeveloped theses. One was that Christ's actions as Mediator were motivated by some unrecorded deal made among the Trinity. "Christ did not make satisfaction by fulfilling the first Covenant [made with Adam] but by fulfilling another voluntary Covenant that was made between the Trinity."[7]

A Farther Discussion also shows that Pynchon continued to read assiduously and voraciously on theological topics. Among the newer volumes he cited was the magisterial, multi-volume *Annotations Upon all the Books of the Old and New Testament* (1645). A panel of biblical scholars gathered by the Westminster Assembly produced this comprehensive set of commentaries on the Scriptures. Pynchon called them the "larger Annotations," or even "our larger Annotations."[8]

---

5. Pynchon, *FD*, 47, 109, 40. Pynchon's source regarding the "Albanenses" was Merbecke, *Common Places*, 20. His remarks on Socinianism and Manichaeism are found in Pynchon, *Covenant of Nature*, 130 and 154; hereafter cited as *CN*. See O'Collins and Farrugia, *Concise Dictionary*, 5 (Albigensianism), 18 (Arianism), 36 (Cathars), 149–50 (Manichaeism), 246 (Socinianism).

6. "The excellent temper, and tender constitution of Christs human nature, made him more sensible of shame, fear and pain, then other men can be" ("The Table," Pynchon, *FD*, e4r, referring to 294). See also Pynchon, *FD*, 20, 393. The Geneva Bible note at Psalm 22:1 that Pynchon found so offensive reads, "Here appeareth that horrible conflict, which he [Christ] sustained betweene faith & desperation."

7. Pynchon, *FD*, D2v. See ibid., 122, 133–136, 227, and 308. See also ibid., 145–46, 228, 331, 339, 358–59; and ibid., *CN*, 348. Pynchon cited only one biblical reference concerning an imagined inter-Trinitarian conference: a marginal reading at Isa 53:6 in the 1611 Authorized (King James) Bible, which he read as "caused him to meet."

8. The unnamed authors of the *Westminister Annotations* included several whose other works were also cited by Pynchon: William Gouge, Thomas Gataker, Edward Reynolds, John Richardson, Thomas Taylor, and John Downame, the editor (Neal, *History of the Puritans*, 2:78). The series was reprinted in three successive editions through

Pynchon also cited two giants of the era. One was the noted Dutch legal philosopher Hugo Grotius (1538–1645). A leader of the Arminian "Remonstrance" in the Netherlands—a movement that emphasized personal, free choice rather than the focus on God's sovereignty found in classical Calvinism—Grotius authored the first Protestant textbook on apologetics, which is the practice of offering theological explanations and reasons to believe. In spite of the tense relationship between Calvinists and Arminians, Pynchon quoted appreciatively from Grotius' *Two Discourses* (1652) and *Of the Law of Warre and Peace*, which had come out in English in 1654. According to Pynchon, Grotius was "a man excelling . . . though I find him to be much out of the way in some things."[9]

Additionally, Pynchon cited Antony Wotton's *De Reconciliatione Peccatoris*, "On the Reconciliation of a Sinner" (1624). Like Hugh Broughton, Wotton (ca. 1561–1626) was a controversial scholar of the prior generation who appealed to Pynchon. He was the first professor of divinity at Gresham College in London. A paper trail of Wotton's various tracts, some of them at the edges of Puritan orthodoxy, reveals how he plunged into numerous theological controversies. *De Reconciliatione Peccatoris* was too hot to handle for the Low Countries publishers who usually printed the works of Puritan authors at a time when the royal government controlled book production in England. The culminating work of Wotton's career had to be printed in Switzerland.[10]

Wotton accepted the classic Protestant doctrine that standing in God's good graces is imputed to sinful humankind by faith.[11] But he dismissed the imputation of sin to Christ, the doctrine Pynchon so despised. No doubt Pynchon also appreciated Wotton's frequent mention of obedience, which Wotton made central to his theology:

> It is my supposition that there is another righteousness, in addition to forgiveness of sins, which is required for justifying the unrighteous, as formal in the act of justifying as those which we are proving by reasons. It turns out that we know what that righteousness is. It is Christ's obedience imputed to the sinner. People mean by Christ's righteousness, which they say is not something

the 1640s and 50s.

9. Pynchon, *FD*, 215. Grotius' work was published in 1627 and by 1652 had been translated into English as *Hugo Grotius His discourses*. The Latin original, *De Jure Belli*, was printed in Paris in 1625.

10. For more on Wotton, see *ODNB* 60:371–72.

11. McGrath, *Reformation Thought*, 119.

earned, not a fruit or a benefit of it passed on to us, but the works themselves, the very actions of Christ, in which that obedience of his is to be found.[12]

Pynchon had known Wotton personally. In 1655, he wrote warmly of him in an assessment that reveals the scholarly qualities that most appealed to Pynchon:

> Mr. Wotton was a man of approved integrity, one that suffered much for Christ, through the iniquity of the times, a man of great reading in all kinds of Writers, both Ancient and Modern, and a man of deep judgment; And his book of Reconciliation, was print-ed in his old age, after much debate, and study, and revising; and therefore what he saith in this point of Imputation, ought not, and will not be slighted of the Judicious. The wise will understand.[13]

Some have suggested that Wotton was Pynchon's mentor, but any re-lationship like that remains unsubstantiated.[14] Pynchon gave some slight indication that he may have met Wotton in 1619 or 1620; he linked Wotton and Robert Smith, who inspired much of *The Meritorious Price* at about that time.[15] Wotton died in 1626, four years before Pynchon emigrated.

Wotton may well have planted an anti-imputation seed in Pynchon's thinking, and Wotton's final book turned out to be a quotable authority to bolster Pynchon's own positions. But Pynchon extrapolated in his own directions. As Christiaan de Jong has observed, Pynchon's "juridical mind dominates his attempts to clarify the mysteries of justification."[16] Begin-ning from a magistrate's sense of simple fair play in the courtroom, Pyn-chon argued from the lesser to the greater: what is fair and just in human society must be the way it is with God. Certainly anything that would never be allowed in the Springfield magistrate's court should never be attributed to God. Even in his first volume, Pynchon contended that "I hold it a point of gross injustice for any Court of magistrates to torture an inocent person for the Redemption of a gross malefactor." He added,

---

12. Wotton, *De Reconciliatione Peccatoris*, Part 2, Lib. 1, ch. 3, 116. My translation.

13. Pynchon, *FD*, 220–21.

14. Winship, "Contesting Control," 795–822.

15. Pynchon connected Wotton and Smith (Pynchon, *FD*, 382–83).He may have conversed with both about how they agreed with one another when Wotton served as Lecturer at Allhallows Barking and Smith at Trinity Minories, both in the Tower of Lon-don neighborhood.

16. de Jong, "Christ's Descent," 136.

I never heard that ever any Turkish Tyrant did require such a double satisfaction of any redeemer for the redemption of Galley-slaves, I never heard that ever any Tyrant did require any redeemer to pay both the full price which they demanded for their redemption of their Galley-slaves, and to bear the punishment of their curse, slavery also in their stead: I think no cruel Tyrant did ever exact such a double satisfaction; therefore I cannot chuse but wonder at the common doctrine of imputation, because it makes God the Father more ridged in the price of our redemption, than ever Turkish Tyrant was . . . [N]o creditor ever did or could by any law of justice exact such a double satisfaction of any surety for the redemption of his debter, why then doth the doctrine of imputation make God the Father to be a harder creditor in the point of satisfaction, then ever any ridged creditor was among men?[17]

At different times both Wotton and Pynchon were charged with Socinianism. That term served as the biggest theological insult of the seventeenth century. But Pynchon's own views were sharply at odds with Socinian tenets. Socinians emphasize the New Testament at the expense of the Old, but as one scholar remarks, "with Pynchon the tables are turned, the Old Testament overshadows the New and provides the framework for understanding it."[18] Socinians also devalued the Trinity and understood Christ to be a human being only, whose perfect moral life served to exalt the mortal into immortality. Pynchon disagreed strongly on both counts.[19] He did not, as one scholar has alleged, "[emphasize] the redemptive nature of Christ's life instead of His death."[20] Pynchon did sparingly cite one author, John Goodwin, who was occasionally linked with Wotton and charged with Socinianism, and who critics called "Socinian John." But Pynchon never referred to those who have been called "England's first avowedly Socinian writers," Paul Best and John Biddle. After several paragraphs on English Puritans charged with "Socinianism," Philip F. Gura concluded that "there is no overt proof of [Pynchon's] association with any" of them.[21]

17. Pynchon, *MP*, 81, 84.

18. Ibid., 66, 61; de Jong, "Christ's Descent," 139.

19. For a classic outline of Socinian teachings see Harnack, *Outlines*, 535–41.

20. Innes, *Labor*, 15.

21. Gura, *Sion's Glory*, 313–15, 317. Even so, Gura claimed that Pynchon "was arraigned for purportedly Socinian beliefs" (ibid., 306). Winship presents a detailed analysis of where Pynchon might fit into the Arminian, Socinian, Antinomian, Trinitarian, High Calvinist, and latitudinarian mix of Puritan argumentation in the early 1600s (Winship, "Contesting Control," 795–822).

Those who have sought to place Pynchon's thinking in wider contexts have identified him as Socinian on the basis of possible connections with Wotton, or Arminian thinking, via Grotius. But Pynchon was no more Socinian than was Wotton, and he roundly criticized Arminians.[22] Neither label fits, because Pynchon belonged to no school. The considerations that most shaped Pynchon's perspective were sociological, not ideological. He spoke from his own privileged role in society, from his position in Commonwealth and community, using whatever comments and references he could mine from his extensive reading to buttress his own previously formed convictions.

In his retirement years, Pynchon, now a full-fledged controversialist, was focused totally on vindicating his original theses. His goal was simply to sharpen the arguments he had previously made. He was addressing no real audience and receiving no response. But that did not deter him.

One final volume in belated response to *The Meritorious Price* appeared in 1656 when Nicholas Chewney (c.1609–1685) published *Anti-Socinianism; or, A brief Explication of some places of holy Scripture*. Chewney's work is vague and highly polemical. In replying to Pynchon's view that Christ as God-man was Mediator because he obeyed "the Law of Mediatour-ship," Chewney said,

> *Monstrum horrendum, informe!* What a piece of stuffe is here?
>
> *Rank Socinianism. The dialogue denies the hypostical Union of the two natures in Christ, which must not, cannot be severed one from the other.[23]

But Chewney was basically mistaken. His misdirected tirade ends with an eloquent condemnation of the church in England: "What distemper doth possesse thee, that thou shouldst so willingly return to thine own, so eagerly pursue, so greedily lick up the vomit of other Churches?"[24] That "vomit," of course, included Pynchon. Still, Chewney's largely irrelevant criticism remains entertaining to read.

---

22. Winship, "Contesting Control," 795–796, persuasively critiques McLachlan's conclusions that Pynchon was "a Socinian without knowing it" (McLachlan, *Socinianism*, 239). McCulloh, "Influence of Arminius" 70, links Pynchon by a tenuous chain to Arminius through Grotius. For Pynchon on Arminians and their "dangerous errors," see Pynchon, *MP*, 89.

23. Chewney, *Anti-Socinianism*, 64.

24. Ibid., 122.

16

Frost Fairs and Finales

EARLY OCTOBER, 1657. AUTUMN winds blew across the landscape with a bitter warning of frigid months to come. Winters over the previous half-century had been unusually cold during what has come to be called the "little ice age." In 1655, the Admiralty office at Deptford was told that ships could not sail because the Thames had frozen across, which provided the opportunity for a "frost fair." These impromptu festivities became possible only rarely in the coldest winters. Sales booths, makeshift dining facilities, a variety of pavilions, ragtag menageries, and numerous entertainment venues would suddenly appear as a virtual mall on the ice spanning the river upstream of the old London Bridge. The winter of 1656 to 1657 was almost as frigid. Snow fell on some hills on May Day, though the summer later turned hot and dusty. The question that concerned everyone this fall was, would the unseasonably cold cycle continue?[1]

As the days shortened and temperatures cooled, Frances Sanford Pynchon died on October 10, 1657, on the eve of the coldest winter in memory. A short while later, William was supposed to have written, "I am the more solitary as Son Smith is of a reserved melancholy disposition, and my daughter [Ann] is crazy [meaning "fragile"]."[2]

At the time, John Pynchon was on his way home from the only visit he made to see his father and stepmother and his sister Ann and her family.

1. Lamb, *Climatic History*, 568–70; Currie, *Frosts*.

2. The death of Frances Sanford Pynchon is recorded in Green, *Springfield*, 122. On the "landmark winter" of 1657 to 1658, see Parker, *Global Crisis*, 6. Pynchon's reputed letter is quoted in Lockwood, *Western Massachusetts*, 1:110.

He had come to England to strengthen business connections as well. John had left Massachusetts before November 1656 (possibly September 10) on an expedition that lasted just about a year. Depending on when he arrived back in the Connecticut River Valley, he would have been faced with the sad news that his only living sister in America, Mary Pynchon Holyoke, was either mortally ill or had also died that same October, on the twenty-seventh, at the age of thirty-five.

The Covenant of Nature

During the next five years, in the winter of his own life, William Pynchon penned his last volume. His books were getting longer. This final work was a self-published tome of more than 530 pages of text, plus indexes and other apparatus, called *The Covenant of Nature made with Adam Described, and Cleared from sundry great mistakes*, which originated "From my study in Wraysbury, Feb. 10, 1661."

The "sundry great mistakes" were the criticisms Pynchon found in John Norton's rebuttal, with its eight "Propositions," four "Questions," and five "Distinctions." Pynchon revived the themes he had brooded over since writing *The Meritorious Price*, including the old controversy with Norton, whom he now accused of "meer fallacies and fictions of his own brain."[3]

The *Covenant of Nature* consisted of a series of loosely connected segments that rehashed themes from his previous writings. It is a pastiche of the words of others and Pynchon's own previous prose. He filled his text with quotations, and repetitions abounded as his mind seemed to wander.[4]

Pynchon cited an expanding armory of sources, but now less from the Independent/Congregational wing of Puritanism and more from authors who expressed the Westminster Assembly's Presbyterian positions. Three whose books Pynchon mentioned had been politically moderate in

---

3. Pynchon, *CN*, 133.

4. Two segments of *CN* may possibly have originated as sermons: ch. 7–10, 196–258, and ch. 14, 380–424, a conclusion based on the classic "plain style" sermonic structure. A citation from Luther's *Commentary on Galatians* continued for more than three pages; a series of citations from Hugh Grotius' *Of the Law of Warre and Peace* (1654) covered four pages. He took another two-page excerpt from *The Covenant of Life* (1655) by Samuel Rutherford, the Westminster Assembly delegate whose advocacy of Presbyterian governance was vigorously opposed by Thomas Hooker on behalf of New England Puritans. A favorite quotation from Baxter appeared on both pages 263 and 279, and one from Gataker was printed on both pages 254 and 281.

the turbulent times of the Cromwellian Revolution. Thomas Gataker supported episcopacy; he also authored a pamphlet on behalf of forty-seven London clergy who opposed the trial of Charles I. William Gouge chaired the committee to draft the Westminister Assembly's Confession. Benjamin Needler joined in petitioning for the life of King Charles just before he was executed in January 1649.[5] As an indication that Pynchon was adapting to the shifting religious climate in England, he cited the six English bishops in his index by the honorific "B.B.," a gesture of respect for the Episcopal Church, which was quickly emerging as the official church of his homeland.

Pynchon continued his problematic reliance on Hugh Broughton's quirky biblical studies. He made much of Broughton's re-translation of Daniel 9:24–27, which Christianized Daniel's terminology by turning "anoint the most Holy" into "shew Christ to be the Holy of Holy," "the Messiah the Prince" into "Christ the King," "Messiah be cut off" into "Messiah shall suffer," and "consummation" into "final judgement."[6]

As in his other works, Pynchon focused on word studies of key Hebrew terms. But this time they were all words he had previously analyzed. He was going in a circle. As a result, he ended his theological career where he began: his next-to-last chapter reprised his studies of Isaiah 53:5, the verse with which he had launched *The Meritorious Price*, while his final chapter probed the meaning of *tzedek*, "justification," with the help of his constant standbys—Kircher, Ainsworth, and Broughton.

While Pynchon's convoluted cross-references and multiple repetitions cause considerable complexity, so too do his increasingly tortuous arguments. An example of his abstruse language gives the flavor of his thinking towards the end of his life. To anyone who might wonder what in the world he was talking about, Pynchon offered a clarification that probably made things worse:

> Lest anyone should stumble at this phrase ["the concreated life of God's image"] he may see it to be a necessary phrase if he do but first consider the Antithesis; namely, the kind of death that God did threaten in the Covenant of nature, which was no other but the deprivation of Adams said concreated life which was conjoined only as an adjunct to his essential life: and thence it followes by necessary consequence, that seeing the deprivation of his said

5. For more on Gouge and Needler, see *ODNB* 23:36–39 (Gouge) and 40:335–336 (Needler). Gataker's pamphlet was *A serious and faithfull Representation*. Names of the signatories are listed in ibid., 13–14.

6. Broughton, *Daniel*, 57, 63.

concreated life is called death, that joining of it as an adjunct to his essential soul must needs be called his concreated life.[7]

Though *The Covenant of Nature* is admittedly somewhat unwieldy for the purpose, the book could serve as a culmination and recapitulation of all of Pynchon's theology. In it, he enlarged upon notions sprinkled in rudimentary and even cryptic form throughout *The Meritorious Price*. In fact, many of the most curious assertions he discussed in full in his final work can be found in his first, though sometimes in a barely recognizable, fragmentary form. These claims include:

1. The fall and redemption of Adam and Eve occurred on the same day they were created;

2. A special covenantal arrangement between the Father, the Mediator, and the Spirit was made at the time of Adam and Eve's fall;

3. Christ's time of death was governed by Gabriel's announcement to Daniel.[8]

Reading this rambling discourse seems like listening to Pynchon reminiscing in his old age as he rehashed all the minutiae of his theological pursuits.

Just months after his final volume appeared, William Pynchon died on October 29, 1662. He was buried in the Wraysbury parish cemetery, which adjoins St. Andrew's Church, on November 7.[9]

Several authors, following Pynchon's descendent, the educator Thomas Ruggles Pynchon, report that he died "in entire conformity with the [Episcopal] Church of England." But there are strong reasons for doubt. Like all of his previous writings, Pynchon's final volume in the last year of his life quoted almost exclusively from Puritan-friendly sources. Considering his caustic warnings about elaborate liturgical practices, it seems just as likely that in those chaotic years for both church and state, he remained on the side of the Commonwealth until the end. Shortly after returning to England in 1652, he wrote (echoing a sentence from Hugh Broughton),

7. Pynchon, *CN*, 36.

8. Ibid., *MP*, 105–106, 122, 152–53 (same-day fall and redemption), 148–49 (deal among the Father and Mediator), 124 (Christ's time of death predicted in Daniel).

9. "A fragment of the old parish register proves that [Pynchon] was interred here 7th November, 1662" (Gyll, *Parish of Wraysbury*, 20). Regarding the Pynchon family's return and his death, see Smith, *CR*, 29.

St. Andrews Church, Wraysbury, England

the Father of Rome doth counterfeit all [ancient Levitical sacrific-
es], He will have a Candlestick, Cope, Linen-Garments, Precious-
Stones, Miter, Girdle, &c. He will have Sacrifice, Priest, and Altar,
and Jubilees, &c . . . seeing [the High Priest's] office is extinguished
[extinct], it is a most high contempt of God to revive it by imita-
tion from mans brain; and therefore such Reformed Churches as
retain any of these Popish Jewish Rites, ought speedily to repent
and reforme, or else God will surely purge them by sharp trials, to
provoke them to repentance and reformation.[10]

10. The speculation about Pynchon's religious orientation at the time of his death is
quoted in the *ODNB*, 1949–1950 ed., 47:85. It was taken from the article on "Pynchon"
written by a great-great-great-great-great-grandson of William in Wilson, *Appleton's
Cyclopaedia*, 5:144. Thomas Ruggles Pynchon of Hartford, Connecticut, was himself an
Episcopalian, and in fact, a priest and President of Trinity College, Hartford, from 1874
to 1883. Pynchon's comments on ceremony and religious reformation in Pynchon, *JS*,
25–26, were adapted from Broughton: "yet the father of Rome will counterfaite: he will
have a Candlesticke, Cope, Linen garments, precious stones, mitre, girdle Priest, sacrifice, Altar: Sathan taught him so, to dally with Gods Law" (Broughton, *Apocalyps*, 109).
Similar phrasing is also to be found in ibid., 211.

Pynchon's surviving correspondence from those years mentions only Puritan preachers. The only known portrait of Pynchon was painted in 1657, the year of John's visit and five years before his death. It depicts him in Puritan garb, wearing dark clothes and a magistrate's skullcap over a short "Roundhead" haircut.

Pynchon's will was dated October 4 and proved December 8, 1662. Its somewhat jumbled arrangement bears the marks of being hastily composed.[11] Always the businessman, he had kept careful accounts to the end and settled his estate largely out of money others owed him. Through his will, he collected on a £220 debt from Henry Smith in order to provide legacies of £10 apiece for his three Davis grandsons in Massachusetts, who ranged in age from nine to seventeen, and £20 dowries for his three unmarried Smith granddaughters in Wraysbury, who were nineteen, eighteen, and thirteen, and the same amount for the Smiths' twelve-year-old son, Elisha. His own son, John, received £106 from a bond John owed his father.

Other assets specified in his will illustrate the wide range of Pynchon's business interests. These included debts owed by others to Henry Smith, which he had in turn promised to Pynchon. One of those debts was a financial interest in "about" 18,000 pounds of tobacco and other assets related to the estate of Nicholas Ware of Virginia. The Pynchons participated in trade with Barbados both for financial gain and for kinship reasons. Ware had married Anna, the daughter of William Vassall of the "Roxwell Group." Before Ware died in 1661, he recorded a bond to John Vassall, his brother-in-law in Barbados, in the amount of 17,234 pounds of tobacco, 8,627 pounds of which were compensation to Vassall for the purchase of "four good negroes" for Ware's Virginia plantation.[12] Pynchon's part in the transaction seems to have involved turning the tobacco into cash as repayment for funds advanced to the Wares. Pynchon also had a share in a horse belonging to Henry Smith in Barbados. Anything realized from the tobacco and the horse he bequeathed to his late daughter Mary's children back in Springfield. His agent for both the tobacco transaction and the Ware legacy was Capt. Samuel Pensax, a successful shipper who worked southern transatlantic routes, crossing from England to ports anywhere between Maryland and Barbados. Given the very low prices of tobacco at the time, Pynchon's interests would have amounted to £300 at the most. Investment in the Barbados trade ultimately proved so unsatisfying that

11. Pynchon's will appears in Appendix 5.
12. Withington, "Virginia Gleanings," 303.

John Pynchon remarked in 1663, "I have found so little profit by [it] that unless I find readier and better returns I shall leave it off."[13]

Pynchon also bequeathed some clothes to the granddaughters who lived with him. Finally, he gave £3 to the poor of Wraysbury—a little less than his grandfather John had left the poor of Writtle ninety years before.

Since Pynchon's chief executor, his son, remained in Massachusetts, he placed matters in the hands of his stepson, Henry Smith, and a friend, the girdler John Wickins of London, who was a long-term trade associate and purchaser of Pynchon pelts for his belt-making business. In a letter of consolation written on February 20, 1663, to his stepbrother (and brother-in-law), John Pynchon, Smith mentioned that he had relied on Wickins to have Pynchon's will proved at the Prerogative Court in London. He also mentioned a few commercial loose ends: the otherwise unknown business of "Carletons administration" was left hanging, and so were deals with "Mr [Daniel] Bridge & partners," who felt that the authorization that John Pynchon had given his father to act on his behalf could not be transferred to Smith, but expired with William Pynchon's death. John Pynchon found his way clear to go to England to settle his father's estate only over a year after his father's death, in late November 1663. The errand took more than half a year. He arrived back in Springfield by late July 1664.[14]

Charles II was restored to the throne when the republican government collapsed in 1660. Two years later, in the very year that William Pynchon died, Charles approved the Act of Uniformity. This law of May 16, 1662, was designed to test the ecclesiastical and political reliability of English clergy by requiring episcopal ordination and a loyalty oath. In the final blow to the

13. See Bruce, *Economic History of Virginia*, 1:389. "From 1655 to 1662, the average value of a pound of tobacco in Virginia would seem to have been barely two pence, and when sold in England brought hardly four pence." Daniell, ed., Calendar of State Papers, 267, called Pensax "the only merchant that uses" Bermuda. John Pynchon's assessment of the Barbados trade is in Bridenbaugh, *Pynchon Papers*, 1:43.

14. John Wickins was a prominent practitioner of the girdler's art and was elected Master of the Girdlers' Guild in 1665 and 1673 (Smythe, *Historical Account*, 255). He did business at the sign of the "Meremayd in Milk-street," on the corner of Cheapside (Bridenbaugh, *Pynchon Papers*, 1:84, 2:43). On Wickins as executor, see Massachusetts Historical Society, "Letter Relating to William Pynchon," 309–11. A letter from John Pynchon dated May 8, 1663, refers to Bridge and his partner, Henry Berkingham, and gives their Fenchurch Street address: the "Blue Bee." See Bridenbaugh, *Pynchon Papers*, 1:43. On the chronology of John Pynchon's second trip to England, see ibid., 1:47–50.

Puritan Commonwealth, over two thousand dissenting ministers who refused to sign on to the king's terms were expelled from their parishes. This ejection occurred on August 24, St. Bartholomew's Day, two months before Pynchon's death. Pynchon's neighbor William Reeves, who had served St. Andrews in Wraysbury since at least 1659, was one victim. At All Saints' Church in Springfield, England, the parish Pynchon had served as churchwarden, one of the two rectors, John Reeve, was forced to leave the Springfield Boswell parsonage; he was later imprisoned at Newgate. George Moxon, Pynchon's pastor in Springfield, New England, was evicted from Astbury in Cheshire. Moxon's son, also named George and also a minister, was ejected from Radwinter in Essex. Anthony Burgess, Pynchon's courteous critic, was ejected from Sutton Coldfield in Birmingham. John Sheffield, who had signed an endorsement of Pynchon's *Holy Time* treatises, was dismissed from St. Swithin's in London. Samuel Slater, who had also signed an introduction to *Holy Time*, was discharged from his lectureship at Bury St. Edmunds. Thomas Walley, a third signer, was ejected from London's St. Mary Whitechapel before moving to a new ministry at Barnstable, Massachusetts. Authorities Pynchon had relied on in his final volume were also ejected: "Socinian John" Goodwin from his Colman Street congregation, William Gouge from Inkpen in West Berkshire, and Benjamin Needler from St. Margaret Moyses on Friday Street in London. Thomas Clendon, Pynchon's vocal supporter, had quietly resigned his less than effective ministry near the Tower of London earlier that year, and the Allhallows Barking parish welcomed back its popular pre-Puritan era pastor. The celebrated Richard Baxter, who exercised a strong influence in many segments of English church life, technically could have fulfilled the king's conditions. But he refused to accept what he considered sectarian requirements and resigned.[15]

15. Calamy, *An Account*, 24, 32–34, 38–39, 53, 100, 110, 128–29, 304, 313, 739–40; ibid., *A Continuation*, 897–932. Regarding John Reeve, see also Grieve, *Sleepers*, 1:85; and Fitch and Fell-Smith, *Essex Review*.

Part II

The Plight of William Pynchon
A Magistrate and His Religion

Behind the Pynchon Saga

WHAT LAY BEHIND WILLIAM Pynchon's censure at the hands of his fellow Magistrates, his abrupt removal from office, and his ignominious return to England?

Beyond the continued one-sided campaign to restate his original thesis, other subjects Pynchon discussed in subsequent publications provide clues to what happened to him because of *The Meritorious Price*, and why. Pynchon's own observations from the later years of his life offer keys for interpreting his ideas and his work as a theologian, and also help to make sense of the sad personal outcome of his New World adventure. His view on church government, as it was outlined in *The Jewes Synagogue*, is one factor. His remarks on theological method in *A Farther Discussion* point to another, as do his reflections on "heresy" in the preface to his final work. Pynchon's later comments also illuminate several factors that played an important role in his case before the Massachusetts General Court: his understandings of church, state, and the relationship between the two.

A persistent tradition about William Pynchon depicts him as a daring innovator who spoke out fearlessly against an inhumane theology. In the late nineteenth century, the Springfield historian Henry M. Burt said that "he alone in all New England dared to proclaim the faith that was in him when that faith was opposed to the lawfully established religion."[1] Website references about Pynchon and banned books continually mischaracterize his theology as an explicit criticism and even refutation of

1. Burt, *First Century*, 1:88. Burt continued: "It [Pynchon's book] was a marked step forward in the evolution of religious truth, and we see in it a glimmering of the great light which many years later was to break over New England and dispel the gloom of an antequated [*sic*] and cruel theology. When he tests the rules of divine Justice by the common standard of man's justice, he makes a bold departure from Calvinism, and one recognizes the same spirit which inspired others in later times" (ibid.).

Puritanism.[2] When other similar commentators are taken into account, we might conclude that Pynchon was an exceedingly rare, if not unique, voice for religious liberalism in what Charles Francis Adams has called the "theologico-glacial period of Massachusetts."[3]

But the champion of "plain common-sense" theology was not a proponent of religious toleration. Pynchon had made himself quite clear on that. He wrote in opposition to Dr. Robert Child and six fellow petitioners who presented a "Remonstrance and Petition" to the Massachusetts Bay General Court in May 1646. The Child case directly concerned the distinctive characteristics of New England life that an immigrant from England would find at that time in Massachusetts Bay.

2. For example, see the discussion of *The Meritorious Price of Our Redemption* in "List of Books Banned by Governments," *Wikipedia*, last modified July 17, 2014, http://en.wikipedia.org/wiki/List_of_books_banned_by_governments.

3. Adams, *Massachusetts*, 64. "The theologico-glacial period of Massachusetts may, therefore, be considered as lasting from the meeting of the Cambridge Synod in September, 1637, to the agitation over the Writs of Assistance in February, 1761, culminating in what is known as 'the Great Awakening;' of the 1740s. As a period, it was singularly barren,—so almost inconceivably somber" (ibid.).

17

The Trouble with Toleration

Dr. Robert Child (1613–1654) came to Massachusetts twice: first between 1638 and 1641, then from October 1646 till the fall of 1647.[1] Although trained as a physician at the University of Padua, he never practiced medicine, but instead focused his efforts on the entrepreneurial possibilities the undeveloped lands of New England afforded. As a natural scientist, he very carefully observed the crops the area produced. As an alchemist, he took an interest in metallurgy, and he became financially involved in several mining operations in Massachusetts. The lead mine at Tantiusques (Sturbridge), the ironworks at Saugus, the trading and prospecting start-up at Nashaway Plantation (Lancaster), and lands on the Saco River in Maine all interested him. He invested heavily in some of these, to the tune of more than £450 at Saugus alone. But by the mid-forties, the severe drop in immigration had precipitated an economic depression. In spite of regulations passed by the Massachusetts General Court specifically to give generous preferential treatment to these entrepreneurial ventures, all were economic failures.

---

1. For more on Robert Child, see *ODNB*, 11:433–434. Various perspectives on the Remonstrants and Dr. Child may be found in: Kittredge, "Dr. Robert Child," 1–146, which depicts Child as an advocate for the Presbyterian Parliament; Morison, *Builders*, 244–68, which understands him to be a champion for freedom of religion and a wider franchise; Wall, *Massachusetts Bay*, which presents him as an accomplice of William Vassall; and Newell, "Robert Child," 223–56, which focuses on Child's economic goals and philosophy. For Pynchon's connection with the Tantiusque exploration and Child's partnership in the venture with John Winthrop Jr., see Woodward, *Prospero's America*, 81, 84, 86–88.

Child blamed the authorities for his crushing financial reversals. The Bay colony's policy discouraged absentee financiers and emphasized the production of finished products for the colony over exports of raw material to England. In the economically difficult 1640s, that policy hampered the development of the kind of natural resources that captured Child's attention. Child also held the authorities responsible for their vision of a society that would consist of congregationally-governed churches for a population largely of godly, Reformed Christians.

On May 19, 1646, Child and his fellow petitioners presented a harsh critique of the Bay colony to the General Court. Its first objection reflected their alleged bewilderment and sharp disagreement at the ways governmental institutions were being reshaped in Massachusetts:

> 1. [W]e cannot, according to our judgments, discerne a setled forme of government according to the lawes of England . . . Wherefore our humble desire and request is, that you . . . unanimously concurr to establish the fundamentall and wholesome lawes of our native country.[2]

The colony's predilection for codifying biblical injunctions like the Ten Commandments into civil law, along with its failure to include longstanding traditional English principles explicitly, made it seem to Child and his associates that Massachusetts had a government of men, not of laws. But the petitioners failed to mention that the General Court had in fact adopted some of the very laws and practices they were seeking. Massachusetts had struggled with creating its own legal code since the late 1630s. Though the magistrates at first resisted the initiative, a "Body of Liberties" was developed in 1641 at the urging of the "commons" delegates to provide a sketchy written systematization of fundamental legal principles. Those included freedom from impressments and seizure of goods, the privilege of appearing and speaking before any court, the right to post bail, and trial by jury, among others. The subsequent 1648 digest of laws, which has been characterized as "the first modern code of the western world," was the text Pynchon had read to his Springfield Court. This more complete version had been under development since 1645, before the "Remonstrance" was presented, but it was held in abeyance until the Remonstrants' case could be

---

2. "Remonstrance and Petition" in Hutchinson, *Collection*, 190.

settled. Fundamentally, it provided a complete digest of the laws the General Court had enacted to that date.[3]

The Remonstrants pointed their second objection more directly at the government's restriction of the franchise:

> 2. We . . . desire that civil liberty and freedom be forthwith granted to all truely English, equall to the rest of their countrymen . . . without imposing any oathes or covenant on them.[4]

The petitioners disapproved of the Congregational state's innovations. They questioned its power to legislate and to tax, and they charged, with some justification, that some even called Massachusetts "a free state, [rather] than a colonie or corporation of England." They sought an expansion in the right to vote. Essentially, the Remonstrants wanted their legal situation to be as they felt it had been in Great Britain. Here as well, a measure to deal with the petitioners' concerns by expanding the franchise was ready for General Court action at the session when the "Remonstrance" was presented, but the legislature delayed action until the petition could be addressed.

The Remonstrants aimed their third objection at the churches:

> 3. We . . . humbly intreat you . . . to give liberty to members of the church of England . . . to be taken into your congregation.[5]

The petitioners disapproved the variety of church covenants, each of which was composed and adopted by the congregation to which it applied. They were baffled by the authority of these locally-created mutual agreements. Indeed, the petitioners rejected the very concept of separate covenanted communities. They wanted churches to accept any English Protestants from the "church of England," which for them meant Presbyterians. They did not like to be required to attend worship. While the colony saw this stipulation as accountability to the community, the petitioners saw it as infringement of their religious rights. They wanted baptism for their children, which in Congregational Massachusetts was usually available only to church members. Ultimately, as the historian David D. Hall has

---

3. See Massachusetts General Court, "Liberties of the Massachusetts Colonie," 261–67. For "the first modern code," see Woolrych, *Commonwealth to Protectorate*, 272.

4. "Remonstrance and Petition" in Hutchinson, *Collection*, 192.

5. Ibid., 194.

pointed out, "[i]nstead of greater freedom for the church, Child demanded greater state control."[6]

The petitioners harbored deep doubts that Massachusetts Congregationalists could "contrive better lawes and customes than the wisest of our nation have with great consideration composed, and by many hundred yeares experience have found most equall and just."[7] They mistrusted the claims to innovation and independence that motivated the Bay colony leadership. They did not share their zeal for bold breaks with the past for the sake of Reformation. The protesters' underlying purpose was to present their "Remonstrance" as a first step towards petitioning the British government—though they never expressed it explicitly that way. Throughout the document they included repeated references to "the honourable houses of parliament" or "appeals into England," clear hints of a threat based on what the British government might say should the petitioners' case come to their attention.[8]

The Court responded to the Remonstrants six months later, in November 1646. The reaction was firm: the protesters had shown disrespect for the colony's charter by appealing to Parliament even before they had been brought to trial, and for that reason they were treated as seditious conspirators. It seemed very clear to the watchful, skittish leaders of the Commonwealth that Dr. Child intended to subvert the Congregational experiment. As George L. Kittredge observed, "the object of the Remonstrants, from the beginning, was to abolish the independence of the Bay Colony, and the object of the General Court, from the beginning, was, in opposing them, to maintain that independence."[9]

On the eve of Child's planned departure for England immediately after the November trial, a last-minute search at the home of one of his fellow petitioners turned up papers that revealed a deeper dimension of their mission. Among those documents was another petition asking that Parliament appoint either a "general governor" or commissioners to regulate Massachusetts Bay. It also called for the imposition of the "Solemn League and Covenant," the one covenant the petitioners would accept, in keeping

---

6. See also Hall, *Faithful Shepherd*, 127. Miller, *Orthodoxy in Massachusetts*, 298–306. The text of the "Remonstrance and Petition" is in Hutchinson, *Collection*, 188–96.

7. Hutchinson, *Collection*, 191.

8. Ibid., 191, 192, 195.

9. Kittredge, "Dr. Robert Child," 69–70.

with the vote of the House of Commons favoring the Presbyterian structure for the Church of England.

In tandem with a petition William Vassal intended to present to the Parliamentary Commissioners for Plantations in England, the Child initiative could have proven devastating for the Congregational Commonwealth. But the Commissioners stood by the Massachusetts government in its order of May 15, 1646, and the threat came to an end.[10]

On March 9, 1647, Pynchon weighed in with an extensive letter to Governor Winthrop.[11] He suggested ways the Bay colony could defend itself by accommodating some of the Remonstrants' concerns. One step would be to conform more clearly to long-established English legal practices. He reasoned that

> as we had the happinesse to be bredd and borne vnder such laws for ciuill gouerment as I conceiue no nation hath better, so it should be our care in thankefulnesse both to god and that state to preserue and adhere to what euer laws or customes they haue except those that be contrary to god.[12]

Pynchon appreciated the tradition of sworn constables, trials by jury, and the other safeguards he had experienced and found described in the two classic writings by Fortescue and Dalton that had guided his own work as a magistrate.[13] In that capacity, Pynchon was especially keen to have warrants issued in the name of the king. In fact, he devoted a full paragraph to that subject, and on one occasion at least issued a warrant in the king's name in 1640. He felt it would offer a kind of insurance against injustice: "for what though the kinge be never so corrupt in Religion and manners," said Pynchon (thinking, no doubt, of the then-current King Charles I), "yet if his subjectes will be faithfull to the lawes of England he cannot hurt [them]."

Massachusetts, after all, *was* England. Governor Endecott had in effect questioned this fact in the summer of 1644. During a tense English Civil War incident that involved two ships in Boston Harbor, with one vessel commissioned by the Parliament challenging another from a Royalist port,

10. Ibid., 48–50; Winthrop, *History*, 2:389–390; ibid., *Journal*, 655–670.

11. Forbes, *WP*, 5:134–36.

12. Ibid., 5:134.

13. Later in 1647, perhaps because of Pynchon's recommendation, the General Court voted to buy two copies of *The Country Justice* for its law library (Shurtleff, *MBCR*, 2:207).

Endecott cagily reserved the right of Massachusetts to become an independent state "if the Parliament should hereafter be of a malignant spirit." But Pynchon looked at circumstances differently. He wrote to Winthrop, "[W]e are not a Free state," reflecting a charge specified in the Remonstrance, "neather do I think it our wisdome to be a Free state[. T]hough we had our liberty," Pynchon insisted, "we cannot as yet subsist without England."[14] The fact that in 1647 Pynchon mentioned the possibility that Massachusetts could "subsist without England" indicates that such an option was actually thinkable, even at that early moment.

However, Pynchon also cricized the Remonstrant petitioners. He wrote from Springfield, "I cannot but be much affected with that malignant spirit that breathes out in their endeuors, bec[ause] by their manner of proceedinge (though they pretend honest reformation, yet) it seemes to me they would destroy both Church & Comonwealth: in laboring for a generall Governor, & in charging treason by Conniuence vppon the Court." He opposed the petitioners' proposal that a "generall Governour" be sent from England because that would strike at the heart of the Massachusetts Bay experiment in independency. Pynchon noticed that the petitioners intended to play the Massachusetts General Court off against the Parliament. He believed that the petitioners' critique of the General Court did not take into account the negative role of Parliament, which he felt permitted the circulation of dangerous notions "which doubtlesse they would not beare if it were a tyme of solid peace." Moreover, he recognized that the petitioners' proposals were an expression of Presbyterian versus Independent arguments raging in England, and he devoted several sentences to that topic. He was convinced that the petitioners' desire for an "inouation in Church" did "not proceed out of zeale of gods glory."[15] He feared the dangerous specter of disorder, a broken church in a broken state.

On another occasion Pynchon was even more explicit about the climate of free inquiry, which he had noticed was infecting New England as it had the Old. Winthrop had noticed it too. On July 1, 1645, Winthrop wrote in his journal about the problem of "liberty of conscience":

> Many Bookes coming out of England, some in defence of Ana-
> baptism & other errors, and for Liberty of Conscience as a shelter

14. For an account of the August 1644 incident, see Mayo, *John Endecott*, 177–79. Pynchon's letter is found in Forbes, *WP*, 5:134–37.

15. Ibid., 5:134–35. See Appendix 6 for Pynchon's comparison of Presbyterian and Independent views on governance.

for their Toleration, &c., others in maintenance of the Presbiterill Government (Agreed upon by the [Westminster] Assembly of devines in England) against the Congregationall waye, which was practized heer: The Elders of the Churches throughe all the Vnited Colonies agreed vpon a meeting at Cambridge this daye, where they conferred their Counsells, & examined the writinges which some of them had prepared in Answeare to the said Bookes, which beeinge agreed & perfected were sent ouer to England to be printed.[16]

Winthrop went on to mention that the United Colonies of New England had commissioned Thomas Hooker to respond to English Puritan concerns about church governance. Echoing the same worry about toleration, Pynchon wrote to the governor on the question of liberty of conscience one year later, in July 1646:

> I perceive by some godly ministers that have wrote into this country: that this is not a tyme of Reformation but of liberty of conscience: I beleeve by that tyme they see a litle more of the lawlessnesse of liberty of conscience, they will change their iudge[men]ts and say that liberty of conscience will give liberty to Sathan to broch such horrid blasphemose opinions as never were the like in any age. [T]he Lord awaken some able men to confute that vi[le] tenent.[17]

An underlying issue was the question of flexibility in Puritan society. In the preface to his *Discussion*, John Norton had framed the dilemma in this way:

> That the care of Religion is the duty of the magistrate, is evident; yet when and how far to bear, in case of errour concerning matters of Religion, is a great Quaery of these times. Unity in judgement is to be endeavoured as much as possible, because truth is one and indivisible, yet some difference touching the truth must be endured, because of the weaknesse of men. To tolerate everything, and to tolerate nothing, are both intolerable.[18]

---

16. Winthrop, *History*, 2:304; ibid., *Journal*, 608–609. The Westminster Assembly met from 1643 to 1649. One of the books was Samuel Rutherford's *The Due Right of Presbyteries*.

17. Forbes, *WP*, 5:91. For Winthrop's thoughts, see also Miller, *Orthodoxy in Massachusetts*, 301.

18. Norton, preface to *Discussion*, A5v–A6r.

Pynchon's experience as magistrate in Springfield seems to have led him to agree—though of course he would scarcely have seen himself as a dangerous deviant from the truth. Certainly Pynchon shared the Puritan conviction that consensus is vital for public order. He probably felt strongly that communities required accord, particularly in frontier situations where their very survival was constantly at stake. But whatever his reasons, and whatever personal experiences as churchwarden in England and magistrate and developer in New England may have shaped his convictions, Pynchon was very much committed to preserving the civic covenant. He assumed the need for a clearly articulated, widely understood, and broadly accepted consensus that would be sustained by shared commitment to the community. Such exercise of covenant was the indispensable basis for Puritan social life.

The irony is that Pynchon was condemned for his own deviant opinions. Did he not realize how his efforts at a theological reconstruction would be received? Should he not have known that the General Court would treat him precisely as he wanted them to deal with the Remonstrants? Did he actually think that his opinions would be any more acceptable than those of any other dissenters from the orthodox norm? And why did the General Court so quickly condemn *The Meritorious Price* without even reading it? Were Pynchon's views really so dangerously heretical that they deserved no hearing at all?

The explanations for what happened hinge in part on the unpalatability of Pynchon's theological notions, but even more on several forces then at work in shaping the emerging life and culture of the Massachusetts Bay colony. Those factors entirely escaped his notice.

18

A Church for the Gentry

IN ITS DESIRE TO develop a commonwealth built around communities of faith, a question that concerned the emerging Massachusetts culture was, "What constitutes a church?"

From the varieties of church polity advocated and practiced in England since the Reformation, the colonists in Massachusetts and Connecticut chose a particular form of congregational governance that they then developed in their unique ways. As Richard Mather emphasized in his 1643 pamphlet entitled *Church-Government and Church-Covenant Discussed*, "We [in New England] do not know any visible Church of the N.T. properly so called, but onely a particular Congregation; . . . There is no true visible Church of Christ, but a particular ordinary Congregation onely." Thomas Hooker offered a clear summary of the New England Congregational objections to Presbyterian structures in the quasi-official pamphlet he wrote at the behest of a gathering of clergy in Cambridge in July 1645:

> 1. A Church in the Gospel is never used only for Elders.
>
> 2. There cannot be a Definition given, that will agree to a congregationall and Presbyteriall Church.[1]

---

1. Mather, *Church-Government*, 9, 10; Hooker, *A Survey*, 127. Hooker wrote in reply to Samuel Rutherford's 1644 volume on Presbyterianism, but his manuscript was lost when the ship carrying it from New Haven to England sank. Hooker could not be persuaded to send another copy, so it was published posthumously in June 1647 (Winthrop, *History*, 2:304–305; ibid., *Journal*, 609).

In this, as in other matters, William Pynchon's views contrasted boldly with those of his neighbor to the south. In the same March 8, 1647, letter to Winthrop in which he criticized the Remonstrants, he maintained that Parliament viewed the plethora of forms of church discipline with a healthy relativism. This assertion is puzzling, because the House of Commons had clearly expressed a preference when it went on record almost exactly a year earlier, on March 5, 1646, to institute a full-fledged Presbyterian system throughout England and Wales.[2]

Whatever the reasons for his claim, Pynchon went on to suggest a criterion for distinguishing authentic churches. He proposed a standard that he argued would be more useful than any well-conceived and well-meaning polity alone:

> But truly where zeale of gods glory and godly wisdome are ioyned together: a world of good hath bin don by godly ministers even in England that haue held no certaine fourme of discipline[.] [O]n the contrary, where a could spirit doth rule in ministers though they may have a good fourme of gouerment there people may be said to haue a name to live, and yet be but dead Christians.[3]

Elsewhere, Pynchon was even more explicit. In *The Jews Synagogue*, he held that early Jewish communities of faith were "true visible churches of Jesus Christ," that the discipline they practiced was revealed by Christ to Moses, and that those practices remained the model for church order. As long as the Jews lived in Canaan, those synagogue-churches were "dependent" on the national ecclesiastical structure—what Pynchon called the "Nationall Church." But of necessity, such faith communities developed independently beyond the Jews' home territory. For this reason Congregational churches suited New England, though they were a deviation from the norm of a "Nationall Church."

Furthermore, Pynchon urged liberality in admitting members into the church. To the objection that laxity would inevitably weaken the doctrinal strength and moral effectiveness of the church, he replied,

> It is true, most outward Professors are but Hypocrites; yet these together with some Godly among them, may well be called The Church of Christ; and by the noblest part they may well be called

2. The vote is recorded in the entry for March 5, 1646, in History of Parliament Trust, "House of Commons Journal," 462–465.

3. Forbes, *WP*, 5:136. See Appendix 6 for the whole passage, including a proposed reconstruction of the words subsequently torn away.

The Kingdom of Heaven, because their profession is of an Heavenly calling.[4]

Under Pynchon's rules, it would be easy to get into a church, but maybe not so easy to stay there:

If none ought to be admitted into a particular Church, until they manifest the Truth of Grace in their souls, then doubtless Christ hath given infallible rules, whereby the Church may discern aright of the Truth of their Grace, and distinguish it from close hypocrisie: But I must confess that I am to seek where to find those rules. For though the Scriptures have perfect rules in general, yet when these rules come to be applied to particular persons, then am I to seek for certainty of judgement. I conceive it is one of the royal Prerogatives of the Lord Jesus, to know what persons have the truth of Grace in their souls. Questionless, all such are the most fit persons that are to be joyned as Members of particular Churches. But yet, if there be any other that do call upon the Name of the Lord, and depart from iniquity, our Lord would have us to esteem them also as fit matter for a particular visible Church; until by their scandalous walking they deserve to be excommunicated.[5]

Others shared his view that entrance standards should be generous and flexible. While preaching at his Windsor church in August 1647, John Warham, Pynchon's former pastor from his days in Dorchester, remarked, "to expect eminency for admission [to the church] is too much. The strong must beare with the weake. The house is a house and all Stones are not big ones."[6]

But Pynchon had in mind something even more sweeping than individual entrance standards for a local church. Admission to one congregation was admission to the whole grand array of Christian assemblies. "All the outward Professors of the Faith through the world do make an universal visible Church of Christ," he said. This entity is "outwardly visible farre and wide over the face of the earth."[7]

---

4. Pynchon, *JS*, 80. Pynchon added: "Yet this I would say, let Churches, both Teachers and Members, be careful that they be not too censorious and pragmatical, lest they turn men upon the stumbling blocks of Anabaptistry, &c" (ibid., 80–81).

5. Ibid., 80.

6. Warham cited in Stout, *New England Soul*, 320. In the course of his long career, Warham held various convictions about baptism, membership, and church discipline; see Lucas, *Valley of Discord*, 38–40.

7. Pynchon, *JS*, 1, 38–41.

A Platforme of Church Discipline adopted at the third and final session
of the Cambridge Synod in August 1648 became, with the subsequent ap-
proval of the General Court, a schema for structuring the Commonwealth's
churches. It maintained that "the Church . . . ought not to be of greater
number then may ordinarily meet together conveniently in one place." For
Pynchon, however, that "meeting" would not require physical presence.
The term "church" refers to

> all visible Professors of the Faith: For though they cannot now per-
> sonally meet together in any one place, as perhaps they did in the
> dayes of Adam and Noah; yet they do dayly meet together in the
> unitie of the Faith, and they do all make the same publick Profes-
> sion of salvation by Christ alone.[8]

In expressing this conviction, Pynchon aligned himself with those whom
Gura called "latitudinarian[s] *within* the English Puritan tradition." Church
was wider for them, and more expandable.[9]

Pynchon's inclusive liberality nicely complemented his convictions
about social order. A more comprehensive church could serve the purpose
of a more comprehensive community of obedience, a more homogeneous
and dutiful body politic. The Massachusetts General Court connected
Christian worship with civic responsibility in a 1646 law requiring church
attendance: "seeing that the word is of generall & comon behoofe to all
sorts of people, as being the ordinary meanes to subdue the harts of hearers
not onely to the faith, & obedience to the Lord Jesus, but also to civill obedience, & allegiance unto magistracy."[10] Obedience is a persistent underly-

---

8. Ibid., 77–78. For the Cambridge Platform see Walker, *Creeds and Platforms*,
194–237. The phrasing cited here is found in ch. 3, para. 4 (ibid., 206).

9. For "Latitudinarian" Puritans, see Gura, *Sion's Glory*, 315–16, 320. It is not clear
that Pynchon exemplified what Gura called "Puritan rationalists," who "argued that the
few truths essential to salvation and recorded in the Scriptures were revealed directly to
the heart of man and corroborated by his reason" (ibid., 316). To connect Pynchon more
closely with rationalism, Gura rephrased Pynchon's words. Where Pynchon had written,
"search [the blessed Scriptures] deliberately, and search them daily" (Pynchon, *FD*, b3r),
Gura loosely rephrased "deliberately" as "by the lights of reason and conscience" (Gura,
Sion's Glory, 319). Gura also tried to link Pynchon and Edward Holyoke as "a small but
active group of Puritan rationalists" in the Connecticut Valley (ibid., 321). Holyoke was
author of a yet to be studied volume, *The Doctrine of Life*, which has much in common with works by Pynchon, whose daughter Mary was married to Edward's son, Elizur
Holyoke. But Edward Holyoke was not "a friend and neighbor in the Connecticut Valley"
(ibid., 320). He lived on the coast in Lynn.

10. Shurtleff, *MBCR*, 2:177.

ing value that is fundamental to *The Meritorious Price*. In a way, the entire volume is a tract on obedience, and that is the one strand of Pynchon's argument that seems most original to him. It was Christ's obedience that led him to offer himself up as a sacrifice. It was obedience that endeared him to the Father and achieved redemption. Many places in Pynchon's repetitive argument make this point:

> [H]e did but say, Father, Into thy hands I commend my spirit; and at that very instant he breathed out his soul . . . and this Mediatorial action of his, was the highest degree of obedience, that the Father required, or that the Son could performe for mans Atonement and Redemption.[11]

> [F]or as the Father delighted to break him [Christ] with stripes, &c. for the tryal of his Mediatorial obedience . . . so the Son delighted to learn obedience, by that which he suffered; and so being found perfect, (through afflictions) he became the Meritorious Author of eternal Salvation, to all that obey him, by believing in him.[12]

> God the Father was more highly pleased with the obedience of the Mediator, then he was displeased with the disobedience of Adam.[13]

> [N]o other thing could procure [our Atonement and redemption] but the highest degree of obedience which the mediator could perform, which was his mediatorial sacrifice of Atonement.[14]

> [T]he sweetness of Christs sacrifice doth [not] ly in his passive sufferings but in his mediatorial obedience, when he did by his own power actually give up his soul to God as a mediatorial sacrifice.[15]

Obedience was the price Christ paid, so obedience becomes the key to living faithfully. Here Pynchon exemplified a feature of the culture Puritans retained from their experience in England, what Hall has called "the everyday experience of accepting the authority of those above you."[16] Pynchon made a virtue of that necessity for orderly community. To be charged with disobedience, as happened in Pynchon's controversy with Hooker in Con-

---

11. Pynchon, *MP*, 55.
12. Ibid., 23.
13. Ibid., 84.
14. Ibid., 86.
15. Ibid., 153.
16. Hall, *A Reforming People*, 9.

necticut, was particularly humiliating and demoralizing. When obedience is salvation, disobedience is the ultimate failure.

Pynchon differed from the definitions and prescriptions of the Cambridge Synod's *A Platforme of Church Discipline* at several other points as well.[17] He did not distinguish between two uses of the word "church," as the *Platforme* did: one for the universal Body of Christ, but another for a congregation of believers. Nor did he agree with the framers of the *Platforme* that since the coming of Christ, the only appropriate mode of church life is congregational. He thought in terms of a second-order church, so to speak: a church of the gentry, a patricians' church, a magistrates' church. He held that to "Tell the Church" could not possibly require opening any issue before the general membership of a congregation, but had to mean instead telling the Elders of the "Sanhedrin," or the national ecclesiastical government, which he believed was ordained by Christ.[18]

Pynchon backed up his contention with a linguistic study of the Hebrew word *kahal*, the meaning of which he narrowed to "church." He noted that the term has multiple applications in the Bible and maintained that "a Court of Magistrates is often called a Church in Scripture," while offering twenty-one examples to substantiate his point. He believed, for instance, that in Deuteronomy 31:30, "And Moses spake in the ears of all the congregation (*kahal*) of Israel," the word could not possibly mean the entire Hebrew people; rather, there the term "Church . . . must be understood of the Elders and Officers of the Church only, which also were the Magistrates of the Commonweal." True to his own judicial calling as the magistrate of Springfield, he was convinced that "the word Church in Matth. 18.17 ["tell it unto the Church"] Must be taken for a Court of Magistrates," and not a congregation of believers.[19] In support of his elastic use of this word, he pointed out, somewhat impishly, that Psalm 26:5 speaks of a "church" of evildoers, and the unbelieving Persian army is called by the same word, "church" or "synagogue," in Jeremiah 50:9!

Finally, Pynchon did not agree with the *Platforme*'s contention that "Church Officers are officers to one church, even that particular, over which the Holy Ghost has made them overseers." He claimed that "Paul was not

17. Walker, *Creeds and Platforms*; see the usages of "Church" in ch. 2, para. 3–4 (ibid., 204–205).

18. Pynchon, *JS*, 69, 42, 70; compare with the *Platforme*, in ch. 2, para. 5, Walker, *Creeds and Platforms*.

19. Pynchon, *JS*, 75, 76, 78, 69; compare with the *Platforme*, ch. 9, para. 6.

made a Minister to any one particular Church, but to the Church of Christ in General."[20]

In Pynchon's view, anyone who confesses a faith in Christ should be at liberty to join the church, but it took the right people—ministers and magistrates—to compose its essential core. Pynchon was willing to call a court of Elders a "Church," and in that sense to affirm, quite contrary to chapter 2, paragraph 4 of the Cambridge *Platforme*, that there is a universal, all-encompassing visible church. This divergent opinion ultimately put Pynchon at odds with the Congregational form of church structure practiced in New England. He preferred a Presbyterian-style polity in which Elders and church officers could be identified as a universal ecclesiastical-political communion, a Church of Christ. His was a more aristocratic understanding of church governance, and that was not the way church polity was developing in Massachusetts Bay.

20. Pynchon, *JS*, 78. The *Platforme* clearly distinguished the extraordinary apostolic era offices of "apostles, prophets, and evangelists" from the subsequent ordinary offices of "elders and deacons" (*Platforme*, ch. 6, para. 3).

19

Governance in Changing Times

AS THE PRACTICE OF Congregational church polity evolved over the first half of the seventeenth century in New England, so also did new patterns in civic governance. In this case as well, Pynchon's position was askance of the emerging Massachusetts culture.

Except for the few years his plantation was aligned with Connecticut, William Pynchon was regularly elected an Assistant in the Bay colony. The Assistants functioned as a fledgling upper house within the General Court, which very early on included Deputies from the various communities. The Court combined legislative and judicial functions. Not only did it create laws and regulations, it also heard judicial appeals. It dealt with a wide range of issues: from diplomatic negotiations with the Dutch and French and the Indians, to boundaries between communities, to individual citizens' petitions for redress. Eventually, the Court morphed into the now bicameral Massachusetts state legislature, which is still called the General Court.

The representative branch of the colony's legislature was sometimes, but not often, called "Commons." It comprised Deputies who were elected by each town. The Deputies had their beginnings in May 1632 when the Assistants, Pynchon included, felt the need to seek popular support for levying taxes for the first time. The Assistants took it upon themselves to name two men from each town to attend their next session and "conferre with the Court about raiseing of a publique stock." Assistants and Deputies met together as a unicameral body for the first dozen years. By 1638, when Pynchon's Agawam was under Connecticut's jurisdiction, the Massachusetts Deputies were no longer appointed, but popularly elected. As the

Commonwealth grew, so did this body: from sixteen in 1632 to thirty-three in 1639, when Springfield was reincorporated into the Bay colony.[1]

For a while Springfield was virtually independent. Then from 1643 to 1650, the General Court resumed its practice of regularly electing Pynchon as one of the Assistants. By this vote, the Commonwealth endorsed and authorized his magistracy on the frontier.

Yet Pynchon seems to have attended the Court's sessions in Boston only when it was in his own or Springfield's interest. There is no indication that he participated in the General Court during a particularly formative time in the Court's development in the 1640s. Those years saw a substantial expansion in the exercise of the franchise; on average, as much as 50 percent of the adult male population had become freemen by 1647.[2] Pynchon does not seem to have been a member of the Court in 1642, when 139 freemen were added to the electoral roles—and the Assistants proposed limiting Deputies to one per town. Nor was he involved when the Deputies and Assistants decided to meet separately in March 1644. Neither was he present in November of 1644, when the upper house tried unsuccessfully to limit the entire number of Deputies to twenty, thus equaling the number of Magistrates, and to require both bodies to meet again as a single, unicameral legislature. This failed proposal was ostensibly presented as a cost-cutting measure. It came at a time of serious economic distress, which led even to the abolition of ballots made of scarce paper in favor of voting by "Indian beanes" (kidney beans). Pynchon was not in attendance in November 1647 when the Court decided to poll the towns to see if they preferred to have only one Deputy each; unsurprisingly, they did not.[3] Throughout all those years when the Deputies struggled to maintain and expand their role of popular representation in the Bay colony, Pynchon was not involved.

The records do indicate that Pynchon showed up for Court meetings in 1645 and 1649. He probably arrived belatedly in May 1645, since he took his oath much later when he happened to be in Boston on a Saturday in July. The business that concerned him at the May General Court was

1. Shurtleff, *MBCR*, 1:95. For an account of the development of the Deputies see "'Arbitrary' or 'Democratical'?" in Hall, *A Reforming People*, ch. 1, especially 24–28, 31–34.

2. Ibid., 92.

3. Shurtleff, *MBCR*, 2:3 (one Deputy only), 58 (Deputies meet separately), 42 (Indian beans), 88 (limit Deputies), 217 (one or two Deputies per town?), 231 (each town to decide).

authorizing magistrates' Court sessions in Springfield.[4] Pynchon was also present at the May 1649 General Court to support Massachusetts' resistance to Connecticut's expansionism. He was eager to ward off both Connecticut's attempt to charge tolls on river freight from Springfield and Hartford's incursions in establishing an outpost at Woronoco. He had an additional purpose in coming to Boston, which was to lobby for the suspension of Bay colony taxes on Springfield for the next six years. He was successful all around. The Court both stood up to Connecticut and gave Springfield tax relief. But Pynchon spent only six days at the Court before leaving early, with the Court's consent.[5]

He was not re-elected an Assistant in 1651, though he did attend, but chiefly in order to deal with the charges pending against him for *The Meritorious Price*. He may not have still been present towards the end of the Court's session that May when it considered a petition signed by sixty-nine women of Boston—including Pynchon's own daughter, Margaret Davis. This appeal sought freedom for an accomplished midwife who had been imprisoned for malpractice. Margaret had no doubt relied on the services of Alice Frost Tilly. Of the reputedly seven children Margaret bore, only three survived to childhood. Benjamin was not quite two at the time of the petition. In response to this appeal and to others like it bearing many other signatures, the Court relented somewhat. The government walked a fine line in its response to a legion of angry women. They allowed Mistress Tilly to practice her art freely, while insisting on the magistrates' authority and the justice of their decision to punish her. In the end, Alice Tilly seems to have weathered the controversy handily and simply continued with her worthy career.[6]

Possibly Pynchon thought that he did not need to attend because John Johnson of Roxbury could adequately represent Springfield's interests. Johnson was the colony's Surveyor General of munitions and arms, a veteran Deputy to the General Court, and Pynchon's long-term business associate. He had acted for Pynchon as his employee in commercial matters; Pynchon called him "my usuall agent in matters that may conserne our plantation" and "my faithfull Agent." The Springfield Court record noted

---

4. Pynchon took the oath on a Saturday in August the following year, but is not recorded as having attended any General or Assistant Court sessions.

5. Shurtleff, *MBCR*, 2:109 (Court in Springfield), 268–70 (Springfield's interests), 3:158 (leaving early).

6. Norton, "Ablest Midwife," 105–134, offers a careful analysis of the case. Concerning Margaret Davis' children, see Whittemore, *Genealogical Guide*, 137.

that residents voted for their Deputy in 1648, apparently for the first time, when they officially elected the non-resident Johnson to represent them.[7]

But even though all adult males could legally vote after May 1647, when the General Court extended the franchise to non-freemen (but for local elections only), Springfield citizens had little say beyond their own town. By 1647, Springfield had forty-three male residents of legal age. Only seven, however, were freemen and therefore eligible to act on colony-wide matters. At 16 percent, this was the lowest proportion of freemen in Massachusetts, and markedly lower than in all other towns, where the percentages of freemen at the time ranged from a low of 26 percent in Gloucester to a high of 65 percent in Charlestown and Concord.[8]

On November 11 of that year, the General Court sought to remedy Springfield's lag in voter enrollment. In order to make the Connecticut Valley settlement conform more closely to the Commonwealth's practices, they voted that

> Mr Pinchin is authorished to make freemen, in the towne of Springfeild, of those that are in covenant & live according to their p[ro]fession; and Springfeild, within twelue months, to bring in a transcript of their land, according to the law in that case p[ro]vided, and a true note of the time of all their births, burials, & marriages.[9]

Records show that in April 1648 Pynchon added six more freemen. They included John, his twenty-three-year old son, Elizur Holyoke, his son-in-law, Deacon Samuel Wright, and an early pioneer and occasional lay preacher at the Springfield church, fifty-three-year-old Henry Burt. Still, Pynchon was quite parsimonious about extending the franchise. Only three more became freemen the following April, bringing the total to sixteen of perhaps forty-five male residents, still a modest 35 percent. This restrictiveness on Pynchon's part was at a time when, as one historian remarked, Puritanism was moving to a "commitment to popular participation in governance."[10]

———— ◁◦▷ ————

7. Forbes, *WP*, 5:137, 271; Smith, *CR*, 216.

8. Wall, "Massachusetts Bay Colony Franchise," 138. See also Foster, "Massachusetts Franchise," 613–23.

9. Shurtleff, *MBCR*, 2:224.

10. Smith, *CR*, 215; Bremer, *First Founders*, 156.

However, Pynchon's incumbency as magistrate and Assistant raised even more questions than his tepid support for the changing patterns of governance that were developing in Massachusetts.

In addition to establishing a constitution for churches, the Cambridge *Platforme* also dealt with the connection between church and state. Puritans considered the roles of governments and faith communities to be complementary. Concerning "the Civil Magistrates powr in Matters Ecclesiastical," the *Platforme*'s chapter 17 declared,

> 6. It is the duty of the Magistrate to take care of matters of religion, & to improve his civil authority for the observing of the duties commanded in the first, as well as for observing of the duties commanded in the second table.[11]

Thus magistrates were to concern themselves with obedience to the first half of the Ten Commandments—the stipulations that concern the individual's relationship to God—as well as the second half, which govern relationships with other people. In that capacity, magistrates were to regulate certain behaviors:

> 7. Idolatry, Blasphemy, Heresy, venting corrupt and pernicious opinions, that destroy the foundation, open contempt of the word preached, prophanation of the Lords day, disturbing the peacable administration & excercise of the worship & holy things of God, & the like, are to be restrayned, & punished by civil authority.[12]

Puritans decisively rejected the continuum of religious and political control that had been their bane in England. Once they arrived in Massachusetts, they instituted a separation of sorts between church and state. Of course, the original form of this entente only partially resembled the system that developed in subsequent American history. But their arrangement did disentangle functions that had been combined under the monolithic power structure in England. It gave churches the sole right to determine the norms of faith, but little power to enforce deportment. By the same token, civil authorities had no right to prescribe articles of faith, patterns of worship, or anything else in the life of congregations. But they did have power to punish any improper behavior and anything that might lead to social instability, including heresy.

11. Walker, *Creeds and Platforms*, 236.

12. Ibid., 237.

As a result of this reconfiguration of religious and secular spheres, the ecclesiastical structure of Massachusetts depended on the magistrates' loyalty to a common doctrine. The General Court saw Pynchon's heterodoxy as a rupture in the solidarity the colony's leadership deemed essential. When Pynchon's orthodoxy came into question, it called the whole system into question, and the leadership felt compelled to act.

The "Epistle Dedicatory" of John Norton's *Discussion* expressed the legislature's concern. Among other things, Norton wrote,

> That licentious and pestilent Proposition, That care of the matters of Religion belongs not to the Magistrate is a Strategem of the Old Serpent and Father of lies, to make free passage for the doctrine of devils . . . The disuse of the Civil Sword as concerning matters of Religion gave opportunity to the rise of the man of Sin; the abuse of it maintained him; and the good use thereof shall help to ruine him.[13]

The Assistants expressed a similar point in their reply to a letter, since lost, which Harry Vane wrote in defense of Pynchon. They maintained that Pynchon's book (which they seem to have read by this time) was "pernicious and dangerous." In affirming his idiosyncratic views so dogmatically, Pynchon in effect condemned everyone else's orthodox convictions. The government found this unacceptable from anyone in Massachusetts, "especially a Magistrate amongst us." In the era's equivalent of "Don't ask, don't tell," they suggested that "Mr. Pincheon might have kept his judgment to himself, as . . . he did above thirty years."[14] Silence would have been tolerable. Going public was not.

Winthrop's diary entry on the "[m]any Bookes coming out of England" is only one of several expressions of a concern—indeed, a fear—that haunted the New England Puritan enterprise, following it like a cloud from behind. Others expressed similar anxiety. In 1640, Thomas Shepard named an objection (which he did not share) to Winthrop's planned history of Massachusetts: "some things may prejudice us in regard of the state of England if divulged."[15] In 1645, John Cotton feared that any corruption in New England could lead to catastrophic consequences. As he warned his Boston

13. Norton, *Discussion*, A3v.

14. The letter was signed by Governor Endecott, Deputy Governor Dudley, and six others; the text is given in Burt, *First Century*, 1:124–25.

15. Forbes, *WP*, 4:183.

congregation, "either all England will judge your reformation but a delusion and an invention of your magistrates, or Elders, or otherwise looke at you, as not sincere but counterfeit."[16] Solidarity was vital. Massachusetts was eager, even anxious, to appear unified in the face of a potentially hostile world. Too much was at stake to allow even the slightest impression that the colony was divided, that the Congregational Way might give birth to peculiar theologies, or that the Puritan experiment in New England was fraying in any manner whatsoever. The clergy letter appended to Norton's *Discussion* noted their concern that "this Book [by Pynchon] being published under the name of a New English gentleman, might occasion many to think, that New England also concurred in the allowance of such Exorbitant Aberrations."[17]

For one thing, the sense of urgency that drove the General Court to condemn Pynchon's book had a simple public relations component. Massachusetts was eager to attract new recruits. After the difficult decade of the 1640s, when the trans-Atlantic population flow reversed and many pioneers returned to England, the colony needed to grow again.

But there was more. The struggle to create a new, covenant-shaped society linking seaboard settlements along the edge of a continent they perceived as unsettled and even dangerous—this was the Puritans' high calling. Such an exalted purpose trumped all niceties. It far outweighed even the slightest gesture of largess toward dissidents.

For its first twenty years, the Bay colony's legislative records did not mention heresy or heretics very often. Only five entries prior to the Pynchon case used those terms. Anne Hutchinson was not among them. As the protagonist of the Antinomian crisis of 1637, she was charged not with heresy, but instead with "traducing the ministers and their ministry." Only Hugh Bewet in December 1640, Samuel Gorton and his followers in October 1643, and Richard Waterman in May 1644 were expressly charged with heresy. The offence in all cases seems to have been Anabaptism. In its next action on heresy, in November 1644, the Court voted to proscribe Anabaptists on the grounds that "they have bene the incendiaries of comon wealths, & the infectors of persons in maine mattrs of religion, & the troublers of churches in all places where they have bene."[18] Since heresy was not

16. Cotton, *Powring out*, 1:23. Also see Stout, *New England Soul*, 49.

17. Norton, *Discussion*, S7v.

18. Shurtleff, *MBCR*, 1:207 (Hutchinson), 312 (Bewet), 2:52 (Gorton), 73 (Waterman), 85 (Anabaptists).

a capital crime in New England, the three were banished, though Gorton and Waterman were first jailed.

The Court's fifth action was the 1646 Massachusetts statute on "damnable heresy," which provided the grounds for condemning Pynchon. With that vote, the legislators denounced any who might "go about to subvert and destroy the Christian faith and religion." The law identified a handful of offensive teachings considered to be particularly dangerous. Denying the immortality of the soul or the resurrection of Christ was punishable, as was denying that regenerate, godly people ever sinned or needed to repent. The statute also forbade "denying that Christ gave himselfe a ransome for our sins, or that we are justified by his death and righteousness."[19] With just a little manipulation, that condemnation could bear on the Pynchon case. After all, Pynchon had maintained that it was not Christ's suffering and dying but rather his obedience that redeemed. So the government acted.

19. Ibid. 2:177. The punishment originally prescribed was 20s. per month, but that was changed to banishment in the Laws of 1648.

20

Dissension in the Court

IT IS SIGNIFICANT THAT the General Court did not condemn William Pynchon unanimously. Six Deputies were willing to tolerate "[t]hat licentious and pestilent Proposition" that Norton had castigated so harshly.

Other related cases dating from the same time period cast further light on the dynamics at work in Pynchon's situation. Voting patterns in the Massachusetts General Court reveal that a determined minority of deputies remained hesitant to apply civil sanctions in cases concerning theology or church discipline. Some of the representatives who voted *for* Pynchon by refusing to censure him also voted *against* the Cambridge *Platforme* one year later. Indeed, four Deputies voted "No" on the *Platforme* twice. In May 1651, they voted against submitting any objections to the *Platforme* to the ministers so that questions could be addressed and problems fixed; five months later, they also voted against approving it. By taking seemingly contradictory stances, they indicated a strong desire for no government involvement whatsoever in church issues.[1]

Votes concerning the situation of Marmaduke Matthews (1606–1683[?]) confirm this further. His case extended over both the spring and fall sessions of the Court in 1651. Matthews graduated in 1627 from All Souls College, Oxford, and immigrated to New England via the West Indies in 1638. In Massachusetts he served as the first settled minister in Yarmouth, but his checkered employment record exhibited an unusual itinerancy in an era when clergy were expected to stay in one congregation

---

1. The recalcitrant Deputies were Leverett, Clarke, Tyng, and Hutchins (Shurtleff, *MBCR*, 4 pt. 1:55).

throughout their careers. After a ten-year ministry on Cape Cod in the jurisdiction of Plymouth colony, he moved to Hull in the Bay colony in 1648. However, because of his "severall erroneous expressions, others weake, inconvenient, & unsafe," the General Court would not let him minister there. He considered moving to New London, Connecticut, in 1649, but chose instead to go to Malden, Massachusetts, in 1650. Even though a petition of thirty-six women from Malden and Charlestown and the male leadership of the Malden Church supported him, in May 1651 the General Court voted censure for what were said to be "vnsafe, if not vnsound, expressions in his publicke teachinge." Matthews was unable to clear his name before the Court—it seems he did not even show up—and in October 1651 the legislature voted to levy a hefty £50 fine against the Malden Church because they had ordained (or re-ordained) Matthews in spite of the negative advice of magistrates, ministers, and other churches. The government kept having to deal with Matthews and his irregular situation. Nobody seems to have wanted him, except the people of Malden. He returned to his hometown of Swansea, Wales, probably in 1654, and ended his ministry there. Though Matthews was constantly criticized for laxity and carelessness in doctrine, it may be, however, that something else really lay behind the controversies that dogged him wherever he went. One observer noted that his problem seems to have been his habit of using "words without much reference to thoughts." The Matthews case, like Pynchon's, proved to be a test for democratic adaptability in the emerging Commonwealth. Several of the same delegates who supported Pynchon and opposed the *Platforme* also refused to censure Matthews and to fine the Malden Church.[2]

Records name the dissenting deputies and their towns in four votes regarding the three theology and politics cases handled by the General Court from late 1650 through 1651:[3]

---

2. Ibid., 2:276, 3:250. For more on Matthews, see *ODNB*, 37:364–65; Hardman Moore, *Pilgrims*, 74–77, 121; and Freeman, *History of Cape Cod*, 1:201–202. The assessment of Matthews' verbal clumsiness quoted by Freeman comes from the Reverend Edmund (Edward) Hamilton Sears (1810–1876).

3. Shurtleff, *MBCR*, 4 pt. 1:29–30 (Pynchon), 42 (Matthews), 3:240 (*Platforme*), 250 (Malden Church fine).

Dissident Deputies in the Massachusetts General Court				
Town	Pro-PYNCHON	Pro-MATTHEWS	Anti-*PLATFORME*	Anti-MALDEN FINE
	October 15, 1650	May 7, 1651	October 14, 1651	October 24, 1651
Salem	Hawthorne	Hawthorne	Hawthorne	Hawthorne
	Bartholomew	Bartholomew	Bartholomew	
Boston		Clarke	Clarke	Clarke
		Leverett	Leverett	Leverett
Braintree	Kingsley	Kingsley	Kingsley	Kingsley
		Tyng	Tyng	
Watertown		Sherman	Browne	Browne
Roxbury			Johnson	
Wenham		Reede	Reede	Reede
Reading	Walker	Cowdry	Cowdry	Cowdry
Sudbury			Haynes	
Hampton, NH			Shaw	
Weymouth		Holbrooke	Holbrooke	
Hingham		Hutchins	Hutchins	Hutchins
		Allen		Allen
Malden	Hills	Hills		
Springfield	Holyoke			
Salisbury, NH		Bradbury		
Haverhill		Clements		

The names of William Hawthorne, Speaker of the House of Deputies, and William Bartholomew (both of Salem), as well as Stephen Kingsley (representing Braintree) appear in all votes in these three cases. So do the representatives from Reading. The representative from Malden voted for Pynchon and Matthews, as did Edward Holyoke of Lynn, representing Springfield at that session. Holyoke was the parent of Springfield's Elizur

Holyoke, who had married Pynchon's daughter Mary, and so was naturally loyal to his son's father-in-law.

Those who sided with Pynchon were veterans of the Court—Hathorne, Bartholomew, Kingsley, Walker, Hills, and Holyoke. But in the succeeding year's divided votes, they were joined (or succeeded) by several newcomers. Clarke and Leverett from Boston, Cowdry in place of Walker for Reading, Sherman for Watertown, Holbrooke for Weymouth, Hutchins for Hingham, and Bradbury of Salisbury, New Hampshire, were all newcomers to the Court. Other veteran Deputies joined them in dissent. John Johnson of Roxbury voted against the Cambridge *Platforme*, but it is hard to imagine that he was present the previous year to vote against Pynchon, since he was Pynchon's associate and often served as the Deputy for Springfield.

The names of those who dissented on other topics in the sessions of 1651 help to characterize the political mood further. In addition to a relatively quaint resolution banning "dauncing in ordinaries [inns]" to celebrate weddings, the May 7 session, which considered the Matthews case, also dealt with a proposal to close a rather glaring tax loophole. The Court decided to tax the holdings of merchants and shopkeepers on the same basis as landholders and farmers. This innovation drew the opposition of ten deputies, including Hawthorne (Salem), Leverett and Clarke (Boston), and Allen and Hutchins (Hingham). To be sure, some voted out of self-interest. William Hawthorne was a merchant; Bozone Allen had a dry goods shop in Boston.[4]

Then in the October session, when the fourteen listed in the table above voted against the *Platforme*, nine of those same Deputies subsequently voted to oppose the fine against the Malden Church. Salem's Hawthorne, both representatives from Boston, Braintree's Kingsley, Watertown's Browne, Reading's Cowdry, Wenham's Reede, and Hingham's Hutchins all opposed the fine, just as they had opposed the *Platforme*.

Clearly a number of the representatives were restive, particularly those from Boston, Salem, Braintree, Hingham, and Reading. Three names turn up repeatedly for Pynchon, for Matthews, and against the *Platforme*: Hawthorne, Bartholomew, and Kingsley.

But the dissenters represented a small minority. In every instance, the establishment position handily prevailed. None of the dissidents were colony officers or Assistants, magistrates and men like Pynchon, gentlemen of higher social standing and greater wealth. All were from the Deputies

4. Allen's extensive inventory is reported in Dow, *Everyday Life*, 244–45.

who represented the towns. If every one of the thirty-nine seated Deputies actually voted, then even at its strongest the opposition remained under one third, and in Pynchon's case, which was the earliest, just 15 percent. (We have only the names of dissenters; even though those who voted not to censure Pynchon asked to have their reasons recorded, they were explicitly prevented from doing so.[5]) Just as the *Platforme* was approved, so too was Pynchon condemned.

Yet there was a minority voice—and it made itself heard.

5. Shurtleff, *MBCR*, 4 pt. 1:30.

21

In His Own Valley

PYNCHON CLEARLY DIVERGED FROM the developing Congregational polity and participatory governance in Massachusetts, but several other factors also played a role in his censure.

Some commentators on Pynchon have argued that he was more liberal than his orthodox adversaries, but that is open to serious question.[1] The very terms "liberal" or "conservative" do not readily fit his situation. He eludes any simple theological classification. Pynchon held a perplexing assortment of convictions: that "liberty of conscience" is a bad thing; that God could never possibly have required Christ to endure the worst pains a human can suffer; that Christ is so genetically different from all humankind that he could never be killed by others but could only die of his own accord; that the Trinity, through some unrecorded get-together, arranged for the redemption of believers on the very same day that Adam and Eve were created; that Christ's obedience to the Law in the course of his life had nothing to do with redemption; that Christ died for the elect only and "pours out his wrath" on those who reject him; and that magistrates comprise a "church." Rather, Pynchon mixed and matched a wide variety of notions from what Gura called "a startling heterogeneity of theological opinion" in seventeenth-century Puritanism.[2]

Pynchon played the theological game without mastering its contemporary rules. As Michael Winship has observed, "[t]here is no indication

1. See, for example, Burt, *First Century*; Green, *Springfield*; Wilbur, *History of Unitarianism*; and *Our Unitarian Heritage*, 392.

2. Gura, *Sion's Glory*, 305.

that he grasped that divines picked their way around theological options with other priorities than his."[3] The tedious reply to Norton in *A Farther Discussion* shows that he did not understand how theological discourse worked in New England. He was quite simply out of his depth when it came to Ramistic logic. Pynchon did make an oblique reference to theological practices he never understood or embraced when he quoted the criticism of John Preston (1587–1628), master of Emmanuel College at Cambridge, against those who end up "framing a model of [their] own" and believing that "god must go by [their] rule."[4] But that is as close as he ever came to naming his intellectual adversary, the logic of Peter Ramus. Consequently, Pynchon's language did not mesh with the theological conversation of others with whom his lot was cast: he offered no "arguments," in the Ramistic sense, and few dualistic divisions. As Michael W. Vella observed,

> If we see Pynchon as an entrepreneur, and above all a magistrate, caught in a conflict of discourses—the discourse of the ministers with its broadly theocratic and communitarian world view, and the discourse of an emerging order of commerce, litigation, and secular law—Pynchon's "heresy" was as much socio-linguistic as it was theological.[5]

It could be said that William Pynchon's real heresy was thinking that there were no linguistic or logical boundaries, or at least any that applied to him. Just as he had achieved some success by learning the language rules of his Algonquian-speaking neighbors, he seems to have felt empowered to cross theological language strictures as well, often on philologically thin ice. But the "native speakers" of theology were not so tolerant.

Additionally, Pynchon chose unwisely in the sources he preferred. He struggled with some success to make use of the original biblical languages, with Kircher's help. He relied extensively on Ainsworth's mainstream scholarship, and he became a master of factoids drawn from Ainsworth's bulky volumes on the Pentateuch and Psalms. But his excessive dependency on Hugh Broughton was much more injudicious. Broughton's etymologies beguiled him, and he cited them with reverence and awe. They seemed exciting, however dubious they may have been. Pynchon's own quirky interpretations also did not prove convincing. His overall result

---

3. Winship, "Contesting Control," 818.

4. Pynchon, *FD*, 103–104. Preston's phrase is in his sermon, "God without causes" (Preston, *Life Eternall*, 143). For more on Preston, see *ODNB*, 45:260–64.

5. Vella, "Heresy and *The Meritorious Price*," in Pynchon, *MP*, xxix.

was unpersuasive. Successive generations rejected the theological solutions Pynchon proposed because his answers did not prove any better than customary ones. He had criticized the sterner elements of Calvinist theories of vicarious, suffering atonement. As Winship remarked, "*Meritorious Price* can be summed up as an audacious effort to improve orthodoxy by inserting a nonpenal atonement into a standard predestinarian framework."[6] But perhaps because Pynchon was himself a judge and was therefore committed to judicial process as well as to order and obedience in society, he could not successfully extricate the entire scenario of Christ's sufferings from a legalistic, forensic framework.

Pynchon's isolation from the rest of New England's culture also contributed to his condemnation at Boston. He was cut off in a number of ways. Pynchon considered himself a member of the church at Roxbury and he appealed to them when he was under attack in the corn controversy in the late 1630s. But it is difficult to see what this connection could have meant, since he lived ninety miles away. He was not expected at General Court or Court of Assistants meetings in Boston. He was not in conversation with any of the ecclesiastical leaders in eastern Massachusetts. And after his crucial break with Hooker in 1638 and his trial by the Windsor Church, he was even more estranged from the Congregationalism that was emerging in Connecticut.[7] As a result, Pynchon was free to enlarge on his basic gentlemanly presuppositions without engaging in the give-and-take of refining, rephrasing, or reframing his arguments. He could proceed without having to face any questions raised or influences exerted by those whose views differed from his own. He could easily assume (though he may not have) that he had always held a mainstream view, and that his ideas on the atonement were actually shared by many others—or, at the very least, should be shared by others—because they were well within the common bounds of Puritan thought. As a matter of fact, most of his ideas can be traced to Puritans of the previous generation.

But because Pynchon lacked direct experience of the concerns that drove the leaders of Massachusetts Puritanism, he did not understand their urgent desire to present a united front. He did not have a clear sense of either the dangers they feared or the possibilities they envisioned. In the potentially precarious environment of the New World, the leaders deemed Pynchon's publication of an even minimally alternative theology a threat

6. Winship, "Contesting Control," 812.

7. See McIntyre, *William Pynchon*, 19–20.

to the integrity of their entire venture. Because the authorities in Boston were convinced that far too much was at risk in the Bay colony experiment, they were driven by an imperative of theological solidarity. They feared that divisions, particularly theological divisions, could scuttle the entire experiment.

Moreover, Pynchon seemed increasingly unenthusiastic about the heady prospect that so excited the Massachusetts Puritans: the opportunity of creating a new kind of society, hearkening back to a pristine world of the biblical era, purified of the constraints of the waning feudal system of their past.[8] He remained committed to traditional English practices other immigrants were willing to jettison. His insistence on issuing warrants in the name of the king, for example, elicited no response from others; instead, Massachusetts practice evolved in precisely the opposite direction. In the Bay colony, there was very little consideration whatsoever for royalty. Because of his isolation from the centers of government and learning, Pynchon had no way to become better acquainted with the culture in which he dwelled and by which his book was judged.

So the entrepreneur from Springfield never understood the spirited rejection of his theological endeavors. In the preface of his final book, Pynchon testily remarked that Norton never bothered to answer the repeated rebuttals he had made to the state-sponsored critique of *The Meritorious Price*. Of course, there is a reason Norton never replied: nobody paid him to.

While all of Norton's criticisms personally hurt Pynchon, he was especially wounded by the charge of heresy. The pain of that censure lasted throughout his life. Pynchon commented on the nature of heresy in his introductory letter "To the Reader" in *The Covenant of Nature*. Norton characterized heresy as "a Fundamental Error, that is, such as he that knowingly liveth and dieth therein cannot be saved." Pynchon offered a different definition, which he adapted from St. Augustine's: a "heretic" is "he, which for the love of Gain or Rule, either bringeth up, or else followeth new Opinions." Pynchon also rightly pointed out the element of choosing that is implicit in the very word "heresy." He described it as "A Choyce, and stubborn defending of Opinions which are against the holy Scriptures, either by Reason of Ignorance, or else contempt of them; to

8. On the Puritan predilection for recovering and reinstituting the earliest, and presumable purest and simplest practices, of the Biblical era and the primitive Christian church, see Bozeman, *Ancient Lives*, 13–50.

the end, the easilier to obtain their own pleasure and Commodities."[9]
Given that definition, Pynchon was convinced that he was not heretical,
though Norton may have been!

Pynchon distinguished "damnable Heresie" from ordinary differences
of opinion, which he maintained are totally benign and quite common
among Christians. More than a little defensively, he complained,

> I cannot but wonder at the sharp censures of some godly ones
> against others that differ in some Particulars from them, seeing
> they are builders together with us by faith on Christ the founda-
> tion of their and our salvation. I think it is an unchristian behavior
> to be so violently transported with passion as some are at such
> differences, as if some new and strange things had befallen unto
> this generation that never did befal any other generation before
> this; seeing I have made it evident that it hath ever been, and ever
> will be the condition of the Church here in this world to have such
> as will differ from others in some point of Faith or other.[10]

Pynchon concluded, "I do not think it meete to thunder out the censure of
damnable Heresie upon Mr. Nortons heterodoxal Tenents, as he doth upon
my sound Scripture Tenents." He further made note of the paradoxical
fact "that it doth often fall out, that such as are affected with great Errours
(which in their deceived Judgment they think to be true) do count such
as hold the contrary Truth to be persistent Hereticks or Sectaries," and he
remarked ironically, "I believe that none are free from some grosse Errour
or other that are most severe in censuring the Errours of others." Finally,
in another "I cannot but wonder" statement (he was fond of the phrase),
Pynchon impugned Norton's competence as a theologian in a markedly *ad
hominem* argument:

> I cannot but wonder that Mr. Norton in his undertaking to prove
> damnable heresie in my Dialogue, doth make such cursory and
> flighty expositions of the Scriptures for the proving of his hetero-
> doxal Tenents: and I make no question but the Judicious Reader
> will find it to be so by my present examination of them; and that
> he doth often times give the sense according to the bare sound of
> the words, and not according to the true sense of them from the
> Context; and I conceive that it is a received Maxim, that he that is
> not a good Text-man, cannot be a sound Divine.[11]

9. "To the Reader," in Pynchon, *CN*, 2r.

10. Pynchon, *CN*, A3r.

11. Ibid., A3v, A4r, a1v.

Norton never rose to this bait. There is no reason to think he ever had the slightest inkling about Pynchon's later writings.

In Pynchon's view, the remedy for the sad animosity among Christians was love. "I confess," he explained, "that bosom Love cannot be well shewed to such as are of an opposite Judgment; yet such a degree of Love must rule over displeased passions, as may evidence that we are the children of God by extending some affections of Love to all such as are begotten of God to believe in Christ." The Devil "laughes in his sleeve," said Pynchon, when there are "distances of Affection between the godly." Divisions among Christians can never be celebrated. People of faith need to stick together.[12]

Pynchon turned to a comment by Hugh Broughton to justify promoting his theologically divergent points of view: "It is no fault to differ from all Churches for the good of all Churches: For Churches (saith he) do carry no sway above the Word of God, but the Word of God (rightly expounded) above all Churches."[13]

Far from rejecting Pynchon for his outlier views about Native peoples, fellow colonists respected him because of his expertise, which became increasingly evident during his years of trading peacefully with the Indians. Even though his point of view was at variance with the common wisdom in the colony, his advice was well-regarded and his intercultural role valued, as when Pynchon convinced Winthrop to stay out of the Quaboag murder case. But at the same time, his fellow Puritans considered Pynchon's outlier views on theology a serious threat.

Pynchon's life spanned most of the Puritan experiment. He sailed to New England with the first big fleet of Massachusetts Bay colony pioneers, and he died not long after the fall of the British Puritan government. Pynchon came to a new land where he founded a city-state and made a fortune. As Vella remarked,

> the text [of *The Meritorious Price*] culminates its author's ascendance in power and wealth, an ascendance whose ultimate reach into theology exacerbated orthodox powers in Boston, provoking stern and quick reaction, and shaping Pynchon's New World biography into a parabola of rise and decline.[14]

12. Ibid., A4v

13. Ibid., A4v, A2r. The Broughton quotation is taken from Broughton, *A Require of Agreement*, 26–27 (Pynchon added the "rightly expounded" phrase).

14. Vella, "Heresy and *The Meritorious Price of Our Redemption* (1650)," in Pynchon, *Meritorious Price of Our Redemption*, xix–xxx.

Pynchon had lived confidently and consistently by his Reformation conviction that "it is more agreeable to the mind of God that every Godly Christian should with their own eys search into the true scope" of the Scriptures.[15] But others around him were discovering new possibilities for church and society from their own understandings of the mind of God. Adapting the words he addressed to Winthrop, it seems that Pynchon himself could not "subsist without England." Isolation in the Connecticut Valley severely limited his participation in the society that was at that very moment developing in unexpected ways at the hands of his fellow Puritans. He had brought aristocratic assumptions with him from Old England to New; he lived out of those suppositions, and he lacked opportunities to acquire a full experience of the emerging cultural patterns in that strange new world. With the exception of the name of the Massachusetts community he left behind in the Connecticut Valley, it is almost as if he had never been there at all.

15. Pynchon, *MP*, 15.

Appendix 1

A Timeline of William Pynchon's Life

1590	Born at Writtle (?), Essex
(1615?)	Married Ann Andrew of Twywell, Nottinghamshire
1619–1620 and 1624	Churchwarden, All Saints Church, Springfield
1620	Inherited lands in Springfield, Essex
1628	Became active in the Massachusetts Bay Company
January 1630	Sold lands in England
April 8–June 12, 1630	Sailed with family to New England
1630–1636	Served as Assistant to the Governor, Massachusetts Bay
1630	Settled in Dorchester (Quincy), Massachusetts Death of Ann Pynchon
1632	Married Frances Sanford Moved to Roxbury, Massachusetts
August 1632–May 1634	Served as elected Treasurer of Massachusetts
Early May 1636	Moved to Agawam, Connecticut River Valley
May 14, 1636	Signed covenant for Agawam community
July 15, 1636	Purchased lands from Agaam Indians

April–August 1637	Opposed the Pequot "War"
March–April 1638	Served as member of Connecticut General Court
February–April 1638	Failed to buy corn at the Connecticut Court's prescribed price
1639–1640	Defended himself against accusations by the Connecticut Court and Windsor Church
February 14, 1639	Elected Magistrate for Springfield, Massachusetts
1643–1650	Served as Assistant to the Governor, Massachusetts Bay
November 4, 1646	General Court enacted law against "Notorious & obstinate heretics"
March 14, 1648	Published *An Endevour After The reconcilement . . .*
July 5, 1648	Letter to Winthrop regarding Quaboag Indians: "an Independent free people"
August 19, 1649	Preached in Springfield
June 2, 1650	Published *The Meritorious Price*
October 16, 1650	*The Meritorious Price* condemned by the Massachusetts General Court
October 17, 1650	*The Meritorious Price* publicly burned in the Boston marketplace
February–March 1651	Took depositions in the Mary and Hugh Parsons witchcraft case
April 17, 1651	Transferred control of Springfield common lands to son, stepson, and son-in-law
May 8, 1651	Met with the General Court to acknowledge his book and with clergy to discuss his "heresy"
September 28, 1651	Transferred all personal Springfield property to John Pynchon
By May 27, 1652	Returned to England

1652	Reissued *An Endevour* as *The Jewes Synagogue* Issued second unrevised edition of *The Meritorious Price*
December 5, 1653	Purchased Wyardisbury House, Wraysbury, Buckinghamshire
November 7, 1654	Published *A Treatise on The Sabbath*
1655	Published *A Farther Discussion* (alternately titled *The Meritorious Price of Mans Redemption*)
November 1656–October 1657	John Pynchon visited England
October 10, 1657	Death of Frances Sanford Pynchon
1662	Published *The Covenant of Nature*
October 29, 1662	Death of William Pynchon
November 7, 1662	Burial at St. Andrew's Church, Wraysbury

Appendix 2

Fealty of William Pynchon at the Springfield Manorial Court

AT THIS COURT WILLIAM Pynchon, gentlemen, came here into the court after the summons given to him and exhibited to the court a charter bearing the date the first day of February in the thirty-ninth year of the reign of the lady Elizabeth[1] formerly Queen of England by which Thomas Durrant and Lawrence Glasscock sold and alienated to John Pynchon, gentleman, late father of the same William, and to his heirs a parcel of land and marsh[2] with its appurtenances, joined into one and built on, called or known by the name of Barneswe . . .[3] Feyldes and Barneswell Moores, containing by estimation twenty-six acres in Springfeild. These tenements with . . . [their appurtenances?] formerly belonged to John Pease late of Springfeild, and were held of the lord of the manor by fealty, suit of court and . . . rent of eight pence as appears in a certain indenture similarly exhibited here in court, bearing the date the eighteenth of May in the twen[tieth year] . . . of the same former queen,[4] made between the aforesaid John Pease and Thomas Wallenger, gentleman, of the one part and Thomas Durrant of the other . . .

AND NOW at this court the same William makes fealty to the lord for the premises. And Robert Browne, the farmer of the said manor and . . . of the rents of that manor confirms here in court that he has received the

1. February 1, 1597.

2. *Mora*: either "moor" or "marsh."

3. Part of the right-hand edge of the document has been lost; the missing portions are indicated by ellipses.

4. May 18, 1578.

aforesaid rent and the arrears arising from it up to the feast of St. Michael the Archangel.[5]

5. September 29.

Appendix 3

The Protestation of the General Court

The declaration & protestation of the Generall Court of the Massachusetts, in New England.

THE GENERALL COURT, NOW sittinge at Boston, in New England, this six-teenth of October, 1650. There was brought to our hands a booke writen, as was therein subscribed, by William Pynchon, gent, in New England, entit-uled The Meritorious Price of our Redemption, Justifycation, &c, clearinge it from some common Errors, &c, which booke, brought over hither by a shippe a few dayes since, and contayninge many errors and heresies gener-ally condemned by all orthodox writers that we haue met with, we haue judged it meete and necessary, for vindication of the truth, so far as in vs lyes, as also to keepe & preserue the people here committed to our care & trust in the true knowledge & fayth of our Lord Jesus Christ, & of our owne redemption by him, as likewise for the clearinge of ourselves to our Christian brethren and others in England, (where this book was printed & is dispersed,) hereby to protest our innocency, as beinge neither partyes nor privy to the writinge, composinge, printinge, nor diuulginge thereof; but that, on the contrary, we detest & abhorre many of the opinions & assertions therein as false, eronyous, & heriticall; yea, & whatsoeuer is contayned in the sd booke which are contrary to the Scriptures of the Old & New Testament, & the generall received doctrine of the orthodox churches extant since the time of the last and best reformation, and for proffe & euidence of our sin-cere and playne meaninge therin, we doe hereby condemne the sd booke to be burned in the market place, at Boston, by the common executionor, & doe purpose with all convenient speede to convent the sd William Pinchon before authority, to find out whether the sd William Pinchon will owne the sd booke as his or not; which if he doth, we purpose (Gd willinge) to proceede with him accordinge to his demerits, unless he retract the same, and giue full satisfaction both here & by some second writinge, to be printed & dispersed in England; all which we thought needfull, for the reasons aboue aleaged, to make knowne by this short protestation & declaration. Also we further purpose, with what convenient speede we may, to appoynt some fitt pson to make a particular answer to all materiall & controuersyall passages in the sd booke, & to publish the same in print, that so the errors & falsityes therein may be fully discoued, the truth cleared, & the minds of those that love & seeke after truth confirmed therein. Per Curiam.[1]

1. Shurtleff, *MBCR*, 3:215–16.

Appendix 4

Books and Authors Referenced in *The Meritorious Price*

SEE BELOW FOR REFERENCES to identifiable authors and their works cited in *The Meritorious Price of Our Redemption*, indicating the pages where citations are to be found, when identifiable, and the page in *The Meritorious Price* where the work is cited.

Authors	Books	References in *The Meritorious Price*
Bibles:		
Tyndale, William	*Bible* (1534)	p. 53
Coverdale, Miles (misspelled "Overdale")	*Bible* (1535)	p. 53
	Geneva Bible (1560)	pp. 24, 26, 119
	Theodore Beza, credited with note at Hebrews 5:7	p. 53
	Rheims New Testament (1582)	p. A3r
	Authorized Version–King James (1611)	p. 53, numerous others
Tremellio, Giovanni Emmanuele	*Testamenti Veteris Biblia sacra* (1618)	p. 18

Authors	Books	References in *The Meritorious Price*
Ainsworth, Henry	*Annotations upon the Five Books of Moses, and the Booke of the Psalmes* (1622)	pp. A3v, 25 (margin), 34, 35, 42, 47, 54, 60 (margin), 65, 66, 69, 86, 90, 94, 104, 139, 156
Authors cited from Ainsworth's text:		
	Ben Manoach, Chizkiya ("Chazkuni")	p. 140
	Iarchi, Schelomo (Raschi) ("Solomon Jarcy")	p. 139
	Maimonides, Moses ("Maymony")	p. 94
Ainsworth, Henry	Personal correspondence	p. A2r, 57
Bastingius, Jeremias	*An Exposition or Commentarie Vpon the Catechisme . . . which is taught in . . . the Lowe Countryes . . .* (1589), p. 160	p. 73
Bellarmine, Roberto, SJ	*An Ample Declaration . . .* (1611)	p. A3r
Broughton, Hugh	*A treatise of Melchisedek* (1591)	p. 92
	Daniel his Chaldie visions and his Ebrew (1597)	p. 124 (margin)
	Two little workes defensive of our Redemption (1604), unnumbered p. 7	p. 74
	An explication of the article [of the Creed] (1605)	p. 74
	Our Lordes Famile (1608), F4, A4	p. 60

Authors	Books	References in *The Meritorious Price*
	Iob: To the King (1610), p. 72	pp. 119–20
	A Require of Agreement (1611), p. 80 (cited as "Req. of Cons.")	p. 60
	An Exposition vpon the Lords Prayer (1613?), p. 3	p. 103
Broughton scribal publications:		
	"An Answer about Hell Torments to Objections, etc."	p. 57
	"Positions Touching the Hebrew Tongue"	pp. 65–66
Other Broughton scribal publications:		pp. 73, 77, 80
Calvin, John	*The Institution of Christian Religion* (1562) 2:14	p. 111
	The Psalmes of David . . . (1571)	p. 60
	A Commentarie . . . upon the first booke of Moses . . . (1578)	p. 7
	The Sermons . . . vpon the fifth booke of Moses . . . (1583), p. 763	p. 69
	A Harmonie vpon the Three Evangelists . . . (1584)	p. 43–46, 48, 51
Carlile, Christopher	*A discourse, Concerning two diuine Positions* (1582) – p. 46	pp. 50, 60

Authors	Books	References in *The Meritorious Price*
Forbes, John	*A Treatise Tending to Cleare the Doctrine of Ivstification* (1616), chs. 9, 19, 23, 24, pp. 47–53	pp. 134, 136, 137, 141, 143–44, 146–47, 150
Foxe, John	*Actes and Monuments of matters most special and memorable* . . . (1583) 1:973, 2:130, 1:85 (from Jan Hus, "Formall Appeal")	p. 49 pp. 58–59
Frith, John	*A boke . . . answerynge vnto M. Mores letter* (1548), p. B2	p. 50
Fulke, William	*A Defence of . . . Transla-tions . . .* (1617), p. 247	p. 53
Gataker, Thomas	*Iereboams Sonnes Decease* (1627)	p. 83
Goodwin, Thomas	*Moses and Aaron, Civil and Ecclesiastical Rites* (1625)	p. 69
	Romanae Historiae Angthologia, An English Exposition (1616) 3:4	p. 71
Hampton, Christopher	*Two Sermons Preached . . . in the Church of Beauly* (1609)	p. 91
Jacob, Henry	*A Defence of a Treatise Touching the Sufferings and Victorie of Christ* (1600), p. 33	pp. A2r, 16 (margin)
Kircher, Konrad	*Concordantiae Veteris Testamenti* (1607)	Passim[1]

1. See Pynchon's personal copy of Kircher, embellished with Pynchon's notes, at the Andover Harvard Library, Harvard Divinity School.

Authors	Books	References in *The Meritorious Price*
Luther, Martin	*A Commentarie . . . vpon the Epistle of S. Paul to the Galathians* (1575)	pp. 25 (margin), 68
Martin, Gregory, SJ	*A Discoverie of the Manifold Corruptions of the Holy Scriptures by the Heretikes . . .* (1582)	p. A2v
Martyr, Peter (Vermigli, Pietro Martire)	*The Common Places of . . . Doctor Peter Martyr* (1583)	p. 119
Niccols, Richard	*A Day-Starre for Darke-wandering Soules* (1613)	p. 101
Authors cited from Niccol's text:		
	Augustine ("Austin"), *Tractates on John*, 116.6	p. 101
Polanus von Polansdorf, Amandus	*The Substanecs* [*sic*] *of Christian Religion* (1600), pp. 141, 154	p. 73
Reynolds, Edward	*An Explication of the Hundred and Tenth Psalm* (1632), pp. 444–45	p. 83
Richardson, John	Scribal publication	
	"Philosophical Annotations"	p. 80
Ursinus, Zacharias	*The Svmme of Christian Religion . . .* (1611), pp. 487, 513	p. 73
Weemes, John	*The Christian Synagogue* (1623), p. 318	p. A3v
Wilmot, Robert	Scribal publication:	
	"Treatise upon the Articles of Christ's Descent into Hell"	pp. 57, 74

Appendix 5

The Will of William Pynchon

MY CHIEF EXECUTOR IS at present absent. To Elizabeth, Mary and Rebecca Smith, daughters of my son Master Henry Smith, and to his son Elisha Smith twenty pounds apiece, to be paid by my son Mr. Henry Smith at the time of their marriage, as he did unto Martha Smith, out of a bond which he owes me, of two hundred and twenty pounds; to my daughter Anne Smith the rest of the said bond (of 220li)[1] with the overplus of interest. To the children of my daughter Margaret Davis, of Boston in New England, deceased, videlicet unto Thomas, Benjamin and William Davis, ten pounds apiece to be paid by my son Mr. Henry Smith. To my son Master John Pynchon, of Springfield in New England (a sum) out of the bond which he owes me of one hundred and six pounds, dated 15 April 1654. Whereas my son Mr. Henry Smith hath promise to pay unto me his debts which have been long due to him in New England and a horse of his at Barbadoes, for the satisfaction of an old debt that he owes me, in my Quarto Vellum Book, in page 112, I bequeath them to the children of my son Master Elizur Holioke in New England &c. To the poor of Wraysberie three pounds. Son Mr. John Pynchon of Springfield in New England to be executor, to whom the residue, provided he pay to Joseph and John Pynchon and to Mary and Hetabell Pynchon twenty pounds apiece. Mr. Wickens, citizen and girdler of London, and Mr. Henry Smith of Wraysbery to be overseers. Friend Mr. John Wickens to be my executor touching the finishing of my administration business concerning the estate of Master Nicholas Ware in Virginia, whose estate is thirty pounds

1. Pynchon's use of "li" here is an alternative to "£."

in a bill of Exchange to Capt. Pensax and about eighteen thousand of tobacco, in several bills made over by Mr. Nicholas Ware to Capt. John Ware of Virginia &c. To beloved sister Jane Tesdall of Abington twenty pounds; to sister Susan Piatt twenty pounds, as a token of my cordial love; certain clothing to Mary, Elizabeth and Rebecca Smith.[2]

2. Waters, *Gleanings*, 2:859.

Appendix 6

William Pynchon on Church Polity

A Response to the Remonstrants,
from a letter to John Winthrop March 9, 1647

But as for their desyre of an inouation in Church . . . [discipline, it does]
not proceed out of zeale of gods glory, neather is the Reform[ation such]
that they can as yet presume what it will be for there . . . [is as much a]
breach betweene Presbuterians about settling the presbute[rian form]
betweene them as betweene the presbeterians and the independa[nts; so]
that if the most ministers in England were for the independa[nts, like these
in]
N. England, that the parliament would as soone establish the indep[endant
form]
for they are a great distance with the Scotish way; for the
parliament doe not hould any certaine fourme of Church gouernment
to be commanded in the particulars thereof as the only way of
Christ: as the Scotts do: for the Scotts say that their fourme
of discipline is the only way of Christ: and the Independants
say that their fourme of discipline is the only way of Christ
But the Parliament say that neather of them is the only way of
Christ, and therefore they have ordained Commissioners to superuise
the conclusions of the presbuterian Courtes.[1]

1. Forbes, *Winthrop Papers*, 5:135–36.

Appendix 7

Books Published by William Pynchon

AN ENDEVOUR AFTER THE *reconcilement of that long debated and much lamented difference between the godly Presbyterians, and [the godly] Independents, About Church-government. In a discourse touching the Iews Synagogues. Proving, 1. That the Jews Synagogue-Assemblies were true visible Churches of Jesus Christ. 2. That their government was ordained by Christ, to be Dependent, when they lived together in the land of Canaan, [to be] Independent, when they inhabited in Heathen Countries. 3 That Schooles of learning were at the first erected by Jesus Christ, For the breeding of a succession of able men for Pastors, Teachers, Elders, Judges, &c. to the worlds end. With many other miscellaneous observations about their Synagogue-Discipline.* (London: Printed by M. S. for John Bellamy at the three golden Lions neare the Royall Exchange, 1648).

Pynchon's first volume was published anonymously and issued by John Bellamy, the premier bookseller of Independent/Congregational literature in London. The publication date was March 14, 1648 (New Style). It was re-issued four years later with the exact same text, but a new title and author identification, as *The Jewes Synagogue*.

The Meritorious Price of Our Redemption, Iustification, &c.: Cleering it from some common Errors; and proving, Part I. 1. That Christ did not suffer for us those unutterable torments of Gods wrath, that commonly are called Hell-torments, to redeem our soules from them. 2. That Christ did not bear our sins by Gods imputation, and therefore he did not bear the curse of the Law for them. Part II. 3. That Christ hath redeemed us from the curse of the Law (not

*by suffering the said curse for us, but) by a satisfactory price of attonement;
viz. by paying or performing unto his Father that invaluable precious thing
of his Mediatoriall obedience, wherof his Mediatoriall Sacrifice of attonement
was the master-piece. 4. A sinners righteousnesse or justification is explained,
and cleered from some common errors. By William Pinchin, Gentleman, in
New-England.* (London: Printed by J. M. for George Whittington and James
Moxon, and are to be sold at the blue Anchor in Corn-hill neer the Royall
Exchange, 1650).

"J. M." was probably James Moxon, son of the well-known printer
and print designer Joseph Moxon, brother of the Reverend George Moxon.
George Whittington sold books at the sign of the Blue Anchor in Cornhill
from 1643 to at least 1649.

*The Jewes Synagogue: or, A Treatise Concerning The ancient Orders and man-
ner of Worship used by the Jewes in their Synagogve-assemblies. Gathered out
of the Sacred Scriptures, the Jewish rabines, and such modern authors, which
have been most conversant in the study of Jewish customes. Wherein, by com-
paring the Scriptures in the Old and New Testament together, many truths
are fully opened, and sundry controversies about church government truly
and plainly stated. By William Pinchion of Springfeild [sic] in N. England.*
(London: Printed for J. Bellamie, 1652).

During his apprenticeship with Nicholas Bourne, stationer, John Bel-
lamy joined the independent church in Southwark where the Reverend
Henry Jacob was pastor. In 1622 he set up his own outlet at the sign of the
Two Greyhounds in Cornhill, where he sold works by the Pilgrims' pastor
John Robinson, the Pilgrims William Bradford and Edward Winslow, the
theologian Henry Ainsworth, Governor John Winthrop, and Revs. Thomas
Sheppard, Thomas Hooker, and John Cotton. By 1623 his business was
located at the Three Golden Lions, a location on Cornhill near the Royal
Stock Exchange and "over against the Conduit," which was opposite the
north end of Change Alley at the eastern side of the Royal Exchange. He
became a ruling elder of St. Michael's Church, which was just to the east of
his shop on Cornhill. Bellamy also served as a London City Councilman.
He retired about 1653. At the time of his death in 1654, he had a house and
two shops in St. Paul's churchyard, one of which was the White Lion.

*The Meritorious Price of Our Rdemption [sic], Iustification, &c.: Cleering it
from some common Errors; and proving, Part I. 1. That Christ did not suffer
for us those unutterable torments of Gods wrath, that commonly are called*

Hell-torments, to redeem our souls from them. 2. That Christ did not bear our sins by Gods imputation, and therefore he did not bear the curse of the Law for them. Part II. 3. That Christ hath redeemed us from the curse of the Law (not by suffering the said curse for us, but) by a satisfactory price of attonement; viz. by paying or performing unto his Father that invaluable precious thing of his Mediatoriall obedience, wherof his Mediatoriall sacrifice of attonement was the master-piece. 4. A sinners righteousnesse or justification is explained, and cleered from some common Errors. By William Pinchin Gentleman, in New-England. (London: Printed for William Ley at PAULS Chain neer Doctors Commons, 1652).

William Ley (or Lee) had a store at Paul's Chain, on the way from St. Paul's to Doctors' Commons (which was in Great Knightrider Street), from 1640 to 1646. This second edition of *The Meritorious Price* is identical to the first edition, but with typological variations and the spelling "Rdemption" on the title page only. It was assembled from surplus pages from the original printing that were simply issued in new packaging.

A Treatise of the Sabbath. Wherein is contained the Time of the first Institution of it. The Manner how the first Sabbath was Ordained. Whereunto is annexed A Treatise of Holy Time: and therein The great Question about the beginning and ending of the Lords Day is largely discussed: And in both Sundry Cases of Conscience are handled, and Many Texts of Scripture are opened, The Practice of the Churches in New England are inquired into. By William Pynchon, late of New England. (London: Printed for Thomas Newberry, and are to bee sold at his shop, at the signe of the three Golden Lyons in Corn-hill near the Royall Exchange, 1655 [1654]).

While the type on this title page bore the date 1655, an annotation on the British Library copy gives the publication date as "Nouemb. 7. 1654"; the second "5" in 1655 has been crossed out.

I The Time when the First Sabbath was Ordained. Negatively, Not in the Time of Adams Innocency, as many say it was. 2 Affirmatively, It was Ordained after the Time of Adams Fall and Re-creation. II The Manner how the First Sabbath was Ordained. 1 By blessing the Seventh Day with many Spiritual ordinances, both for publick and private use. 2 By Sanctifying that Day for the Exercise of the said Ordinances. 3 By Sanctifying the outward Rest of that Day, to be a Typical Sign both of Gods Resting, and of mans Resting in the Seed of the Woman, that was promised to break the Devils Head-plot, namely, by his Propitiatory Sacrifice. And hence it follows, 1 That as the Sabbath was

Ordained to be a Typical sign, so it must be abolished, as soon as Christ had performed his said Propitiary Sacrifice. 2 As it was Ordained to be the Sanctified Time, for the Exercise of the said blessed Ordinances; so the next day of the week, into which it was changed, must continue without intermission to the end of the world. Part II. III A Treatise of Holy Time, concerning the true limits of the Lords Day, when it begins, and when it ends, is hereunto annexed. By William Pynchon, Esq. Published by Authority. (London: Printed by R. I. and are to be sold by T. N., 1654).

Holy Time: or, The True Limits of the Lords Day. I. Proving, That the Lords Day doth begin with the Natural Morning, and that the Morning of the Natural day doth begin at Mid-night; and so consequently that the Lords Day must both begin with the Natural Morning at Mid-night, and end with the Natural Evening at Mid-night. II. Proving, That the Jews beginning of the Day at Sun-set Evening was only in relation to the date of the Person purified from his Levitical uncleanness. III. That The Jews themselves did not hold, That the Natural day did continue after Sun-set till Mid-night. By William Pynchon, Esq. Published by Authority. (London: Printed by R. I. and are to be sold by T. N. at the sign of the three Lions in Cornhil, near the Royal Exchange, 1654).

These two tracts were placed together under a single title page, *A Treatise of the Sabbath*. Thomas Newberry, identified only as "T. N." on the separate title pages of both tracts, was successor to John Bellamy at the Three Golden Lions on Cornhill. "R. I." seems to have been Robert Ibbitson, one of the premier printers of the era. These two booklets are the only of Pynchon's works to bear the phrase "Published by Authority."

A Farther Discussion of that Great Point in Divinity the Sufferings of Christ: and the Questions about his Righteousnesse, Active / Passive, and the Imputation thereof: being a Vindication of a Dialogue Intituled [The Meritorious Price of Our Redemption, Justification, &c.] from the exceptions of Mr. Norton and others. By William Pynchon, late of New England. (London: Printed for the Author, and are to be sold at the Signe of the three Lyons in Cornhill, over against the Conduit, MDCLV [1655]).

The same book was also issued as *The Meritorious Price of Mans Redemption; or, Christs satisfaction discussed and explained* (London: Printed by R. I. for Thom. Newberry, and are to be sold at his Shop in Cornhil over against the Conduit near the Royal Exchange, 1655).

The Covenant of Nature made with Adam Described: and Cleared from sundry great mistakes. And thereby proving, I. That the kind of death that was threatned in that covenant, in Gen. 2.17. ought not to be understood of any other kind of death but of a double spiritual death, 1. By depriving Adam of Gods concreated image: and 2. By corruption of nature that followed thereupon. II. Proving that the said covenant was totally extinguished and made utterly null, as soon as Adam had but tasted of the forbidden fruit, and received the said threatned punishment. III. Expounding Gal. 3.10. and proving that the curse therein threatned must not be understood of the curse of the said covenant of nature, but of that curse that is threatned in the covenant of grace to the fallen posterity of Adam, for their not doing of Moses law by faith in Christ, which was given to them for the covenant of grace and reconciliation only . . . VIII. Expounding Rom. 8.1, 2, 3, 4, 5, 6, 6, 8. in ch. 25. By William Pynchon. (London: Printed for the author, and are to be sold at the Bishops-head in St. Pauls Church-yard, 1662).

The Bishop's Head was operated by Sam Thomson from 1659 to 1661, and by J. Thomsen in 1663.

Bibliography

Adams, Charles Francis. *Massachusetts: Its Historians and Its History.* Boston: Houghton Mifflin, 1893.

Adams, James Truslow. *Dictionary of American History.* New York: Scribner's, 1940.

———. *The Founding of New England.* Boston: Atlantic Monthly, 1921.

Adamson, J. H., and H. F. Folland. *Sir Harry Vane: His Life and Times (1613–1662).* Boston: Gambit, 1973.

Ainsworth, Henry. *Annotations upon the Five Bookes of Moses, and the Booke of the Psalmes.* London: Iohn Haviland and Iohn Bellamie, 1627.

Alley, William. *ΠΤΩΧΝΟΜΟΥΣΕΙΟΝ. The poore mans Librarie: Rapsodiae G.A. byshop of Exceter vpon the first Epistle of S. Peter.* London: Iohn Daye, 1571.

Ames, William. *The Marrow of Divinity.* Translated with an introduction by John Eusden. Boston: Pilgrim, 1968.

———. *The Marrow of Sacred Divinity Drawne Out of the Holy Scriptures, and the Interpreters thereof, and brought into Method.* London: Edward Griffin for Henry Overton, 1642.

Anderson, Robert Charles. *The Great Migration Begins: Immigrants to New England, 1620–1633.* Boston: NEHGS, 1995.

Armytage, Frances, and Juliette Tomlinson. *The Pynchons of Springfield: Founders and Colonizers (1636–1702).* Springfield, MA: Connecticut Valley Historical Museum, 1969.

Ashton, Robert. *Counter-Revolution: The Second Civil War and Its Origins, 1646–48.* New Haven: Yale University Press, 1994.

Bailyn, Bernard. *The Barbarous Years: The Peopling of British North America: The Conflict of Civilizations, 1600–1675.* New York: Knopf, 2012.

Baldwin, Simeon E. "The Secession of Springfield from Connecticut." *Publications of the Colonial Society of Massachusetts* 12 (1908) 55–82.

Ball, Timothy Horton. *Francis Ball's Descendants; or, The West Springfield Ball Family, from 1640 to 1902.* Crown Point, IN: Wheeler, 1902.

Bangs, Jeremy Dupertuis. *Indian Deeds: Land Transactions in Plymouth Colony, 1620–1691.* Boston: NEHGS, 2002.

Banks, Charles Edward. *The Winthrop Fleet of 1630: An Account of the Vessels, the Voyage, the Passengers, and Their English Homes from Original Authorities.* 1930. Reprint, Baltimore, MD: Genealogical Publishing, 2003.

Bartlett, John Russell. *Records of the Colony of Rhode Island and Providence Plantations, in New England, 1636–1663.* Vol. 1. Providence, RI: Greene and Bro., 1856.

Baxter, Richard. *A Sermon of Iudgement, Preached at Pauls before the Honourable Lord Maior and Aldermen of the City of London, Decemb. 1, 1654.* London: R. W. for Nevill Simmons, 1656.

Beard, Darren. "A Millennium of British Solar Eclipses (1501–2500 AD)." *Journal of the British Astronomical Association* 111 (2001) 88–98.

Bidwell, Percy Wells, and John I. Falconer. *History of Agriculture in the Northern United States, 1620–1860.* 1925. Reprint, Clifton, NJ: Kelley, 1973.

Bilson, Thomas. *The Survey of Christs Sufferings for Mans redemption and of his Descent to Hades or Hel for our deliuerance.* London: Melchisedech Bradwood for John Bill, 1604.

Bozeman, Theodore Dwight. *To Live Ancient Lives: The Primitivist Dimension in Puritanism.* Chapel Hill: University of North Carolina Press, 1988.

Bradford, William, ed. *A Relation or Iournall of the beginning and proceedings of the English Plantation setled at Plimoth in New England, by certaine English Aduenturers both Merchants and others ("Mourt's Relation").* London: J. Dawson for Iohn Bellamie, 1622.

Bremer, Francis J. *First Founders: American Puritans and Puritanism in an Atlantic World.* New England in the World. Durham: University of New Hampshire Press, 2012.

———. *John Winthrop: America's Forgotten Founding Father.* Oxford: Oxford University Press, 2003.

———. *The Puritan Experiment.* New York: St. Martin's, 1976.

———. *Puritanism: A Very Short Introduction.* New York: Oxford University Press, 2009.

Bridenbaugh, Carl, ed. *The Pynchon Papers.* 2 vols. Publications of the Colonial Society of Massachusetts 60–61. Boston: Colonial Society of Massachusetts. Distributed by the University Press of Virginia, 1982–1985.

Broughton, Hugh. *An Aduertisement of Corruption in our Handling of Religion.* [Middelburg: Richard Schilders],1604.

———. *A Censure of the late translation for our Churches: sent vnto a Right Worshipfull knight, Attendant vpon the King.* Middleburg: Richard Schilders, [1611?].

———. *Daniel: With a Brief Explication.* Hanaw [Hanover, Germany]: Daniel Aueri, 1607.

———. *An Epistle to the Learned Nobilitie of England: Touching translating the Bible from the original, with ancient warrant for euerie worde, vnto the full satisfaction of any that be of hart.* Middelburgh: Richard Schilders, 1597.

———. *An explication of the article* κατηλθεν εις 'αιδου: *of our Lordes soules going from his body to paradise.* [Amsterdam?]: s.n., 1605.

———. *An Exposition vpon the Lords Prayer, compared with the Decalogue.* [Amsterdam?]: s.n., [1613?].

———. *Iob: To the King. A Colon-Agrippina studie of one moneth, for the metricall translation: but of many yeres for Ebrew difficulties.* Amsterdam: Giles Thorp, 1610.

———. *Our Lordes Famile and Many Other Poinctes depending vpon it.* Amsterdam: s.n., 1608.

———. *Positions of the VVord Hades: That it is the generall place of Soules: and holdeth as vvell the Godly vvhich are in Paradise, as the vvicked that are in Tartarus.* [Amsterdam?]: s.n., 1605.

———. *Principal Positions for groundes of the holy Bible: A Short Oration of the Bibles translation.* [Amsterdam: Giles Thorp], 1609.

———. *A Replie vpon the R.R.P. Th. VVinton for Heads of his Divinity in his Sermon and Survey: Hovv he taught a perfect truth, that our Lord vvent he[n]ce to Paradise: But adding that he vvent thence to Hades, & striving to prove that, he iniureth all learning & Christianitie.* [Amsterdam?]: s.n., 1605.

———. *A Require of Agreement to the Groundes of Divinitie Studie.* Middelburg: Richard Schilders, 1611.

———. *A Reuelation of the Holy Apocalyps.* Middelburg: Richard Schilders, 1610.

———. *Two little workes defensiue of our Redemption, That our Lord went through the veile of his flesh into Heaven, to appeare before God for vs.* Middelburg: Richard Schilders, 1604.

Bruce, Philip Alexander. *Economic History of Virginia in the Seventeenth Century: An Inquiry into the Material Condition of the People, Based upon Original and Contemporaneous Records.* Vol. 1. New York: Macmillan, 1896.

Burgess, Anthony. *The True Doctrine of Justification Asserted & Vindicated From the Errours of many, and more especially Papists and Socinians.* London: Thomas Vnderhill, 1654.

Burt, Henry Martyn. *Cornet Joseph Parsons, One of the Founders of Springfield and Northampton, Massachusetts.* Garden City, NY: Parsons, 1898.

———. *The First Century of Springfield: The Official Records from 1636 to 1736, with an Historical Review and Biographical Mention of the Founders.* Vol. 1. Library of American Civilization 23893. Springfield, MA: H. M. Burt, 1898.

Byington, Ezra Hoyt. "Sketch of William Pynchon." *Andover Review* 6 (1886) 239–55.

———. "William Pynchon, Gent." In *The Puritan in England and New England,* 185–218. 3rd ed. Boston: Roberts, 1897.

Calamy, Edmund. *An Account of the Ministers, Lecturers, Masters, and Fellows of Colleges and Schoolmasters, who were Ejected or Silenced after the Restoration in 1660.* London: J. Lawrence, 1713.

———. *A Continuation of the Account of the Ministers, Lecturers, Masters, and Fellows of Colleges and Schoolmasters, who were Ejected or Silenced after the Restoration in 1660.* London: J. Ford, 1727.

Carvalho, Joseph, III. *Black Families in Hampden County, Massachusetts, 1650–1855.* Boston: NEHGS, 1984.

Cave, Alfred A. *The Pequot War.* Native Americans of the Northeast. Amherst: University of Massachusetts Press, 1996.

———. "Who Killed John Stone? A Note on the Origins of the Pequot War." *The William and Mary Quarterly,* 3rd ser., 49 (1992) 509–21.

Chewney, Nicholas. *'ΑΙΡΕΣΙΑΡΧΑΙ,' or a Cage of Unclean Birds. Containing the Authors, Promotorers, Propagators, and chief Disseminators of this damnable Socinian Heresie.* London: 1656.

———. *Anti-Socinianism; or, A brief Explication of some places of holy Scripture, for the confutation of certain gross Errours, and Socinian Heresies, lately published by William Pynchon, Gent. in a Dialogue of his, called, The Meritorious Price of Our Redemption.* London: J. M. for H. Twyford and T. Dring, 1656.

Christ-Janer, Albert, Charles W. Hughes, and Carleton Sprague Smith. *American Hymns Old and New.* New York: Columbia University Press, 1980.

City of Boston. *Fourth Report of the Record Commissioners, Dorchester Town Records.* Boston: Rockwell and Churchill, 1880.

Clapp, Ebenezer, and the Dorchester Antiquarian and Historical Society. *History of the Town of Dorchester, Massachusetts.* Boston: Ebenezer Clapp, 1851.

Clendon, Thomas. *Justification Justified; or, The Doctrine of Justification: Briefly and clearly explained.* London: Robert Ibbitson, 1653.

Cogley, Richard W. *John Eliot's Mission to the Indians Before King Philip's War.* Cambridge: Harvard University Press, 1999.

Collinson, Patrick. *The Elizabethan Puritan Movement.* Oxford: Clarendon, 1987.

Connecticut Historical Society, and "A. C. B." *Some Early Records and Documents of and Relating to the Town of Windsor Connecticut, 1639–1703.* Hartford, CT: Connecticut Historical Society, 1930.

Cooper, James F., Jr. *Tenacious of Their Liberties: The Congregationalists in Colonial Massachusetts.* Religion in America Series. New York: Oxford University Press, 1999.

Cotton, John. *God's Promise to His Plantation.* London: William Jones for John Bellamy, 1630.

———. *The Powring Out of the Seven Vials; or, An Exposition of the 16 Chapter of the Revelation, with an Application of it to our Times.* London: R. S., 1642.

Currie, Ian. *Frosts, Freezes and Fairs.* Coulsdon, UK: Frosted Earth, 1996.

Dalton, Michael. *The Countrey Iustice: Conteyning the practise of the Iustices of the Peace out of their Sessions. Gathered for the better helpe of such Iustices of Peace as haue not beene much conuersant in the studie of the Lawes of this Realme.* London: Adam Islip for the Societie of Stationers, 1618.

Daniell, Blackburne F. H., ed. *Calendar of State Papers, Domestic Series, of the Reign of Charles II, December 1671 to May 17th 1672.* London: Eyre & Spottiswoode, 1897.

Dean, John Ward, ed. *The New-England Historical and Genealogical Register.* Vol. 48. Boston: NEHGS, 1894.

de Jong, Christiaan G. F. "'Christ's Descent' in Massachusetts: The Doctrine of Justification According to William Pynchon (1590–1662)." In *Gericht Verleden*, edited by Christiaan G. F. de Jong and J. van Sluis, 129–58. Leiden: J. J. Groen en Zoon, 1991.

Delbanco, Andrew. *The Puritan Ordeal.* Cambridge: Harvard University Press, 1989.

Demos, John Putnam. *Entertaining Satan: Witchcraft and the Culture of Early New England.* New York: Oxford University Press, 1982.

Dixon, Philip. *'Nice and Hot Disputes:' The Doctrine of the Trinity in the Seventeenth Century.* New York: T. & T. Clark, 2003.

Dolin, Eric Jay. *Fur, Fortune, and Empire: The Epic History of the Fur Trade in America.* New York: Norton, 2010.

Dow, George Francis. *Everyday Life in the Massachusetts Bay Colony.* 1935. Reprint, Bowie, MD: Heritage, 2002.

Drake, Samuel G. *Annals of Witchcraft in New England, and Elsewhere in the United States; from Their First Settlement.* Woodward's Historical Series 8. 1869. Reprint, New York: B. Blom, 1967.

———. *The Book of the Indians; or, Biography and History of the Indians of North America, from its First Discovery to the Year 1841.* Boston: Benjamin B. Mussey, 1845.

Dugdale, William. *The History of St. Pauls Cathedral in London From its Foundation untill these Times: Extracted out of Originall Charters, Records, Leiger Books, and other Manuscripts: Beautified with sundry Prospects of the Church, Figures of Tombes and Monuments.* London: Tho. Warren, 1658.

Duniway, Clyde Augustus. *Freedom of the Press in Massachusetts.* New York: Longmans, Green, 1906.

Dunn, Alastair. *The Great Rising of 1381: The Peasant's Revolt and England's Failed Revolution.* Stroud, UK: Tempus, 2002.

Eliot, John. "Record of Church Members, Roxbury, Mass." In *A Report of the Record Commissioners Containing the Roxbury Land and Church Records,* 73–100. Boston: Rockwell and Churchill, 1884.

Emmison, F. G. *Elizabethan Life: Home, Work and Land.* Vol. 3. Chelmsford, MA: Essex County Council, 1970–1980.

Fischer, David Hackett. *Albion's Seed: Four British Folkways in America.* New York: Oxford University Press, 1989.

Fitch, Edward Arthur, and Charlotte Fell-Smith. *The Essex Review.* Chelmsford, MA: Durant, 1908.

Forbes, Allyn B., ed. *Winthrop Papers.* 5 vols. Boston: Massachusetts Historical Society, 1929–1947.

Forbes, John. *A Treatise Tending to Cleare the Doctrine of Iustification. Written by Io. Forbes, Pastour of the English Church at Middelburgh, for the Instruction of His Flocke.* Middelburgh: Richard Schilders, 1616.

Ford, Worthington Chauncey. "Letters of William Pynchon." *Proceedings of the Massachusetts Historical Society* 48 (1915) 35–56.

———. "Supplies for Massachusetts Bay, 1631–1632." *Proceedings of the Massachusetts Historical Society* 47 (1914) 343–47.

———. "Winthrop in the London Port Books." *Proceedings of the Massachusetts Historical Society* 47 (1914) 178–90.

Fortescue, John. *A Learned Commendation of the politique Lawes of England: wherein, by most pithie reasons and euident demonstrations, they are plainelye proued farre to excell, . . . all other Lawes of the world.* Translated by Robert Mulcaster. London: Thomas Wight and Bonham Norton, 1599.

Foster, Frank Hugh. *A Genetic History of the New England Theology.* 1907. Reprint, New York: Russell & Russell, 1963.

Foster, Stephen. "The Massachusetts Franchise in the Seventeenth Century." *WMQ,* 3rd ser., 24 (1967) 613–23.

———. "New England and the Challenge of Heresy, 1630 to 1660: The Puritan Crisis in Transatlantic Perspective." *WMQ,* 3rd ser., 38 (1981) 624–60.

Freeman, Frederick. *The History of Cape Cod: The Annals of Barnstable County.* Vol. 1. Boston: Geo. C. Rand & Avery, 1860.

Gardener, Lion, and William Newnham Chattin Carlton, ed. *Relation of the Pequot Warres (1660).* Acorn Club of Connecticut Publication 4. Hartford, CT: Acorn Club, 1901.

Gataker, Thomas. *A serious and faithfull Representation of the Judgements of Ministers of the Gospell Within the Province of London, Contained in a letter from them to the Generall and his Councell of Warre, Delivered to his Excellency by some of the subscribers, Jan. 18, 1649.* London: M. B. for Samuel Gellibrand and Ralph Smith, 1649.

Gillett, Charles Ripley. *Burned Books: Neglected Chapters in British History and Literature.* Vol. 1. New York: Columbia University Press, 1932.

Goddard, Ives, and Kathleen Joan Bragdon. *Native Writings in Massachusett.* Memoirs of the American Philosophical Society 185. Philadelphia: American Philosophical Society, 1988.

Goodwin, Nathaniel. *Descendants of Thomas Olcott.* Hartford, CT: Case, Tiffany, & Burnham, 1845.

Grandjean, Katherine A. "New World Tempests: Environment, Scarcity, and the Coming of the Pequot War." *WMQ*, 3rd ser., 68 (2011) 75–100.

Green, Mason Arnold. *Springfield 1636–1886, History of Town and City*. Springfield, MA: C. A. Nichols, 1888.

Grieve, Hilda Elizabeth Poole. *The Sleepers and the Shadows: Chelmsford, a Town, Its People and Its Past*. 2 vols. Essex Record Office 100, 128. Chelmsford, MA: Essex County Council and Chelmsford Borough Council, 1988–1994.

Grotius, Hugo. *Hugo Grotius, His Discourses: I. Of God and His Providence. II. Of Christ, His Miracles and Doctrine: With Annotations and the Authors Life: An Appendix concerning his Judgment in sundry points controverted*. London: James Flesher for William Lee, 1652.

———. *The Illustrious Hugo Grotius Of the Law of Warre and Peace: With Annotations, III Parts, and Memorials of the Author's Life and Death*. Translated by Clement Barksdale. London: T. Warren for William Lee, 1654.

Gura, Philip F. *A Glimpse of Sion's Glory: Puritan Radicalism in New England, 1620–1660*. Middletown: Wesleyan University Press, 1984.

Gyll, Gordon Willoughby James. *History of the Parish of Wraysbury, Astkerwycke Priory, and Magna Charta Island*. London: Henry G. Bohn, 1862.

Hall, David D. *The Faithful Shepherd: A History of the New England Ministry in the Seventeenth Century*. New York: Norton, 1972.

———. *A Reforming People: Puritanism and the Transformation of Public Life in New England*. New York: Knopf, 2011.

———. *Witch-Hunting in Seventeenth-Century New England: A Documentary History, 1638–1692*. Boston: Northeastern University Press, 1991.

———. *Worlds of Wonder, Days of Judgment: Popular Religious Belief in Early New England*. New York: Knopf, 1989.

———, ed. *The Antinomian Controversy, 1636–1638*. Durham: Duke University Press, 1990.

———, ed. *Puritans in the New World: A Critical Anthology*. Princeton: Princeton University Press, 2004.

Hampshire County. *The Register Booke ffor Birthes Marriages & Deaths*. MS records for Hampshire County, 1638–1696, in the collection of the Springfield History Library and Archives of the Lyman & Merrie Wood Museum of Springfield History.

Hankins, Jeffrey B. "Papists, Power, and Puritans: Catholic Officeholding and the Rise of the 'Puritan Faction' in Early-Seventeenth-Century Essex." *Catholic Historical Review* 95 (2009) 689–717.

Haraszti, Zoltán, ed. *The Bay Psalm Book*. Chicago: University of Chicago Press, 1956.

———. *The Enigma of the Bay Psalm Book*. Chicago: University of Chicago Press, 1956.

Hardman Moore, Susan. *Pilgrims: New World Settlers and the Call of Home*. New Haven: Yale University Press, 2007.

Harnack, Adolf. *Outlines of the History of Dogma*. Translated by Edwin Knox Mitchell. 1893. Reprint, Boston: Beacon, 1959.

Hazard, Ebenezer. *Historical Collections; Consisting of State Papers, and Other Authentic Documents; Intended as Materials for an History of the United States of America*. Vol. 2. Philadelphia: T. Dobson, 1795.

Hill, Christopher. *Society and Puritanism in Pre-Revolutionary England*. London: Secker & Warburg, 1964.

History of Parliament Trust. "House of Commons Journal, 5 March 1646." *Journal of the House of Commons* 4:1644–1646 (1802) 462–65.

Holyoke, Edward. *The Doctrine of Life; or, Of Mans Redemtion, by the Seed of Eve, the Seed of Abraham, the Seed of David, &c.* London: T. R. for Nath. Ekins, 1658.

Hooker, Thomas. *A Survey of the Summe of Church-Discipline. Wherein, the Way of the Churches of NEW-ENGLAND is warranted out of the Word, and all Exceptions of weight, which are made against it, answered.* London: A. M. for John Bellamy, 1648.

Hunt, William. *The Puritan Moment: The Coming of Revolution in an English County.* Cambridge: Harvard University Press, 1983.

Hutchinson, Thomas. *A Collection of Original Papers Relative to the History of the Colony of Massachusets-Bay.* 1769. Reprint, Carlisle, MA: Applewood, 2009.

Innes, Stephen. *Creating the Commonwealth: The Economic Culture of Puritan New England.* New York: Norton, 1995.

———. *Labor in a New Land: Economy and Society in Seventeenth-Century Springfield.* Princeton: Princeton University Press, 1983.

Jacob, Henry. *A Defence of a Treatise Touching the Sufferings and Victorie of Christ in the Worke of our Redemption.* Middelburg: Richard Schilders, 1600.

———. *A Treatise of the Sufferings and Victory of Christ, in the work of our redemption.* Middelburg: Richard Schilders, 1598.

Jennings, Francis. *The Invasion of America: Indians, Colonialism, and the Cant of Conquest.* Chapel Hill: University of North Carolina Press, 1975.

Jones, David. *Chelmsford: A History.* Stroud, UK: Phillimore, 2003.

Jones, Mary Jeanne Anderson. *Congregational Commonwealth, Connecticut 1636–1662.* Middletown: Wesleyan University Press, 1968.

Jonson, Ben. *The Alchemist.* Edited by Charles Montgomery Hathaway Jr. Yale Studies in English 17. New York: Henry Holt, 1903.

Judd, Sylvester. "The Fur Trade on the Connecticut." *New England Historical and Genealogical Register* 11 (1857) 217–19.

Kamensky, Jane. *Governing the Tongue: The Politics of Speech in Early New England.* New York: Oxford University Press, 1997.

Karr, Ronald Dale. "The Missing Clause: Myth and the Massachusetts Bay Charter of 1629." *NEQ* 77 (2004) 89–107.

———. "'Why Should You Be So Furious?' The Violence of the Pequot War." *The Journal of American History* 85 (1998) 876–909.

Katz, Steven. "The Pequot War Reconsidered." In *New England Encounters: Indians and Euroamericans, ca. 1600–1850,* edited by Alden T. Vaughan, 111–35. Boston: Northeastern University Press, 1999.

Kawashima, Yasuhide. *Puritan Justice and the Indian: White Man's Law in Massachusetts, 1630–1763.* Middletown: Wesleyan University Press, 1986.

Keeble, N. H., and Geoffrey F. Nuttall. *Calendar of the Correspondence of Richard Baxter.* 2 vols. Oxford: Clarendon, 1991.

Kenyon, John, and Jane Ohlmeyer, eds. *The Civil Wars, a Military History of England, Scotland, and Ireland 1638–60.* Oxford: Oxford University Press, 1998.

Kircher, Konrad. *Concordantiae Veteris Testamenti: Ebraeis Vocibus Respondentes.* Frankfurt: Claudium Marnium and Heredes Iohannis Aubrii, 1607.

Kittredge, George L. "Dr. Robert Child the Remonstrant." *Publications of the Colonial Society of Massachusetts* 21 (1920) 1–146.

Kupperman, Karen Ordahl. *Indians and English: Facing off in Early America*. Ithaca: Cornell University Press, 2000.

Lamb, H. H. *Climatic History and the Future*. Vol. 2 of *Climate: Present, Past and Future*. London: Methuen, 1977.

Lightfoot, John. *The Harmony of the Four Evangelists: Among themselves, and With the Old Testament*. London: R. C. for Andrew Crook, 1650.

Liu, Tai. *Puritan London: A Study of Religion and Society in the City Parishes*. Cranbury, NJ: Associated University Presses, 1986.

Lockwood, John H. et al., eds. *Western Massachusetts: A History 1636–1925*. 4 vols. Genealogy and Local History LH8811. New York: Lewis Historical Publishing, 1926.

Lucas, Paul R. *Valley of Discord: Church and Society along the Connecticut River, 1636–1725*. Hanover, NH: University Press of New England, 1976.

Manegold, C. S. *Ten Hills Farm: The Forgotten History of Slavery in the North*. Princeton: Princeton University Press, 2010.

Massachusetts. *The Book of the General Lawes and Libertyes Concerning the Inhabitants of the Massachusets*. 1648. Reprint, Cambridge: Harvard University Press, 1929.

Massachusetts Court of Assistants. *Records of the Court of Assistants of the Colony of the Massachusetts Bay, 1630–1692*. Boston: County of Suffolk, 1904.

Massachusetts General Court. "The Liberties of the Massachusetts Colonie in New England, 1641." Boston: Directors of the Old South Work, 1905.

Massachusetts Historical Society. "Letter Relating to William Pynchon." *Proceedings of the Massachusetts Historical Society* 11 (1869–1870) 309–11.

———. "Pincheon Papers." *Collections of the Massachusetts Historical Society*, 2nd ser., 8 (1826) 227–37.

———. "Winthrop Papers." *Collections of the Massachusetts Historical Society*, 5th ser., 1 (1871) 1–509.

Mather, Cotton. *Magnalia Christi Americana; or, The Ecclesiastical History of New-England: From Its First Planting in the Year 1620 unto the Year of our Lord, 1698*. 7 vols. London: Thomas Parkhurst, 1702.

Mather, Richard. *Church-Government and Church-Covenant Discussed, In an Answer to the Elders of the severall Churches in NEW-ENGLAND To two and thirty Questions*. London: Benjamin Allen, 1643.

———. *The Summe of Certain Sermons upon Genes: 15.6 VVherein not only the Docrine [sic] of Justification by Faith is Asserted and Cleared, and sundry Arguments for Justification before Faith, discussed and Answered*. Cambridge, MA: Samuel Green, 1652.

Matthew, H. C. G., and Brian Harrison, eds. *Oxford Dictionary of National Biography*. Oxford University Press, 2004.

Mayo, Lawrence Shaw. *John Endecott: A Biography*. Cambridge: Harvard University Press, 1936.

McCulloh, Gerald O. "The Influence of Arminius on American Theology." In *Man's Faith and Freedom: The Theological Influence of Jacobus Arminius*, edited by Gerald O. McCulloh, 64–87. New York: Abingdon, 1962.

McGrath, Alister E. *Reformation Thought: An Introduction*. Oxford: Blackwell, 1999.

McIntyre, Ruth A. *William Pynchon: Merchant and Colonizer, 1590–1662*. Springfield, MA: Connecticut Valley Historical Museum, 1961.

McLachlan, H. John. *Socinianism in Seventeenth-Century England*. Oxford: Oxford University Press, 1951.

Merbecke, John. *A Booke of Notes and Common Places, with their expositions, collected and gathered out of the workes of diuers singular Writers, and brought Alphabetically into order.* London: Thomas East, 1581.

Miller, Perry. *The New England Mind: The Seventeenth Century.* 1939. Reprint, Boston: Beacon, 1961.

———. *Orthodoxy in Massachusetts, 1630–1650.* Boston: Beacon, 1959.

Morgan, Edmund S. "The Case against Anne Hutchinson." *NEQ* 10 (1937) 635–49

Morison, Samuel Eliot. *Builders of the Bay Colony.* Boston: Houghton Mifflin, 1964.

———. *The Intellectual Life of Colonial New England.* Ithaca: Cornell University Press, 1956.

———. "William Pynchon." In *The Dictionary of American Biography*, edited by Allen Johnson et al., 15:292–93. New York: Scribner's, 1935.

———. "William Pynchon, Frontier Magistrate and Fur Trader." In *Builders of the Bay Colony*, 337–75. Boston: Houghton Mifflin, 1964.

———. "William Pynchon, the Founder of Springfield." *Proceedings of the Massachusetts Historical Society* 64 (1931) 67–110.

Neal, Daniel. *The History of the Puritans, Or Protestant Nonconformists.* 2 vols. New York: Harper, 1863.

Nelson, William E. "The Utopian Legal Order of the Massachusetts Bay Colony, 1630–1686." *The American Journal of Legal History* 47 (2005) 183–230.

Neuman, Meredith M. *Jeremiah's Scribes: Creating Sermon Literature in Puritan New England.* Philadelphia: University of Pennsylvania, 2013.

Newell, Margaret E. "Robert Child and the Entrepreneurial Vision: Economy and Ideology in Early New England." *NEQ* 68 (1995) 223–56.

Nichols, Charles Lemuel. "Letter of William Pynchon, 1638." *Proceedings of the Massachusetts Historical Society* 58 (1925) 386–88.

Norton, John. *The Answer to the Whole Set of Questions of the Celebrated Mr. William Apollonius, Pastor of the Church of Middleburg.* Translated by Douglas Horton. Cambridge, MA: Belknap, 1958.

———. *A Discussion of that Great Point in Divinity, the Sufferings of Christ; and the Questions about his Righteousnes—Active/Passive: And the Imputation thereof.* London: A. M. for George Calvert, 1653.

———. *The Orthodox Evangelist; or, A Treatise Wherein many Great Evangelical Truths (Not a few whereof are much opposed and Eclipsed in this perilous hour of the Passion of the Gospel) Are briefly Discussed, cleared, and confirmed.* London: John Macock for Lodowick Lloyd, 1654.

Norton, Mary Beth. "The Ablest Midwife That Wee Knowe in the Land: Mistress Alice Tilly and the Women of Boston and Dorchester, 1649–1650." *WMQ*, 3rd ser., 55 (1998) 105–34.

O'Collins, Gerald, and Edward G. Farrugia. *A Concise Dictionary of Theology.* New York: Paulist, 2000.

Ong, Walter J. *Ramus, Method, and the Decay of Dialogue: From the Art of Discourse to the Art of Reason.* Cambridge: Harvard University Press, 1958.

Osborne, Francis. *Historical Memoires on the Reigns of Queen Elizabeth and King James.* London: J. Grismond, 1658.

———. *The Works of Francis Osborne, Esq.: Divine, Moral, Historical, Political, in Four several tracts.* London: R. D. for A. Bancks, 1673.

O'Shea, Marty. "Springfield's Puritans and Indians: 1636–1655." *Historical Journal of Massachusetts* 26 (1998) 46–72.

Page, William, ed. *The Victoria History of the County of Buckingham.* Vol. 3. Victoria History of the Counties of England. London: St. Catherine, 1925.

Pareus, David. *In divinam ad Romanos S. Pauli apostoli epistolam commentaries.* Heidelbergae [Heidelberg, Germany]: s.n., 1613.

Parker, Geoffrey. *Global Crisis: War, Climate Change, and Catastrophe in the Seventeenth Century.* New Haven: Yale University Press, 2013.

Paynter, Helen I. *Short History of All Saints' Church, Springfield, Essex.* Chelmsford, MA: John Dutton, 1949.

Perley, Sidney. *The Indian Land Titles of Essex County, Massachusetts.* Salem, MA: Essex Book and Print Club, 1912.

Phillips, Paul Chrisler. *The Fur Trade.* With concluding chapters by J. W. Smurr. 2 vols. Norman: University of Oklahoma Press, 1961.

Platt, Stewart. *All Saints Writtle, A History and Guide.* Chelmsford, MA: Printing Place, 1992.

Plomer, Henry R. *A Dictionary of the Booksellers and Printers Who Were at Work in England, Scotland, and Ireland from 1641 to 1667.* 1907. Reprint, London: Bibliographical Society, 1968.

Preston, John. *Life Eternall; or, A Treatise of the knowledge of the Divine Essence and Attributes: Delivered in XVIII. Sermons.* Edited by Thomas Goodwin and Thomas Ball. London: R. B[adger], 1632.

Pulsifer, David. *Records of the Colony of New Plymouth, 1620–1651.* Vol. 12. Boston: William White, 1861.

Pynchon, John. "John Pynchon Moxon Sermon Notes (1640)." Unpublished manuscript. Springfield History Library and Archives of the Lyman and Merrie Wood Museum of Springfield History, Springfield, MA.

———. "Notes of the Rev. Mr. Moxon's Sermons by the Hon. John Pynchon of Springfield (1649)." Unpublished manuscript. Simon Gratz Collection, Historical Society of Pennsylvania, Philadelphia, PA.

Pynchon, Joseph Charles. *Record of the Pynchon Family in England and America.* Revised by William Frederick Adams. Springfield, MA: Old Corner Book Store, 1898.

Pynchon, William. *The Covenant of Nature made with Adam Described, and Cleared from sundry great mistakes.* London: s.n., 1662.

———. *An Endevour After The reconcilement of that long debated and much lamented difference between the godly Presbyterians, and Independents; About Church-government.* London: M. S. for John Bellamy, 1648.

———. *A Farther Discussion of That Great Point in Divinity, the Sufferings of Christ; or, The Meritorious Price of Mans Redemption, or Christs Satisfaction discussed and explained.* London: Thomas Newberry, 1655.

———. *Holy Time; or, The True Limits of the Lords Day.* London: R. I. for T. N., 1654.

———. *The Jewes Synagogue; or, A Treatise Concerning the ancient Orders and Manner of Worship used by the Jewes in their Synagogue-Assemblies.* London: J. Bellamie, 1652.

———. *The Meritorious Price of Our Redemption, Iustification, &c. Cleering it from some common Errors.* London: J. M. for George Whittington and James Moxon, 1650.

———. *The Meritorious Price of Our Redemption.* With notes by Michael W. Vella, Lance Schachterle, and Louis Mackey. Worcester Polytechnic Institute Studies in Science, Technology, and Culture 10. New York: Peter Lang, 1992.

————. *The Time when the First Sabbath was Ordained*. London: R. I. for T. N., 1654.

Pynchon, William, and John Pynchon. "Record of Accounts with Early Settlers and Indians." In unnamed MS notebook, 1645–1650. Forbes Library, Northampton, MA.

Roberts, Strother E. "Changes in the Water: Beaver Ecology and the Fur Trade in the Connecticut Valley." Paper presented at the Boston Environmental History Seminar, Massachusetts Historical Society, Boston, MA, December 11, 2012.

Roberts-Miller, Patricia. *Voices in the Wilderness: Public Discourse and the Paradox of Puritan Rhetoric*. Tuscaloosa: University of Alabama Press, 1999.

Robinson, John, and George Francis Dow. *The Sailing Ships of New England, 1606–1907*. Salem, MA: Marine Research Society, 1922.

Rose-Troup, Frances James. *The Massachusetts Bay Company and Its Predecessors*. New York: Grafton, 1930.

Ryves, Bruno. *Mercurius Rusticus; or, The Countries Complaint of the Murthers, Robberies, Plunderings, and other Outrages committed by the Rebells on His Majesties faithfull Subjects*. Oxford: s.n., 1643.

Scott, Jonathan. *England's Troubles: Seventeenth-century English Political Instability in European Context*. Cambridge: University of Cambridge Press, 2000.

Schechter, Stephen L., ed. *Roots of the Republic: American Founding Documents Interpreted*. Madison, WI: Madison House, 1990.

Shadrack, Alan. *Historical Notes of All Saints' Church, Springfield, Essex*. Chelmsford, MA: s.n., 2000.

Shurtleff, Nathaniel B. *Records of the Governor and Company of the Massachusetts Bay*. Boston: William White, 1854.

Smith, Joseph H. *Colonial Justice in Western Massachusetts (1636–1702): The Pynchon Court Record, an Original Judges' Diary of the Administration of Justice in the Massachusetts Bay Colony*. Cambridge: Harvard University Press, 1961.

Smythe, W. Dumville. *An Historical Account of the Worshipful Company of Girdlers, London*. London: Chiswick, 1905.

Stout, Harry S. *The New England Soul: Preaching and Religious Culture in Colonial New England*. Oxford: Oxford University Press, 1986.

Taylor, Robert J. *Colonial Connecticut: A History*. History of the American Colonies. Millwood, NY: KTO Press, 1979.

Temple, J. H. *History of North Brookfield, Massachusetts*. North Brookfield, MA: Town of North Brookfield, 1887.

Thomas, Peter A. "Bridging the Cultural Gap: Indian/White Relations." In *Early Settlement in the Connecticut Valley*, edited by J. W. Ifkovic and M. Kaufman, 5–21. Westfield, MA: Historic Deerfield and Westfield State College, 1984.

————. "Contrastive Subsistence Strategies and Land Use as Factors for Understanding Indian-White Relations in New England." *Ethnohistory* 23 (1976) 1–18.

————. "In the Maelstrom of Change: The Indian Trade and Cultural Process in the Middle Connecticut River Valley, 1635–1665." Ph.D. diss., University of Massachusetts, Amherst, 1979.

Thompson, Roger. *From Deference to Defiance: Charlestown, Massachusetts, 1629–1692*. Boston: NEHGS, 2012.

Trumbull, J. Hammond, ed. *The Public Records of the Colony of Connecticut, 1636–1776*. Vol. 1. Hartford: Brown & Parsons, 1850.

Valeri, Mark R. *Heavenly Merchandize: How Religion Shaped Commerce in Puritan America*. Princeton: Princeton University Press, 2010.

Vaughan, Alden T. *New England Frontier: Puritans and Indians, 1620–1675*. Boston: Little, Brown, 1965.

Vincent, Philip. *A Trve Relation of the Late Battell fought in New England, between the English, and the Salvages: VVith the present state of things there*. London: M[armaduke] P[arsons] for Nathanael Butter and Iohn Bellamie, 1637.

Von Frank, Albert J. "John Saffin: Slavery and Racism in Colonial Massachusetts." *Early American Literature* 29 (1994) 254–72.

Walker, George Leon. *History of the First Church in Hartford, 1633–1833*. Hartford: Brown & Gross, 1884.

Walker, Williston. *Creeds and Platforms of Congregationalism*. 1893. Reprint, Boston: Pilgrim, 1960.

Wall, Robert Emmet, Jr. "The Massachusetts Bay Colony Franchise in 1647." *WMQ*, 3rd ser., 27 (1970) 136–44.

———. *Massachusetts Bay: The Crucial Decade, 1640–1650*. New Haven: Yale University Press, 1972.

Warden, G. B. "Law Reform in England and New England, 1620 to 1660." *WMQ*, 3rd ser., 35 (1978) 668–90.

Waters, Henry F. *Genealogical Gleanings in England*. 2 vols. Library of American Civilization 22478–79. Boston: NEHGS, 1901.

Weisman, Richard. *Witchcraft, Magic, and Religion in 17th-Century Massachusetts*. Amherst, MA: University of Massachusetts Press, 1984.

Westminster Assembly. *Annotations Upon all the Books of the Old and New Testament*. London: John Legatt, 1645.

Wilbur, Earl Morse. *A History of Unitarianism in Transylvania, England, and America*. Cambridge: Harvard University Press, 1952.

———. *Our Unitarian Heritage*. Boston: Beacon, 1925.

Williams, George H., ed. *Thomas Hooker: Writings in England and Holland, 1626–1633*, Harvard Theological Studies 28. Cambridge: Harvard University Press, 1975.

Williams, Roger. *The Bloody Tenent yet More Bloody*. London: Giles Calvert, 1652.

Wilson, James Grant, and John Fiske, eds. *Appleton's Cyclopaedia of American Biography*. New York: Appleton, 1888.

Whittemore, Henry. *Genealogical Guide to the Early Settlers of America*. Baltimore: Genealogical, 1967.

Winship, Michael P. "Contesting Control of Orthodoxy among the Godly: William Pynchon Reexamined." *WMQ*, 3rd ser., 54 (1997) 795–822.

———. "William Pynchon's The Jewes Synagogue." *NEQ* 71 (1998) 290–97.

Winthrop, John. *The History of New England from 1630 to 1649*. Edited by James Savage. 2 vols. 1853. Reprint, Baltimore: Clearfield, 1996.

———. *The Journal John Winthrop, 1630–1649*. Edited by Richard S. Dunn, James Savage, and Laetitia Yeandle. John Harvard Library. Cambridge: Harvard University Press, 1996.

Winthrop, Robert C. *Life and Letters of John Winthrop*. Boston: Ticknor & Fields, 1867.

Withington, Lothrop. "Virginia Gleanings in England." *The Virginia Magazine of History and Biography* 12 (1906) 297–310.

Woodward, Walter E. *Prospero's America: John Winthrop, Jr., Alchemy, and the Creation of New England Culture, 1606–1676*. Chapel Hill: University of North Carolina Press, 2010.

Woolrych, Austin H. *Commonwealth to Protectorate*. Oxford: Clarendon, 1982.

BIBLIOGRAPHY

Wotton, Antony. *De Reconciliatione Peccatoris*. Basileae [Basel, Switzerland]: s.n., 1624.

Wright, Harry Andrew. *Indian Deeds of Hampden County*. Springfield, MA: s.n., 1905.

Wright, Michael. "Jews Trumps and Their Valuation, 1545 to 1765." *Journal of the International Jew's Harp Society* 2 (2004) 41–46.

Younge, Richard. *A Christian Library; or, A Pleasant and Plentiful Paradise of Practical Divinity: In Ten Treatises*. London: James Crumpe, 1655.

Index

Page numbers in **boldface** refer to illustrations. Numbers followed by n refer to footnotes.